The Universities We Need

Increasing numbers of young adults go to university. This book explores contemporary understandings of what universities are for, what impact they might be having on their students and what visions of life and society are driving them. It criticises a narrow view of higher education which focuses on serving the economy. It argues that, for the sake of the common and individual good, universities need to be about forming citizens and societies as well as being an economic resource. It does so in the light of theological perspectives, mainly from the Christian but also from the Muslim faith, and has a global as well as a British perspective. It brings together key thinkers in theology and higher education policy – including Rowan Williams, David Ford, Mike Higton and Peter Scott – to present a unique perspective on institutions which help shape the lives of millions.

Stephen Heap is a Baptist minister who spent most of his ministry in University Chaplaincy in London and Bedford, where he was also Director of a Christian education centre. From 2008 to 2014 he was the Church of England's National Higher Education Adviser. He is now a Visiting Professor at the University of Winchester, engaged in theological reflection on what it means to be an Anglican university, and has a consultancy role at the Cardiff Centre for Chaplaincy Studies. He is the author of the Grove Booklet *What are Universities Good For?* (2012) and various articles on higher education.

The Universities We Need
Theological perspectives

Edited by Stephen Heap

 Routledge
Taylor & Francis Group

LONDON AND NEW YORK

First published 2017
by Routledge
2 Park Square, Milton Park, Abingdon, Oxon OX14 4RN

and by Routledge
711 Third Avenue, New York, NY 10017

Routledge is an imprint of the Taylor & Francis Group, an informa business

British Library Cataloguing in Publication Data
A catalogue record for this book is available from the British Library

Library of Congress Cataloging-in-Publication Data
Names: Heap, Stephen, editor.
Title: The universities we need : theological perspectives / edited by Stephen Heap.
Description: 1 [edition]. | New York : Routledge, 2016. | Includes bibliographical references and index.
Identifiers: LCCN 2016023490 | ISBN 9781472477286 (hardback : alk. paper)
Subjects: LCSH: Education (Christian theology) | Universities and colleges.
Classification: LCC BT738.17 .U55 2016 | DDC 261.5—dc23
LC record available at https://lccn.loc.gov/2016023490

ISBN: 978-1-472-47728-6 (hbk)
ISBN: 978-1-315-54748-0 (ebk)

Typeset in Sabon
by Apex CoVantage, LLC

Printed and bound in Great Britain by
TJ International Ltd, Padstow, Cornwall

To the Memory of Malcolm Fisher 1954–2015

Table of Contents

Foreword

The title of this book implicitly poses two questions: what kind of universities do we need? And: how might theological perspectives help us here? In answer to the first question, both a national and – more importantly – a worldwide horizon are set before us. It is observed that the world faces considerable challenges of inequality, of poverty and of living together and of an undue reliance on the economy and markets in deriving policies intended to help in meeting its main challenges. The universities that we need, accordingly, are going to be universities that are prepared seriously to grapple with the very large issues of the contemporary world. And examples are offered of universities around the world which are beginning more and more to do just that.

It is, perhaps, in relation to the second question – how might theological perspectives help us here? – that this timely volume wins its spurs. And it does so, in the first place, simply by putting the matter of theological perspectives on the table, so to speak, as a matter of significance and deserving of serious consideration. It is not that we live in an increasingly secular age – for the reverse may be the case, that is, it may be that adherents to some kind of religion are increasing and that interest in religion is intensifying. And, indeed, some refer to the present time as a 'post-secular age'. It is an age in which secular reason and the religious traditions are being brought up against each other.

In higher education, however, matters are rather different. Here, higher education policymaking across the world seems to be taking place in a secular space. The discourse of higher education has its feet rooted in the here-and-now (or, at least, not far off) horizons and in the material world.

Concern is voiced over students' employment six months after their graduation. That a comparable concern might be voiced about students' lifelong development and the ways in which they might acquire the foundations of personal resources for living through the twenty-first century as human beings seems rarely to trouble the writers of government policy statements. After all, some students entering higher education today will be alive in the twenty-second century. What changes might they encounter and what challenges over values and fundamental frameworks for understanding the world might they have to address in their lifetimes? In *this* secular context (of higher education debate and policy-making), to pose the matter of theological perspectives and their potential in throwing light on the universities that we need is a radical move.

Over the last decade or so, Jurgen Habermas – whose work is touched upon here – has turned his attention to religion and has raised the issue directly as to how religion might gain a purchase in today's world. His response (Habermas, 2008; 2010; 2011), in a nutshell, is that religion does indeed contain resources on which the world can draw. He adds two provisos: that neither 'secular reason' nor religion should impose their beliefs on each other and that, since the two regimes – let us use that term – will then exist alongside each other, there need to be processes of 'translation', as he terms it, between them. How does this set of ideas help us here? In two ways, one positive and the other more critical.

Positively, the university can act as a space in the world in which religious and secular traditions and perspectives can be held together and engage with each other in respectful conversation. More critically, and here is where things get really interesting and what is in question here, as this volume's title indicates, is the matter of theological perspectives rather than religious beliefs per se.

I wish to be a little assertive here. I would say that the main value of this volume lies not in any proposition that it contains but, and more subtly, in its language. In short, its value lies in its expressing and advancing a theological language, as we may term it. In reading the manuscript of this book, I made a note of words and phrases that one rarely if ever sees in government policy documents, and I have a list of nearly 50 such words and phrases beside me as a result. Just indicative of the terms on that list are 'spirituality', 'righteousness', 'faith', 'belief', 'incompleteness', 'sin', 'gift', 'hope', 'holiness', 'receiving', 'sharing', 'conversation', 'soul', 'transcendent' and 'civility'. Ideas include those of 'public theology', 'the public mind', 'prophetic voice' and a 'disruption of cohesion'. There are yet other terms here, certainly on occasions to be seen in some of the educational literature, but still rarely to be seen or heard in the public debate. These include 'virtue', 'trust', 'human flourishing', 'wisdom', and 'wellbeing'.

In other words, what this volume is doing is to help to put into circulation a language that runs counter to the dominant discourses of our age, which are in play in relation to universities and higher education. This is, therefore, a properly subversive book; properly so, in that it implicitly calls to account the ways in which universities are characteristically described and understood. More than that, however, this language in itself helps to answer the first of the two earlier questions: what universities do we need? And the answers should surely include the proposal that our universities should be such that they offer a space for such a discourse. But, and more fundamentally, they should be institutions that are disposed to being and acting in the world in ways in which such a language seems appropriate.

This may seem unduly formal and abstract; but this volume offers ready testimony to such university presences. Within its pages are all kind of proposals – in the form of actual examples and case studies as well as practical suggestions – as to actions and stances that universities might take where such a language would make very good sense, of universities having a care for the world and acting to enhance wellbeing in all manner of ways and at all levels, personal and societal.

Two footnotes, as it were, may be warranted. First, and picking up the earlier observations about Habermas, the theological perspectives in view here are not those of substantial theological ideas and concepts as such, still less any religious belief system. Rather, what is being held out for here is implicitly an institutional stance on the part of universities which can be understood through a language that resonates theologically. What this volume points us towards, I believe, are *institutional dispositions* on the part of universities that call for the public language and concepts of the higher education discourse to be substantially widened, and with that widening, a larger sense as to the possibilities for universities in the world.

The second footnote is that reflections such as these do not open the way to any straightforward idea of the university for the twenty-first century, and for two reasons. The language and glimpses of possibilities for the university contained within this volume have to be worked through for each university, in its own time and space, wherever it may be in the world. And different possibilities will emerge for each university and will also call for an imagination at once sensitive to the particularities of a specific institution as well as the larger and even universal horizons. Moreover, those possibilities will, in any university, be characteristically contentious. And so a further implication here is not just that universities have to be spaces in which dissent and even conflict may be handled with mutual respect – a point made often enough – but also that the university should become a space large enough to accommodate quite different traditions of thought and belief and, on occasions, their mutual non-comprehension. To draw on a phrase in this volume, the universities that we need have in part to provoke and to live with and act with a 'disruption of cohesion'.

This, then, is a considerable book precisely in the sense that its messages deserve to be discerned and given serious consideration. And if taken seriously, it could have significant impact – to use a word of our times. Adroitly shepherded by Stephen Heap, the contributions here collectively amount to a distinctive and worthwhile voice. It remains to be seen as to what extent others might listen.

Ronald Barnett
University College London, Institute of Education

References

Habermas, J., 2008. *Between Naturalism and Religion*. Cambridge: Polity.

Habermas, J., 2011. 'The Political': The Rational Meaning of a Questionable Inheritance of Political Theology, in Mendieta, E., and Vanantwerpen, J., eds. *The Power of Religion in the Public Sphere*. pp. 15–33. New York and Chichester: Colombia University.

Habermas, J., et al, 2010. *An Awareness of What Is Missing: Faith and Reason in a Post-Secular Age*. Cambridge: Polity.

Acknowledgements

Stephen Heap

The road to this book has covered many territories. I am grateful to all who have helped shape the thinking which has led to it. They include my own tutors in various universities over many years of mainly part-time study, the people of Blackbird Leys, students and staff in universities I have worked in, those I worked with during my time as the Church of England's National Higher Education Adviser, current colleagues in the University of Winchester and elsewhere.

Jon Nixon offered significant encouragement to publish in this area. My thanks to Jon, and to David Ford and Mike Higton for early conversations. I am grateful too to all who willingly agreed to write chapters and who have devoted time, energy and their own gifts to producing what has become this book. They have been amenable, stimulating and scholarly travelling companions. So has Ronald Barnett, whose books and wisdom I, along with many others, have benefitted from, and who in the midst of a busy schedule gave time to writing the Foreword for us. Thanks to him. Thanks also to the staff at Routledge for all their help.

Andrew Bradstock, Elizabeth Stuart and Jeremy Law kindly read drafts of my own chapter and did much to improve it. Any remaining inadequacies are entirely my own.

I am particularly fortunate to have benefitted from the generosity and commitments of the University of Winchester, which is funding me to read, think and write on these issues. My thanks to the Vice-Chancellor and others for opportunities granted, and to John Gay for good colleagueship and many stimulating conversations.

Most important of all, my thanks to my wife, Liz. We have journeyed far together. Much would have been impossible without her willingness to share life with my various projects.

Introduction

Stephen Heap

In recent years in Britain, as in other parts of the world, going to university has become part of life for increasing numbers of young adults in particular, and the sector has expanded enormously, both here and worldwide. Why do people go to university? What is a university? What are universities for?

Such questions have been faced within and without universities down the years. This book asks what it means to be a university today. It asks the question mindful of the history and traditions of what is involved in being a university. It sets the question in the context of the needs of society (as has often been done before): what does contemporary society need of its universities?

The book is in part a response to rather narrow understandings of those needs in present higher education policy, but it is not, or not only, a tract against the times. Rather, it seeks to offer positive visions of what universities can offer to society. No claim for comprehensiveness is made in saying that, but some key themes are highlighted which might resource readers in further thinking and even action.

The book begins with a chapter from Susan Durber offering perspectives on issues the world faces. She captures something of the possibilities and potential of the present time. The worldwide web puts vast amounts of information at the fingertips of anyone with access to a computer and enables instantaneous communication, unfiltered by hierarchies. Scientific advance means a longer life and a better quality of life for millions, and, at least potentially, a less fossil fuel-dependent economy. The numbers living in absolute poverty have fallen. Education can be a tool for learning to live together for the good, and even the fact that what is good is contested can mean, as Suzy Harris argues, that a dynamic is released into society as debate takes place about what is and what could, or should, be. Humankind has many rich resources for engaging in such debate, including, as David Ford suggests, both secular and religious wisdoms. This is not a book which preaches doom!

It does, however, recognise the world faces challenges, again outlined in Durber's chapter. Providing for an ageing population is something some societies have to work on; others have to deal with a large younger age cohort, including resourcing their education. Contemporary methods of communication open up new worlds, but they may be shaping the way human beings relate in ways not yet fully grasped and pose a challenge about how what is communicated is to be evaluated. Climate change, if not adequately addressed, risks the very future of the planet. Continuing economic woes suggest searching for a better way of ordering economic life is needed. Population movements, along with other factors, such as the way people express identity, make learning to live with difference a matter of vital and immediate importance. In Britain, there is not always the engagement with democracy there might be, with a demise of participation even at the basic level of voting. The very pace of change can mean making sense of what is happening in a variety of arenas is difficult.

Living as part of this world is humankind, with all its failings, and with vast resources of wit, learning, wisdom and ingenuity, which it can choose to apply or not to make the best use of the opportunities and rise to the challenges.

Such is the context in which today's universities do their work, universities which have traditionally been, and can still be, one particular focus for the development and application of human wit, learning, wisdom and ingenuity, universities which are inheritors of traditions and debates about what it means to be a university. What sort of universities does a world such as this need? What roles should universities aspire to perform in and for the world?

This book faces those questions with the help of theological perspectives. They are offered in the belief that theological wisdom has resources to offer, alongside others, as thinking is done about both society and universities. That is not a novel approach. Religious communities have long engaged in theological reflection on society, including on education, and have, indeed, been a driving force in the creation of a significant number of universities or their antecedent institutions.[1] Religions continue to care about education and society and do so at a time when, as Durber and Ford indicate, religion has an important and, in many parts of the world, resurgent, presence. There may also be some commonality of role between religious groups and universities which helps bring them together; both, for example, are 'critical friends' to wider society, as Rowan Williams puts it in his chapter.

It is mainly Christian theology which is drawn on here, as the religious tradition which has been most active in Britain in shaping universities. There is also a chapter offering Islamic perspectives, for there are now Islamic institutions of higher education in Britain and, on a global scale, Islam has a very long involvement indeed. The university usually hailed as the oldest in the world, al-Qarawiyyin in Morocco, was founded by Muslims.

Such is the rationale for the approach taken. At the same time, it is freely recognised that there are many other voices to be heard in contemporary Britain, which, to use a phrase from Ford, is 'multi-faith and multi-secular'. That can be seen in figures from the 2011 census; of those who responded to the voluntary question 'What is your religion?', 59% described themselves as Christian, 25% as having no religion, 5% as Muslim, 1.5% Hindu, 0.8% Sikh, 0.5% Jewish and 0.4% Buddhist.[2] A larger project embracing such voices would be enriching, and certainly some of the groups there have an involvement in universities at least somewhere in the world, as can be seen from John Wood's chapter, which refers to Hindu foundation universities, amongst others.

The book draws on theology, but it is not written only for people of faith. It is for any who are concerned about the wellbeing of society and the role of universities in society. That includes those who research and write on such things, those who have a particular professional interest, such as university chaplains, politicians, and those who from various academic or more general interest bases wish to think about the nature and purpose of higher education and the shape of society.

To facilitate addressing questions about what sort of universities the world needs, the book begins with the chapter, already mentioned, from Durber. She draws attention to some major issues in a way which invites the reader to contemplate how reality looks from different perspectives, asking and considering what challenges and opportunities lie before the world and how they might look to people in various situations. Such realities form a context for thinking about universities and what they are for.

Universities are themselves part of society, formed, amongst other things, by societal trends and higher education policy. Peter Scott gives an overview of those policies and trends and their effect on universities. He considers in particular what has happened from the mid-1980s, but also looks further back, helpfully giving a longer perspective. Amongst recent developments, he highlights the expansion of student numbers, the increased international standing of UK research, developments in the curriculum, the use of new methods of communication in delivering the curriculum, moves towards 'market-oriented forms of higher education', the introduction of fees and the development of an audit culture which seeks to measure how universities perform against goals often set by the state and often to do with the economy. He discerns an increasingly interventionist attitude on the part of governments and increasing 'managerialism' within universities. Some of those developments Scott sees as more beneficial than others. His chapter roots our thinking about universities in the immediate framework within which universities work.

The first two chapters thus set the context. They treat of the issues the world faces and the forces shaping universities in particular directions. There then follows a series of chapters discussing how universities might offer things wider society needs and what impact present trends around universities have on them offering what is needed.

Williams writes about the need for good citizens and the work of universities in nurturing citizens. That work is important because a healthy democracy needs citizens who are engaged and participatory. It is perhaps doubly important in days when, as Durber puts it, there is 'a growing disengagement from traditional politics', including disengagement from voting.

Williams shows how universities have traditionally been about preparing people for public life, including leadership in society. He suggests that in a democratic society where 'every student becomes potentially someone with significant political views and capacities in the democratic system', universities are needed which equip students for being mature citizens, concerned not just with immediate skills, but with the quality of the public realm and with living wisely. Today that means living wisely in diverse societies, whose citizens need to be nurtured in 'civility', equipped for patient conversation with the other, even for that love of the other which says conflict is not the last word. He laments the challenges universities face in doing such work, some arising from those trends in society and policy Scott has pointed to which, in Williams's words, risk universities being dominated not by the sort of work he emphasises, but by 'external pressure to produce and to offer functional training'.

Citizens are individuals who operate in wider society. There is a strand in the history of universities which says universities are about the nature, and the good, not just of individuals, but of society.[3] This is turned to in the next chapter, in which Harris considers the work of universities in envisaging and working for the good of society. Her particular concern is 'the kind of university which meets the needs of a pluralistic and democratic society'. She addresses issues around pluralism in particular; again one of the key issues Durber points to which the world needs to face.

Harris asks what role universities have in helping to form democratic and pluralistic societies towards what might be considered 'the good'. She does so with reference to two giants of Catholic thinking about universities, John Henry Newman and Alasdair MacIntyre, and brings the writing of the Protestant Henry David Thoreau into dialogue with Newman and MacIntyre. She finds things in Newman's and MacIntyre's work which are of continuing value: the idea that universities are places for asking fundamental questions, and that university education should shape people in such a way that they are equipped to make good judgments, for example. Both Newman and MacIntyre, however, seek communities which are marked by common ends and traditions. Harris thinks it unlikely that such communities can be fostered in today's diverse societies. What may be more creative is facing the diversity and following Thoreau in recognising that it is not only what is held in common in human life which matters, but the 'uncommon'. That may be a better way forward than seeking to recreate the commonality of the past. The passing of more homogenous societies may create a sense of loss, says Harris, but it may also create a dynamism in which there is much questioning and evaluating of society and its possibilities.

Universities have their contribution to make to societies at that place of loss, dynamism and questioning. They will make their contribution not through an easy acceptance of the idea that 'commonality and cohesion are necessarily virtues of the community', but rather as they engage in conversation with 'the other', those who bring diversity and plurality, and do so with openness to 'the other' and the different ways of thinking they bring. Such is part of education, and in such encounters the university can 'extend and enrich the language' society has to speak about how it lives with diversity, thus facilitating dialogue more widely across society. In such ways, universities can support pluralistic and democratic societies as they shape ways forward for themselves.

If universities are to help society face the issues it does around citizenship and diversity, they need to be ordered in particular ways. Mike Higton considers something of this in his chapter on 'Education and the Virtues'. He opens with: 'For universities to be seats of learning they must be schools of virtue', or at least they must be, he says, 'if they are in any way committed to the exploration of truth for the sake of the common good'. Higton clearly thinks universities should be about the good, or 'living well', to use a phrase he also uses. He does so on the basis of a theological understanding of education based on the Biblical Epistle to the Ephesians, from which he draws, amongst other things, the view that there is a connection between understanding and 'living well'. There is also, for Higton, a connection between living well and the Christian gospel, or 'Learning Christ'. Whilst not all will take that last step and turn to Christianity for guidance, it is, as will be shown in various parts of this book, a common idea that universities are about the good of individuals and society, so there is overlap between a position arrived at from the basis of Christian theology and one more widely held; universities are to seek the good of society.

There is also some commonality around Higton's thesis that if universities are to be about such things, they need to be about discovering the virtues. Not unusually for those who consider the workings of universities from various perspectives, Higton argues that universities need to be about the virtues not only in connection with their impact on wider society, but certain virtues are needed within the academic process if it is to be done well. That means part of being a university is nurturing people in those virtues needed to do the core academic work: patience, honesty, integrity, humility, courage and trust. Whilst such virtues may be seen simply in terms of what is needed to do the work of the university well, they are often 'given a decidedly more ethical cast', seen as 'constituents of a good human life' and associated with 'contributions to the common good', says Higton. As universities help form people in such virtues, they make a fundamental contribution to the good of the world.

The next chapter, from Ford, considers what a religiously plural world might need of its universities. He writes about universities as places of 'public theology' which engage in an 'academically mediated' way with various aspects of the religions. He argues for universities engaging with religious voices speaking into the public realm, with relations between the religions, with the peace of societies which are religiously and secularly diverse and where religious (and other) groups can have good and bad impacts and with the wisdoms the religions can bring to wider society.

Ford argues universities can engage with such issues best if they embrace both religious studies, which considers religions from a variety of academic disciplines, and theology, defined as 'the various ways in which religious traditions do their thinking, pursuing the questions that are important for them, and also the discourses that study this religious thought historically, critically, comparatively, or with a view to contributing constructively to current discussions (including those of public life)'. Universities which embrace both have a rich resource for consideration of religion and its place in society, for they can facilitate both the study of and the engagement between the religions.

Ford continues with recommendations 'distilled from a lifetime of personal involvement in the field' which bring together 'what I consider the main elements of "best practice" that might lead to lively, intelligent and wise university-based public theology'. He argues for universities having departments dedicated to the study of theology, for religion to be studied in other departments also and for universities themselves to be 'religiously literate'. Such universities might, as well as being foci themselves for wise treatment of the religions, also resource the religions for wise engagement in public life. He offers a rationale for university-based public theology based on his own Christian theology, making use of understandings drawn from Christianity of what it is to be a university. In doing so, he invites others to offer their own 'rich theologies'. He concludes with some guidelines for those who have responsibility for shaping the future study of religions in universities, suggesting such study can help create 'wiser religion and wiser understanding of religion in plural societies' and that it can draw on the wisdom the religions themselves have for the good of society.

Chapter 7 is a reminder that there are actually existing Church foundation universities and colleges within the English public higher education system; pieces of lived theology, perhaps. How far are they the sorts of universities and colleges society needs? Two senior managers from such institutions, Elizabeth Stuart from the Anglican University of Winchester and Michael Holman from the Catholic Heythrop College University of London, bear witness to how a Christian foundation can help shape a particular higher education offer. Stuart writes of Winchester as a university which aims to live out its Anglicanism through being committed to 'inclusivity, hospitality and diversity' and through a set of values which the university seeks to live towards. Those values mean the university is committed to, for example, widening participation, Fair Trade and Stonewall. They also shape the style of education on offer. Perhaps key to the latter is that within the education offered at Winchester are the facing of issues about values, ethics, wisdom, creating global citizens, as well as equipping students with the skills needed for work. Stuart gives examples of how that works out in practice. These are themes which fit well with what previous chapters say about the sorts of universities society needs. Stuart also suggests the present policy environment, whilst a stimulus to Winchester to be distinctive, is also a hindrance to an approach based on the values Winchester has adopted.

The second part of Chapter 7 is about Heythrop College University of London. Holman tells the story of the recent history of the college as a small and specialist institution specialising in philosophy and theology. He, like Stuart, finds the marketisation of the sector creates challenges. Holman writes about Heythrop as much as a small and specialist institution as a Church foundation. The difficulties it is presently facing have more to do with the former than the latter. He does speak of how the nature of education offered is shaped by the Catholic foundation. The college offers Church Degrees as well as those from the University of London; it brings theology and world issues into dialogue; it provides 'education for service'; there is a concern for the moral and spiritual development of students alongside the intellectual; and it all happens 'within an active faith community'. In what this says about concern for the world, service and holistic development, it fits well with the themes of earlier chapters. It does not sit easily with current priorities and, sadly, Heythrop is not to continue in its present form. One choice at present open to students will, therefore, be lost to them, as will this particular centre for the study of theology and religious studies, subjects which are, as Ford suggests, rather important at present.

As well as Church foundation universities, there are Islamic higher education foundations in England. Two of them (Markfield Institute of Higher Education and Islamic College of Advanced Studies) have validating relationships with universities. Alison Scott-Baumann and Sariya Cheruvallil-Contractor give us a philosophical and Islamic perspective on what society needs from its universities. They offer a timely reminder of the long intellectual tradition of Islam, which embraces both depth and width of subject areas, which from early days was owned by women and men and which helped to form Western culture, not least through preserving and developing the thought of ancient Greece and Rome through the European Dark Ages. Scott-Baumann and Cheruvallil-Contractor reflect on what has happened to that tradition within Islam, how it is received by the wider community and what place it might have in the university. They argue for a role for the 'faithful voice' in discussions about the nature of society, consider how the voice of Islam is treated, and suggest Islam can help identify issues which need challenging in the contemporary British university with a view to protecting the values of dignity and mutual self-respect that Muslims and non-Muslims hold dear in Western society and universities.

Sadly, the intellectual contribution of Islam is rarely recognised in wider society. A tendency to think and speak (violently) of Muslims as 'the different other' and as a security threat is noted and explored. Government programmes designed to tackle 'extremism' and the impact of those programmes on universities and Muslims are considered out of the authors' extensive work on this area, with knowledge and feeling. The reality of security threats is recognised, as is what Scott-Baumann and Cheruvallil-Contractor describe as, 'in effect . . . religious and often racial profiling', which can stigmatise minority groups and may go unnoticed and unremarked on by the majority. In the light of those threats, what needs to happen, what society needs, the authors suggest, is for universities to be places of debate about difficult issues. Anti-terrorism legislation, the attitude to universities within it, misunderstandings of anti-terrorism guidance and legislation in universities, coupled with the general shifts in higher education policy, and, indeed, trends towards not allowing a platform for speakers on a range of subjects are all making such debate more difficult. Society needs universities which face difficult societal issues but is not always supporting universities in that task. Freedom of speech and academic freedom 'must be protected in a democracy as a unique public and safe space for discussion of difficult subject matter and complex issues'.

Whilst the book is mainly about England, it is important to see the local in the context of the global, for this is an interlinked world facing common challenges. In Chapter 9, Wood, who writes out of great experience of universities in different parts of the world, helps us do that.

He shows how individual universities are part of a global system. Globally, as nationally, the sector is diverse. He illustrates that, including with the help of mission statements from universities in different contexts. The sector is also expanding; 'never before has there been such growth' he says. A significant part of that is the rise of privately funded universities and those he describes as 'mono-subject'.

Universities also face some common challenges across the world. For example, governments tend to see the role of universities as being to support economic growth, and fund them for such, yet such growth may not be sustainable. What is the prophetic role of universities in a world where individuals and governments may need to learn to live with less? Should universities 'teach and motivate' students for a 'future where their quality of life and aspirations will have to be less than we have'? The global context sharpens the questions this book poses about the sorts of universities the world needs.

Wood also shows how universities are global institutions. Students and staff move between universities and countries. Universities are not limited by national boundaries, but have campuses in different countries. Massive global research projects, such as CERN, involve academics from many countries and universities. In some cases, that may mean academics have primary responsibilities elsewhere than in their universities. Open access to data and increased interconnectivity, including in the 'internet of things', mean academics from many institutions and people totally outside the university sector can engage in conversation and research, contributing thoughts and findings into projects. These things mean universities may lose control and become increasingly permeable institutions. Such is the permeability that the very concept of the university may be breaking down. That clearly raises questions for managers. It also raises questions about how universities can respond to societal needs and sharpens questions about ethics, values and responsibilities. Somehow universities still need to be, says Wood as he quotes a previous Vice-Chancellor of Oxford, 'the bulwark against systems of pseudo-knowledge based on unverified sources and fantasies of meaning'. To do that, universities need solid value bases which express what they are about.

A final chapter draws on the themes developed earlier in the book to argue that society needs universities which are about the good of society and individuals. It shows that, whilst there are various views of what it means to be a university, a view that they are about the good keeps re-emerging. That can be seen in history, in contemporary thinking and in the actual work of universities. Today, society faces challenges which universities can help society address. Sadly, contemporary higher education policy, certainly in England, but in other places also, tends not to support universities in such work. Rather, it represents a narrow view of what it means to be a university, focused on serving the economy and social mobility. Whilst both are important in themselves, such a narrow focus may create universities which fail both individuals and societies. There are those, both within and without universities, who are fighting back against that. The final chapter alludes to some of their work. It also puts arguments, including from specifically theological perspectives, for universities which self-consciously seek to offer an education which prepares students for citizenship and tackles the questions the world actually faces, for the sake of the good, that the universities we have might be the universities we need.

Notes

1 In Britain, universities which have their origins in whole or part in institutions founded by the churches or individual Christians include the universities which are part of the Cathedrals Group of Church Foundation Universities (http://www.cathedralsgroup.org.uk/ accessed January 24th 2016) and others such as Durham, Northumbria, Manchester, University College and King's College London. In the case of the founding of University College London, Jews and free thinkers associated with Jeremy Bentham were also involved. More is said about such faith involvements in the final chapter.
2 http://www.ons.gov.uk/peoplepopulationandcommunity/culturalidentity/religion/articles/religioninenglandandwales2011/2012–12–11 (accessed 24th March 2016).
3 Themes I will return to in the final chapter, discussing the difficulties around ideas of the 'good' and illustrating the point about universities seeking the good from various sources.

1 The needs of the world

Susan Durber

How do we know what the needs of the world are? In an amusing and revealing TED talk given in June 2014 in Berlin, Swedish researchers Hans and Ola Rosling revealed to a stunned audience how ignorant about the world most of us really are (TED, 2014). According to their research, most people give less accurate responses than even a random set of answers would be to questions about global issues like economic inequality, literacy rates among women or rates of vaccination for measles. Most of us, they argue, draw conclusions about the world based on our personal prejudices, emerging from our very particular and unrepresentative backgrounds. We, all of us, draw on largely outdated facts, and we often have no idea how to draw generalised conclusions from the few facts that we do know. In short, we have a high level of ignorance. In multiple-choice tests, we perform worse than random (worse, in the Roslings' presentation, than chimps). The Roslings go on to offer their audience advice about 'how not to be ignorant about the world' and point out that those who are going to shape the world for the future need to do so on the basis of knowledge.

But the question of what it would mean to escape ignorance is much deeper than a question about facts, about 'knowing stuff'. If the world is going to find those who can really respond to its needs, we need people who can do more than search for facts, more than those who know how to 'Google'. We need those who can interpret such facts with something like wisdom. The more we think about this, the more we see that 'facts' are never straightforward or objective, that the place where you stand in the world shapes even the facts that you light on or discover and shapes what you do with them and why. A wise person will know that questions about what the world is like cannot be answered alone, but in conversation with others, with those who will see the world from a very different place. Wisdom comes from recognising that the world and its needs look different depending on where you stand. This does not mean that there is nothing we can say together with a degree of confidence, but it does show that finding what we can say and know about the world is more complex than simply 'unveiling the facts'.

There is also a question of authority. Whose voices have authority to speak and to be heard as anyone asks what the world is really like, or what it needs? Can the World Bank answer the question? May the Pope? Do academics and intellectuals really know the answer? Will we find the truth about the world in the writing of poets? Is it those who are in the place where the world hurts most? Will it be those with the broadest global view or those who experience a particular place and context in depth? What about the voices of those who live in poverty? Or the voices of any who claim that their experience, counter to the usual ways of the world, has a particular witness to bring? Do we listen to those who hold power or to those who have little power in this world? Do we listen to our own experience and, if we do, how do we test it against the experience of others? How do we judge between the voices competing for a hearing in the many-layered space of mass communication today? Who can tell us what the world is 'really like'? How will we know, and how will we know that we know?

Most people can tell of moments in their own lives when an experience of meeting another person, or a community, or a different context or place, changed their sense of what it means to live in the world, or at least provided a sense of their own previously, and perhaps always inevitably, partial view. Such experiences don't only teach us different 'facts', give us different knowledge, but they re-shape the frames by which we make sense of the world, the ways in which we deepen wisdom and insight. Many people can also speak of moments in their lives when the 'frame' they had placed around their understanding of the world suddenly changed or the 'lens' through which they had come to see it changed forever. In the field of knowledge and understanding, people sometimes speak of a 'paradigm shift' (Kuhn, 1962), a moment when something radical moves in how the world is understood, when our previous way of looking, thinking and making sense was suddenly overwhelmed, and we see clearly that 'knowing what the world is like' is no simple task.

As a constant reminder of the complexity of knowing what the world is like and what its needs might be, an appendix to this chapter includes some short (fictional) pen portraits of people who sit in very different places around the world. They can hardly be representative, but they can work to alert us constantly to the need to keep wrestling with the 'ignorance' of the world that besets us all, even while we are well intentioned, willing and searching hard.

This chapter will present some reflections on some of the things which, by many accounts, are judged to be the challenges the world is facing at the moment, some of them evident to most people if they think for a moment, but some of them not so immediately obvious. It must be vital, as well as fascinating and compelling, that we constantly work at understanding and interpreting our experience of the world, bringing together witnesses we hope we can trust, to make judgements about what is happening around us and to us and to others, in the hope that the world isn't only happening despite us, but might also be shaped for good. A proper modesty and humility about our own ignorance and partiality might temper what we want to say, but might also better equip us to search well for insight and help us to say some important things about the key issues for the world in which we live so that we might seek to live a good (in the sense of virtuous), engaged and useful human life.

People and population

The world is not only about people, and indeed one of the most significant challenges of our time (in view of what climate change is teaching us) is that wisdom lies in finding a much less anthropocentric view of the world. We need to think about people, but also to find a way of seeing the place of humankind within 'nature' rather differently. This is one response to what has been termed the 'Anthropocene', an age when human beings have the kinds of power which in previous eras were only attributed to gods, the power to destroy even the planet on which we live, to determine the weather and the harvests, the storms and droughts. This in itself makes it all the more important that we notice and consider the pattern of human life on planet earth and our impact on each other, on other creatures and on the natural world itself.[1]

The human population is presently around seven billion, and is forecast to be more than nine billion by the middle of the 21st century and 11 billion by the end of the century (United Nations, 2015a). But it is significant that all the predicted growth is to be within less developed countries and most of it within sub-Saharan Africa (where the population is predicted to triple by 2100). Meanwhile, the population is predicted to decline in Europe, China and Australia, for example (though China is seeking to address this by rescinding the one-child policy, because there are now not enough people to care for the oldest generation). So while there is to be growth in the number of people, it is growth in the numbers of those who are poorest in the world. The predicted increase invites a question about how we can feed that rising population, but the recognition that most of this rise will happen in the poorest parts of the world makes that question more acute. Of the seven billion people in the world right now, about one billion are thought to be undernourished.

Populations are also not only growing (overall and in some particular places), but growing older. By 2050, the number of people over 60 will have doubled. The patterns of ageing are, of course, not uniform around the world, and there are huge differences in terms of life expectancy around the world, but the overall trend is certainly clear. An ageing population is a positive sign in so many ways (testimony to improved health and better living conditions), but also presents challenges since more older people will present new economic demands, change the care needs we have throughout life, the illnesses we fear and the ways in which we die. In some countries, where there is a large young population, there are different challenges. In Malawi, where 65 per cent of the population is under 25 and 45 per cent under 15, we might ask how basic education, let alone higher education, will be provided for those who should have it.

People are also changing *where* they live. An increasingly higher proportion of people, particularly in middle-income countries, now live in an urban environment, and the trend is for more people to move to cities. Many of the world's urban centres are in coastal areas, subject to high levels of risk from rising sea levels. Urban populations are more vulnerable to crime and more dislocated from traditional family structures, networks and support. A movement of populations to cities has consequences about the way we live together as human beings.

Populations in the world today are also, in many places, moving. Migration, its causes and consequences, is one of the biggest issues facing the world today. There are vast population movements within countries as people are displaced by poverty or by conflict. There are also movements from one country to another as people seek to escape from persecution (in places where ethnic or religious cleansing is real) and as people seek what they hope will be a better life. According to Act Alliance, a coalition of church agencies acting to overcome poverty, in 2011, 4.3 million people were displaced by conflict or persecution alone (Act Alliance, 2013). In 2015, as this chapter is being written, it is clear that increasing numbers of people are being displaced by conflict and persecution and also by economic pressures and climate change.

It is not easy to grasp what the trends in human population might mean, especially when presented only in terms of statistics. But sometimes very significant changes come into focus. If we ask questions like, 'What language should our children be learning in school?' we might conclude that, if we simply choose the language most spoken, it would need to be a Chinese language. If we ask, 'Who is a typical Anglican?' we would find that she is a layperson from Nigeria. If we visit El Salvador, we would ask where all the old people are. If we go to Calais, or to Lesbos in Greece or to South Sudan, Iraq or Syria, we will find ourselves moving with people who are seeking a new home.

A question of power

There are many signs at the moment that significant shifts of power are taking place in the world. Most people may be barely aware of them, from day to day, but at moments when we stand back, insofar as we can, and look at the world we are experiencing, something remarkable comes into view.

It can be argued that what is happening is the globalisation of power. Whereas power used to be held by nation states, by democratically elected governments and parliaments, there is now a rapidly increasing sense that the 'greatest' power is not held or held to account there anymore. There are now multinational corporations, for example, which hold total budgets greater than some middle-sized countries. This means sometimes that, however much some nation states want to use their power to shape their life, they find it impossible to do so. Of course, many nations, and an increasing number of them in some contexts (the G20 is now, arguably, the key body in the way that the G8 once was), can still exert considerable power (if they so choose) over markets, international agreements, the regulation of emissions into the atmosphere and the movements of peoples. But at the same time, there are some things that cannot be changed unless key corporations (or organisations) are acting too, corporations that are situated and which act globally. On some key issues, like, for example, tax regulation, there have been calls for a global body to act in that newly global space, but this is being resisted. There is then a lacuna in which power is negotiated and wielded without sufficient accountability. Agreements on many such global issues may happen through world 'treaties', but such agreements are not 'governed' in the same way as in a national space. There is no governance, in the traditional sense, in the global space. Yet we are all increasingly aware that we live in a more connected global space. Whether we think of infectious disease, of financial crises or of the world of children's stories (Disney), the world is becoming much more connected.

The presence of hugely powerful organisations of so many kinds in this often-ungoverned global space reduces the power of the nation state and the citizen, though some will argue that the internet restores or provides another kind of power potentially to each person in the world (see 'A networked world', below). Power seems both more dispersed (across a much broader space) but also further away (always somewhere other and somehow 'higher' than where I live). This has several disturbing effects. It challenges our sense that states should have sovereignty over their own affairs. In many contexts, this new globalisation of power means that people are losing faith in the processes of democracy. If the parliament for which I vote seems to have little or no power to effect change, why should I bother voting? Or, if the parliament for which I vote can only have local power, then would it be better somehow to reinforce the local or the regional and to reassert its power? Is it this feeling that power has moved that lies behind the development in many places of strong nationalist movements, as people rebel? And is it this that leads people to opt out of the traditional ways of participating in and regulating power, and to find new ways of doing so? Much of this feels both destabilising and frightening, as the chance to have a real say over the way life works seems to be diminishing. If power is shifting in the world, if there are new regimes, regimes that no one seems to be controlling or restraining, in ways that put them beyond governance, then people are either alarmed or simply disengaged.

Shifts in power also impact on poverty. Indeed, Christian Aid defines poverty as being rooted in a lack of power, as follows:

> Christian Aid's analysis of poverty is that at its root is lack of power: the power, for example, to have your say and be heard, or to know your

rights and demand them; the power to have access to essential services or to share fairly in the world's resources or to live in the security not only of surviving, but also of thriving . . . Christian Aid is clear that poverty can be eradicated through the empowerment of individuals and communities.

(Christian Aid, 2012, p. 3)

If power is really this fundamental, then major shifts in where power is held are profoundly important. Some shifts and even radical changes in the holding of power could clearly be very welcome indeed for those who are living in poverty. But the changes the world is seeing (or sometimes not noticing) do not very often seem to work in their favour. As it becomes increasingly hard to identify where power is held or how change can happen, the world stands in a fragile place.

Economics

Everyone, it seems, is talking about economics in today's world. Pope Francis, in his most recent encyclical, *Laudato Si* (2015), argues that the climate crisis is in itself a symptom of a broken economic system, one that is destroying nature, one that depends on creating and exploiting human desire for more things, and one that leaves many of the world's people in poverty. Many find it hard to envisage real alternatives to the economic system that is now dominant, though many also argue that it is not 'working'. Even after the financial crisis of 2008, with its many devastating impacts, we are still operating, as a global community, with this same system, even if some try to moderate it and ameliorate its worst effects. Those who benefit from the present global economic system are, unsurprisingly, unwilling to change it, and there is no real consensus about what a true alternative would look like.

The approach you take to the global economy and how it is doing depends on where you sit. At the time of writing, the UK economy is reported to be growing by 0.7 per cent, which might suggest that the present system can deliver growth and prosperity. During the last two decades, the world GDP has nearly doubled, and the volume of world trade has increased fourfold. It is also true that, in recent decades, many people have moved out of extreme poverty. There is now a smaller proportion of people in the world living on less than US$1.25 a day, though extreme poverty of this kind has been much slower to decline in places like sub-Saharan Africa. But this is not the whole story, and there are many who believe that what they refer to as 'neo-liberal globalisation' is killing millions and causing great suffering. For example, the World Council of Churches has been engaged in a long term project called the Economy of Life, which aims to bring together diverse global voices who can speak from very different experiences about the impact of the global economy (WCC, 2014). The writings of Douglas Meeks on economics and theology have been remarkable in bringing into the discussion the experience of those who live in the Global South, those who can speak as those who suffer, as they would argue, at the hands of the present global system. He argues, 'The starting point for economic thinking should be the suffering caused by the present household arrangements. Why can we not see what is before our eyes?' (Meeks, 1989, p. 17).

One very striking thing about the economic landscape in the world most recently is the deepening of extreme inequality. The Oxfam report *Even it Up: Time to end extreme inequality* (2014) brought the deepening nature of global economic inequality to public attention in the UK. An introduction to the report on the Oxfam website (2015) says

> . . . today, just 80 people now own as much wealth as half the world's population, while nearly a billion people can barely afford to feed their families.

And inequality is rising: *the combined wealth of the richest one per cent will overtake that of the other 99 per cent of people next year* unless the current trend is checked.

Such extreme economic inequality is threatening to undo much of the progress made over the past 20 years in making sure millions more people have food on the table, a decent education and health care.

Rising levels of extreme inequality invite reflection, even if your first instinct is not simply to be outraged because such inequality seems fundamentally unfair. Many had thought that economic growth, where it happened, would benefit all of us, that wealth would trickle down. But, in many places, what seems to have happened is that growth has not benefitted those who have least, but has become concentrated in the hands of those who have most. So inequality challenges the success of the economic growth model. Extremes of inequality (by contrast with societies where inequality rates are low) seem to have a number of negative impacts. Inequality makes trust evaporate. It erodes a sense of common purpose. Interaction between increasingly separated and 'unequal' communities becomes more difficult. Inequality is not just about the figures, but about the sense of 'unfairness', resentment and distrust that this creates. Many of the countries in the world with the highest levels of inequality are also those with the highest levels of violence and homicide (there are many examples in Latin America, for example).

Of course, inequality is not a simple notion. Do we mean inequality of opportunity, or inequality of outcome? Does it really matter that a few people have way more than most – particularly if, as some argue, the situation that enables a few to be mega-rich might be the very situation that enables most people to *escape* poverty? Is a little inequality actually necessary to incentivise us? Or are we all better off with less though in a more equal society, than in one where a few have significantly more than most? Inequality is also not simply about some having more money than others. Economic inequality intersects with other inequalities; women comprise half of the world's population and yet are also the majority of those living in extreme poverty today, while two-thirds of the people in the world living in extreme poverty belong to an ethnic minority group in the country where they live. As the world becomes more unequal, there are vital questions to be raised, not only for economists, but for all of us. But it seems increasingly clear that poverty and inequality are so connected that you cannot tackle poverty without tackling inequality.

Most people in the world might want us to find ways to trade, to be creative, to buy and sell, that can bring fullness of life to all our citizens, but at the moment there is a dearth of ideas about how to do this. Many argue that the economic model that now dominates the world is the only one that really works, though others argue that it seems inevitably to produce the kind of extremes of inequality which do not end poverty but rather contribute to it. In the UK, the Department for International Development (DFID) in *Growth: building jobs and prosperity in developing countries* (2007) has claimed that '[e]conomic growth is the most powerful instrument for reducing poverty and improving the quality of life in developing countries'. The Oxfam report *Even it Up: Time to end extreme inequality* (2014) tells a very different story.

Perhaps one of the biggest challenges at present is to find something like a new imagination about economics so that the world can find an 'economy of life' that is sustainable (in the sense of ecologically sustainable) and inclusive of all people, an economics that 'leaves no one behind'. In September 2015, the United Nations, after much consultation and discussion, agreed new Sustainable Development Goals, identifying the steps we need to take as a global community to overcome poverty. These, together, highlight the need for a global economy that can address, amongst other things, inequality and climate change, on the way to 'end poverty in all its forms everywhere'. One of the goals seeks '[d]ecent work and economic growth', but it is clear that all 17 goals taken together seek a nuanced kind of growth that is sustainable and inclusive, and certainly not the kind of growth 'at any cost' that many in the world experience as damaging (United Nations, 2015b).

In contrasting parts of the world the weaknesses of global economics are noticed in different ways. In the poorest countries of the world, people despair of their chances of benefitting from a globalised world that sees cash crops being grown on their land for the benefit of the shareholders of a multinational corporation, while they are unable to grow food for themselves. In many of the middle-income countries, like China, Brazil and India, extreme inequality is what ferments dismay, frustration and unrest. Luxury yachts are moored not far from the favelas where the poorest people live, and street children are still blinded to make them better beggars while, in the same nation, a space programme flourishes. Across Europe, since the financial crisis of 2008, a generation of university graduates has discovered that there are not so many graduate-level jobs for them to go to, that they face limited hopes of living in their own homes any time soon and the prospect of working (if they can find work) much, much further into old age than their parents' generation. A report of the Act Alliance says that 'the benefits of globalisation accrue to a minority of the world's people whilst poverty and social exclusion continue to increase' (Act Alliance, 2013, p. 6).

The real impact of that is now being felt not only in the poorest or the middle-income countries, but in the wealthier countries too. Even where governments can boast about an increase in economic growth, there are those people and communities who see that this will not bring *them* benefit. From the crowds protesting on the streets of Greece to the young unemployed in the UK, from those hungry in South Sudan to those in the rural states of the US, there are countless people in today's world for whom the economic model which dominates the globe is not working. What are we going to do?

Politics

'World politics' is always shifting and provides endless scope for analysis and reflection, let alone participation and activism. But just now there are some apparently seismic shifts, leaving even the few previous certainties being questioned.

What has already been described as a 'globalisation of power' means that many now ask where power really lies. When this deep questioning accompanies growing disillusionment or cynicism about the effectiveness or the morals of many politicians, there develops very quickly a growing disengagement from traditional politics. One of the most popular figures (particularly with young people) associated with the public debate in the most recent UK General Election was Russell Brand, an articulate critic of present politics and politicians who was known for encouraging people not to vote. But this kind of 'malaise' or critique of the traditional electoral system could be contrasted with the high level of engagement in the 2014 referendum about Scottish independence. Was the greater level of engagement here indicative of a desire to have a new 'system' in order to bring about a much more radical kind of change? Ruth Fox writes persuasively about a problem that needs addressing in the UK context, but is no less relevant elsewhere in the world (Fox, 2015).

Political life has changed in many places, partly, at least, because of a more general cultural tendency (in Europe and North America at least) to move away from voluntarist and institutional forms of engagements. Many sorts of institutions (churches, political parties, trades unions) have experienced a decline in membership, and many would argue that this indicates not a decline of interest in faith, politics or justice in the workplace, but changes in the ways we relate to one another. This means that it is hard for politicians, for example, to work out whether their ideas are unpopular or whether their ways of engagement, meeting and acting are no longer effective. It does seem in many places that people are more likely to come to a one-off political rally on a political issue but are less likely to join a political party and go to regular meetings. Looking more widely, we have seen governments around the world brought down not by opposition parties or by democratic process, but by people who had rarely engaged in politics before getting onto the streets. Paul Mason, in his book *Why It's Still Kicking off Everywhere. The New Global Revolutions* (2013), describes the political impact of what he calls 'swarms', eruptions of sudden new popular alliances to express a particular protest or to achieve a particular end but which do not always lead to the establishment of anything like traditional political parties and which can sometimes simply end as swiftly as they began. He uses the events of the Arab Spring, of riots in London and of protests in Greece to illustrate his experience of the ways in which political engagement is changing dramatically across the world. He points out that such political movements and action are not always interested in systemic change, are not powerful enough or structured enough to take on power, and thus can be in danger of being ephemeral acts of gesture politics, powerful for a moment, while those who sustain power over time simply regroup.

Traditional ways of marking political difference are also changing and the old ways of defining political allegiances and their differences are shifting; see, for example, a blog post by Peter Franklin on *Conservative Home*, including a reference to F.M. Esfandiary's fascinating analysis of left/right/up/down (Conservative Home, 2013). What does it mean to talk of 'right/left' when you have someone who is 'Blue Labour'? What does it mean when Green politicians can seem both communitarian (and thus left) and also localist and passionate about conservation (and thus right). There is some fascinating thinking going on about present and potential re-alignments of political 'sides'. In a global context, the former political opponents of the Cold War era are now, even if cautiously, often friends, and allegiances and alliances seem to shift far more quickly and unpredictably.

There is a sense of volatility and unpredictability about the political landscape, in the UK and more globally. Election results, political events and new movements are producing some astonishing surprises (at least by former standards) and political commentators are finding a new vocabulary of astonishment. Disillusionment, perplexity and cynicism in some quarters are unsurprising, but the sense of a world without anchors or markers, a world in which political frustration fuels a potent but often unstructured rage, a world in which radicalism (that might belong at both 'ends' of what is or was the political spectrum) erupts and demands to be understood.

What is apparent, however, is that in a time when we need, as a global community, to act together, our politicians are finding this more difficult to do, and people are finding it more difficult to support them. 'Economic and climatic shocks have increased global risk and insecurity, making co-operation more important. However the impact of these shocks at national levels has tended to force politicians to look inward and to close down the space for decision makers to make the policy compromises necessary for collective action' (Act Alliance, 2013, p. 3).

We need political movements and politicians who will bring together popular voices, political and human wisdom and the power to implement change, and for the common good. Some of the volatile, fearful and often weak alliances we have at present seem ill fitted for this task, though it may be that in the present ferment of new ideas, amidst what looks like the dying phase of an old politics, something new will emerge.

Climate change

Climate change is arguably the most significant challenge facing the world at the moment. We are faced with the challenge of how we may continue to live on earth without destroying it, a challenge made all the more difficult because there are those who cannot, will not or are determined not to see what is happening and why. We do know (as surely as we know that there is a link between smoking and lung cancer) that global warming is happening and that it is being caused by human activity.[2] The impacts of conventional industrialisation and the burning of fossil fuels have meant an unprecedented rise in the amount of carbon dioxide in the air we breathe (now at its highest level for 800,000 years), and our planet is getting warmer. There are already more extreme climate events, rising sea levels, more floods in some places and droughts in others and radical threats to life. As Rowan Williams comments, 'for millions of people around the world, living with this sense of fragility is nothing new. Far from being a vague threat in the distant future, a warming world is very much a present reality, with global temperatures already having risen by 0.8°C since before the industrial revolution' (Christian Aid, 2014, p. 4).

Climate change is also a justice issue for the world, since those who are already bearing the brunt of predicted changes are the poorest people in the world. They are losing their land to the sea as low-lying islands are disappearing below the waves, while crops will not grow as they once did and people become more vulnerable to diseases like malaria because mosquitoes can now survive where once they did not. It is in the coastal cities of the world, where many of the world's urban poor now live, that rising sea levels are becoming most evident. Changing weather patterns are already impacting production and food security in the poorest countries in Africa. It was in the Philippines that the strongest recorded storm ever to fall on land has already destroyed lives. And the people who lived in these places are those least responsible for the changes to the climate.

In many parts of the world, people are already learning to adapt to climate change by growing different crops, rearing different animals, living in different kinds of houses, migrating to a different place or making provision for a future with many more emergencies and risks. This kind of adaptation will, no doubt, become a much more prominent feature of life in an increasing number of places.

But there is also need for a different kind of action to mitigate climate change. The whole international community needs to take steps that will tackle the causes of global warming and prevent further rises in temperature. This can only be done by keeping fossil fuels in the ground and changing to new forms of renewable energy. The world needs a low-carbon future, and of course we can only really achieve this if we can work together as an international community, so that the responsibility to create this future is shared. We need to find ways of making it possible for all the people in the world to have a full and flourishing life, but in ways that do not mean that the world's limited resources will be overused or that the earth will be warmed in such a way that the balance of life will be harmed. This need will not be easily met in a world where communities compete for resources or want to 'race to the top'.

Climate change presents a challenge for a world in which politicians find it hard to act for the common good, for the long term or beyond local or national interest. It is also a challenge when so much power is held in the hands of multinational corporations whose share values are closely related to activities or industries which rely on the exploitation of fossil fuels. But it also represents a challenge for local communities and for individuals, indeed for human life at all levels. Climate change presents us with the effects of the ways in which many of us have lived our lives, imagining ourselves as dominant over what we have learned to call 'nature' (as though we were somehow outside it or over it), and desiring ever more in terms of consumer goods. In his encyclical *Laudato Si*, Pope Francis (2015) describes how we are faced with the need for a radical conversion in politics, in theology, in faith and in living. We need to find not only new international agreements and policies, not only new sources of energy and ways of conducting our economy, but also a new spirituality, a new (or renewed) sense of wonder within creation. The crisis asks us to think again about the most fundamental things of all: who we are as human beings, what we are for and what we might hope for, what we are willing to give and where we belong. For this, we need scientists and politicians, but also poets and priests, prophetic exemplars and those who will help us learn again to contemplate and give thanks.

A networked world

One of the most radical changes to human life in recent decades must be the development of the internet and social media like Twitter and Facebook, a change the implications of which we have barely begun to grasp. There is increasingly a recognition that these developments have not only impacted on our working styles, our abilities to communicate and to share information at speed, but also on the ways in which we relate to one another and thus on what it means to live a human life in today's world. Such technology is not only about the means of communication, but has also shaped what it means to communicate at all.

Manuel Castells, the much-cited sociologist, has spent years reflecting on the interaction between internet use, politics and personal identity. He argues

22   *Susan Durber*

that, because of the internet, we now operate largely in horizontal 'network societies' rather than vertical organisations. Networks are 'flat', instant and accessible. They can be created fast and can also disappear quickly. Many of us are part of many such networks and we can thus enter (and exit) virtual communities at speed and for all sorts of reasons. The internet has also contributed significantly in shaping and effecting globalisation. Though the internet has not yet reached every person in the world, it can be argued that it has significantly influenced and shaped the world that almost everyone lives in and experiences (Castells, 1996).

The workplace in many parts of the world has been transformed by the internet, as many of us become accustomed to working with Skype calls and video conferencing. Having a social media presence now becomes a useful tool for advocacy and for creating movements. But our world has been transformed even more profoundly as people engage, make decisions and expect to access knowledge, information and analysis with speed, not only in working life but in politics, culture, faith and personal life. Many people now might access counselling online or pray using an internet site. Even the world of relationships and sex has changed, as the virtual environment becomes a place to meet or to have cybersex. The political events of the Arab Spring have been much analysed as powerful examples of the role of the internet not only in transforming but also making possible political change (Mason, 2013).

It is commonly accepted that in 15th- and 16th-century Europe, the development of a new technology (the printing press) and radical changes in culture and society (Renaissance and Reformation) were closely interrelated in ways that no one could have seen at the time. The development and dominance of the internet will have had similarly far-reaching consequences, for good and for ill. There is no way back from the internet age, even if we wanted one, but the ways in which it is changing all our lives calls for the deepest reflection.

One book that helped many to reflect on what was becoming of human life in present times was Robert Putnam's *Bowling Alone* (2000). His book reflects on the irony that, though we may all be more 'networked' (and even more so since he wrote the book), we are also more alone. We spend more time watching television, less time playing sports than watching them, not only joining fewer institutions, but participating less in the institutions that we join. Even our benevolence, he argues, has become individualised, as we join fewer collective community projects. His book, with its detailed analysis of patterns of behaviour in millennial US society, reflects back to us a way of living human life that is profoundly changed, at least in some parts of the world. Even understanding this kind of change fully presents a challenge. Are we so networked that we have access to untold amounts of knowledge which could make us wise, or are we so isolated from other human beings because we spend so much time in front of our screens? Are we alone with our localised prejudices, or are we stepping into a global

village? What we make of this and how we respond to it are crucial challenges for humankind.

Difference and identity, sex and gender: being human

In the search for understanding for what the world is really like, it may be
revealing to look where there seems to be most tension and even violence,
to the places where people are shocked or uncomprehending of others, to
the places where we find ourselves at odds for reasons we can barely name.

Though the world is becoming, in many ways, a more global community
with more common narratives, products and experiences, it is also becoming
a more divided place and less tolerant of difference. In some contexts, where
different ethnic groups and faith communities may have lived alongside one
another or with one another for centuries in peaceful co-existence, there is
now open conflict, a reassertion of distinct identity and the persecution of
minority communities. For example, in the ancient city of Alexandria, a
centuries-old cosmopolitan multi-culturalism has been replaced by the assertion of one culture as dominant. What some in the West see as 'the persecution of Christians' in the Middle East is but one face of a world in which
identities have become more starkly significant in shaping citizenship and
providing a basis for exclusion or inclusion. It would be naïve simply to
compare a former romanticised peace with today's violence and tension, and
relationships have always been negotiated, but in many parts of the world
there is a reassertion of a kind of identity politics, both in order to assert
power and to resist being overpowered. Just as the nation state is coming
under question, new national, faith or ethnic identities are being asserted.
There are also struggles going on to define what it means to be a true disciple
of a particular faith, or what it means to have a secular state, or to have a
state religion or to guard the rights of minorities. How does an affirmation
of freedom of speech work with the protection against blasphemy? When do
legitimate critique and satire become crass offence? Who can say what it
means to be a citizen in a particular nation? There are many signs that it is
not becoming any easier to find the place where a peaceful consensus can be
found about what it means to live together for the common good, rather than
to leave people within communities and nations competing for hard and soft
power.

For a while it seemed, in Western Europe at least, that the diverse landscape of different religious faiths in the world would soon be replaced by a
secularised world in which any remaining remnants of religion would be held
firmly, and quietly, in the private sphere. The sociologist of religion Peter
Berger believed, along with many others in the 1960s, that religion would
be replaced by a worldwide secularised culture, though he changed his mind
later. One of the great surprises to many in recent decades has been the
resurgence of faith as an important factor in culture and politics almost
everywhere. The great majority of people in the world claim a religious faith,

and it is well testified that more than 85 per cent of people globally identify with a religious group (Pew Forum, 2015). In the world of global development, for example, there was for some decades an expectation that the trajectory would move from faith-led development to more secular models, but even actors like the World Bank now argue that faith, being a key part of life for much of the world's population, cannot be separated from issues of development. As Katharine Marshall (2007) has argued, faith communities do not only supply lots of 'willing hands' and community contact, but also shape the ways in which life is understood to be good.

Alongside the increasing recognition of the public reality and significance of faith, there is also a sense of incomprehension and, in some places, fear about the rise of what some call religious fundamentalism. Many of the world faiths have those within them who have taken a 'fundamentalist turn' and have formed radicalised communities, which, in some cases, are associated with violence. Such fundamentalism is sometimes understood as one kind of reaction to Western secularism, or as a post-colonial reassertion of identity, or as a consequence of an economic system which excludes so many of the world's populations and thus opens a space for choosing a radically different set of values and practices. But whether faith is seen as a dying form of an old world, or as a resurging phenomenon in what is emerging, it has refused to be extinguished from the public square and continues to shape communities, their values and stories, practices and hopes.

There is also something like a revolution going on about sex and gender, and it is in this area that communities across the world often seem most at odds. There is a worldwide conversation bubbling about what it means to be male and female, what sex is for and how sexuality should be lived, experienced, portrayed and understood. As President Obama prepared to visit Kenya in 2015 and to speak for the rights of lesbian, gay, bisexual and transgendered people, his measured words were listened to carefully, but a march was planned for hundreds of people to walk together naked, 'to show Obama the difference between male and female'. Though the march was cancelled, its rationale is revealing. It is today issues of sexuality that threaten to split world church communities (like the Anglican Communion), and it is sexual mores and behaviour that often now become the presenting cause of the breaking of relations between different faith communities.

It is striking, and in many ways tragic, at a time when so many, particularly women and children, around the world are being exploited in a burgeoning sex industry, that we find it hard to have a fruitful and helpful conversation about sexuality. It is urgent, since gender is the strongest determinant of whether or not a person experiences poverty in today's world, that we find ways to reflect together on the significance of gender and the social norms and powerful forces that shape our understanding. In some places these are difficult, though still urgent, conversations. When issues become 'taboo', when even the vocabulary with which to have a conversation across the world seems absent and yet people are suffering, there is a sign that an urgent task waits.

Concluding reflections

So, how do we know what the world is really like and what the needs of the world really are? We can go to the great 'global issues' of our times, the issues discussed in the newspapers and on the internet, and, of course, we need people who can help us understand those and begin to respond to them. We need those who can help us see something of the 'big picture', the inexorable trends, the causes of suffering around the world, the things that we need as a global family to address. We need those who can show us how the world looks different when we stand in another place, particularly those places where people do not form opinions through their writing or their blogging, where people struggle to lift up their voice, where people live precariously in the world as it is now. We also need those who can help us to imagine things differently, those who can touch our spirits with a new kind of hope, those who can remind us that life is not lived in the analysis of statistics but in the most intimate experiences of our lives, in the moments when we find love and courage. And we need those who are simply good at living, at nurturing families, at enjoying creation (sustainably and justly of course . . .), at contemplating and praying and just being. We need not only knowledge, not only to end our own ignorance, but also to find wisdom.

Living well in such a complex world as this one also demands that we find ways to keep looking, keep asking questions, listening to the testimony of those at the sharp end of this world's systems and problems, keep on looking for what we've missed and might never see from where we sit. The world so often seems to get 'stuck' because we are working with narratives that no longer fit or which we have misunderstood or which most of us can no longer speak.

Onora O'Neill's work on trust (2002) is a good example of someone reflecting on a challenge most of us recognise that we face but find hard to address, a challenge that is both global and personal. We sense that trust has declined; opinion polls confirm this (though of course, in one sense, opinion polls simply collect the intuitions of many), and we wonder what it means. We need those who can help us to understand what underlies the intuition and to help us to think clearly. She argues, for example, that what is important is not so much trust as trustworthiness. What we need in all our communities are those who are competent, honest and reliable. We do not only need those who can help us think, but those who will live out the results of the best thinking, those who will embody and inhabit the best hopes we all have for the world.

William MacAskill (2015) argues that, too often, well-intentioned people do the wrong thing because they are ignorant about what might actually be most effective in changing the world. He argues, for example, that if you want to help more children go to school in Kenya then you don't buy books, but you eradicate worms and other parasites. (We might add that providing toilets for the girls would help too, and that reforming tax regimes in developing countries and in multinational corporations would be even better, so that the government can afford to fund good health and education programmes.) He is right to say that we must be constantly asking questions about the world, searching for truth, even truths that might challenge the vested interests of those closest to us. But of course we also need to be and to nurture the kind of people who will respond readily to truth and knowledge when they find it, people who can see the world with new eyes and who will act out of love and justice. That can never be taken for granted. The world needs not only clever people, not only people with a different vision. It also needs kind people and generous people, people ready to give themselves to and for others, people who are committed to the good of all, people who are trustworthy and who love their neighbours.

Notes

1 See, for example, Northcott (2013).
2 See Christian Aid (2014).

References

Act Alliance, 2013. *The Changing Development Paradigm*. [online] Available at: http://www.cws.org.nz/files/ChangingDevelopmentParadigmPaperACTAlliance.pdf. [accessed December 5th 2015].

Berger, P., 1967. *The Sacred Canopy: Elements of a Sociological Theory of Religion*. New York: Doubleday.

Castells, M., 1996. *The Rise of the Network Society: The Information Age: Economy, Society and Culture* Vol. I. Cambridge, MA, Oxford, UK: Blackwell.

Christian Aid, 2012. *Partnership for Change*. London: Christian Aid.

Christian Aid, 2014. *Taken by Storm*. London: Christian Aid.

Conservative Home, 2013. [online] Available at: http://www.conservativehome.com/the-deep-end/2013/11/heresy-of-the-week-the-battle-for-the-future-is-not-red-versus-blue-but-black-versus-green.html [accessed November 5th 2015].

DFID (Department for International Development), 2007. *Growth: Building Jobs and Prosperity in Developing Countries*. [online] Available at: http://www.oecd.org/derec/unitedkingdom/40700982.pdf. [accessed November 27th 2015].

Fox, R., 2015. Improving the Health of Our Representative Democracy in Sentamu, J., ed. *On Rock or Sand?* pp. 185–212. London: SPCK.

Kuhn, T., 1962. *The Structure of Scientific Revolutions*. Chicago: University of Chicago Press.

MacAskill, M., 2015. *Doing Good Better*. New York: Gotham Books.

Marshall, K., and van Saanen, M., 2007. *Development and Faith: Where Mind, Heart and Soul Work Together*. Washington DC: The World Bank.

Mason, P., 2013. *Why It's Still Kicking Off Everywhere: The New Global Revolutions*. London: Verso.

Meeks, M.D., 1989. *God the Economist: The Doctrine of God and Political Economy*. Minneapolis: Fortress Press.

Northcott, M.S., 2013. *A Political Theology of Climate Change*. Cambridge and Grand Rapids Michigan: Wm B Eeerdmans Publishing Co.

O'Neill, O., 2002. *A Question of Trust*, BBC Reith Lectures. [online] Available at: http://www.bbc.co.uk/radio4/reith2002/. [accessed November 22nd 2015].

Oxfam, 2014. *Even It Up: Time to End Extreme Inequality*. [online] Available at: http://policy-practice.oxfam.org.uk/publications/even-it-up-time-to-end-extreme-inequality-333012. [accessed July 15th 2015].

Oxfam website, 2015. [online] Available at: http://www.oxfam.org.uk/. [accessed July 15th 2015].

Pew Forum, 2015. *The Future of World Religions*. [online] Available at: http://www.pewforum.org/. [accessed November 22nd 2015].

Pope Francis, 2015. *Laudato Si*. London: St Pauls Publishing.

Putnam, R., 2000. *Bowling Alone*. New York: Touchstone.

TED, 2014. [online] Available at: http://www.ted.com/talks/hans_and_ola_rosling_how_not_to_be_ignorant_about_the_world?language=en. [accessed November 22nd 2015].

United Nations, 2015a. Department of Economic and Social Affairs. Population Division. *World Population Prospects, the 2015 Revision*. [online] Available at: http://esa.un.org/unpd/wpp/. [accessed November 5th 2015].

United Nations, 2015b. *Sustainable Development Goals*. [online] Available at: https://sustainabledevelopment.un.org/index.php?menu=1300. [accessed November 5th 2015].

World Council of Churches, 2014. *Report of Theological Consultation on Economy of Life, 27–30 October* 2014. [online] Available at: http://www.oikoumene.org/en/resources/documents/wcc-programmes/public-witness-addressing-power-affirming-peace/poverty-wealth-and-ecology/economy-of-life-an-invitation-to-theological-reflection-and-action. [accessed November 5th 2015].

APPENDIX: Pen Portraits

Manju lives in India and is in her early twenties. She is part of the new 'middle class' and has a university degree. She hopes to find a good job, to contribute to the life of her country and to have a good life for herself and her family. She is Hindu, and her recent marriage ceremony was very traditional. She is also active in campaigning against sexual violence.

Edith lives in the UK, in a residential home, and is in her nineties. She has infrequent visits from her family, who all live a long way from her and have busy lives, and she is lonely. She remembers the time when, post-war, it seemed that life was going to get inexorably better, and she is puzzled that now her savings have been used up, she lives with the most basic standard of care. She also worries that the lives of her children and grandchildren seem to be more precarious than hers has been.

Paulo is ten years old and lives on the streets of Sao Paulo in Brazil. He has no parents that he can remember, but he belongs to a gang which takes care of him and teaches him how to survive on the streets. He already has a knife which he keeps to defend himself, and he looks up to the gang leaders and expects that one day their life will be his.

Regina lives in Sierra Leone and is the head of a large household, which includes her own children and the children of relatives who have died in the Ebola outbreak. She has little education and there are few opportunities for work. She manages to grow a few crops and she is part of a women's co-operative, which gives her access to markets to sell what she grows at a better price. She works almost every waking hour, whether on the land or in caring for her family and running the household.

Dwight lives in the US, is a teenager and spends most of his free hours playing computer games or on social media. When he is at college or at family gatherings, he is on his phone, connecting to 'friends' and groups. He is very sociable on the internet, but finds a face-to-face conversation embarrassing. Most of his knowledge about the world, including sex and friendship, comes from the internet.

Jean is CEO of a multinational corporation and lives, during the working week, in Paris. He is one of 'the 1%', one of the most wealthy people in the world. He works long hours, travels frequently and sees his children on family holidays. He has to work hard to make sure his company is competitive – but he also wants his company to pay good wages in the places where it manufactures and to pay honest and appropriate taxes in the countries where it earns its money.

Fatima is a refugee from Syria, living in a camp in the Lebanon, along with thousands of others. Conditions are bad in the camps, even though they are supported by humanitarian aid from the international community. She is caring for her younger siblings and has no idea what the future will be. She is beginning to wonder whether life wasn't better in Syria, despite the bombings.

Ibrahim lives in a village in Iraq, near the Syrian border. He, with most of his peers, is an agricultural worker. But, for the last seven years, the harvests have failed. He monitors the statistics and the forecasts and is convinced that this is a result of climate change. The people in his village are becoming poorer and more desperate, and some of his friends have been tempted to join ISIS.

Mohammed is a high-flying student at a business school within a prestigious university in Germany. He cares deeply about poverty in the world. Like many of his contemporaries, he's wondering what to do next – whether to get a job that will earn him a big salary so he can be a philanthropist, or train to acquire a skill that might enable him to work with a medical NGO. But now he's distracted, because people on the metro and even some of his fellow students are beginning to avoid him.

2 The higher education policy framework

Peter Scott

Introduction

The focus of this chapter is on the development of policy for higher education from the mid-1980s, when what might be called the 'Robbins settlement' first began to crumble, to the mid-2010s, when the drift towards the growth of more market-oriented forms of higher education has become perhaps an irreversible trend. In these three decades, the United Kingdom developed a truly mass system, in 2015 enrolling 2.4 million students (making the UK one of Europe's 'big four' higher education systems, alongside France, Germany and Poland) with a participation rate nudging 50 per cent of all school leavers (more than half in Scotland) (HESA, 2015). The same period witnessed a revolution in the curriculum of higher education, in terms of entirely new subjects (especially in healthcare, information sciences and management), of new course structures (notably with regard to interdisciplinary courses) and of new forms of course delivery (culminating in the growing popularity of Massive Open Online Courses [MOOCs] but also reflecting the revolution in communication technologies and communicative cultures represented by the rise of social networking). It also saw a revolution in research, in extent and depth, in productivity and in performance, with the result that, on most measures, the UK is second only to the United States in standing and esteem. All these, beneficial, changes reflect the impact of 'policy' in its widest sense, national initiatives, institutional strategies and also the deliberate action of disciplinary and professional communities.

There have been other, arguably less beneficial, impacts of 'policy'. Higher education in 2015 is a much more closely managed system than it was in 1985, let alone in the mid-1960s at the time of the 'Robbins settlement'. At a national level, colleges and universities are increasingly seen as responsible for 'delivering' politically determined agendas – for example, meeting the skills needs of a global 'knowledge economy' or focusing on students as 'customers' within a higher education marketplace and also emphasising the social and especially economic 'impact' of research, perhaps at the expense of more speculative and scholarly activities. At institutional level, a more clearly demarcated management cadre has developed, necessarily so because the scale and complexity of institutions demand more sophisticated professional management and a stronger sense of strategic direction. But this 'new management class' has also been criticised for espousing an ideology of 'managerialism' that is regarded by some as incompatible with more traditional collegial values (and which has legitimised a new language of 'modernisation', 'performance' and 'targets'). Higher education in 2015 is also subject to more intensive controls, despite the rhetoric of the 'market', and also more intrusive surveillance. New information systems provide the tools, with the development of performance indicators such as the National Student Survey (NSS) or the Research Excellence Framework (REF) and also of management information systems (MIS) which now allow institutional managers to exercise an enhanced degree of internal control. However, in this respect higher education is far from unique. Nor is the UK unique. Alongside the more familiar idea of the 'knowledge society' has developed the parallel idea of the 'audit society', powered by information systems but also reflecting a more fundamental erosion of professional autonomy and, more fundamentally still, trust (Power, 1997; Engwall and Scott, 2013).

'Policy', therefore, has many faces. It is historically and culturally contingent and often ambiguous and even contradictory in its intentions (and especially effects). For that reason, any claim that it represents a consistent and cumulative flow of change is generally a post-hoc reconstruction. 'Policy' is also multi-lateral and multi-layered, with many different and often competing actors. Even at the national level there are many actors – Whitehall Departments (among which the department responsible for higher education, at the time of writing the Department for Business, Innovation and Skills [BIS] has never been among the most influential), a plethora of agencies (notably, of course the higher education funding councils but also organisations such as the Quality Assurance Agency for Higher Education [QAA]) and, of course, the Scottish and Welsh governments. There is a less strongly articulated regional dimension, although it can still be influential. The major source of funding for the merged University of Manchester came from the (former) Regional Development Agency (RDA), and most universities work closely with Local Enterprise Partnerships (LEPs), which replaced RDAs (Scott, 2014b). Finally, much 'policy' is made at the institutional level, directly through the strategic choices made by universities and indirectly by the ways in which they choose to implement national policies. It would also be highly misleading to imagine that, even at the national level, 'policy' is properly co-ordinated. The most significant example of lack of coordination has been the competing agendas of the Home Office and BIS on visas for international students, the former focused on restricting immigration and the latter eager to promote the internationalisation of higher education (in particular, the recruitment of international students).

This is the first qualification that must be made in any discussion of 'policy' in higher education: it can never be a tidy business. The second is that 'policy' must be seen in its wider context. The French historian Fernand

Braudel made a famous distinction between what he called *histoire événe-mentielle*, in other words, political history (and, by extension, policy making), and the *longue durée*, the deeper changes in social and economic structures and cultural practices which may proceed at a much slower pace but have more fundamental effects. This is clear with regard to higher education in the UK in three important respects:

- It is impossible to imagine the development of mass higher education in the absence of the comprehensive reorganisation of secondary education a generation before. This, of course, could be regarded as the effect of 'policy' – but 'policy' that had little regard for its future impact on higher education and maybe also catch-up 'policy' that merely reflected the radical changes that were already taking place in post-war British society.
- It is equally impossible to imagine mass higher education without the important changes in the structure of the labour market that have taken place over the past half century – the expansion of the public sector with its growing appetite for professional skills (for example, in education and healthcare) but also the development of new para-professional, creative and entrepreneurial occupations.
- The same can be said of the impact of cultural change. Perhaps the single most important influence on the development of higher education has been the radical shift in attitudes to gender roles and aspirations. Without feminism, in a broad sense, it is impossible to imagine contemporary higher education in the UK. Expansion has been fuelled above all by the increasing enrolment of women, now the majority. But other, more diffuse, cultural influences can also be observed. Their cumulative effect is that the UK has become a 'graduate society', which raises serious questions about the status and prospects of non-graduates.

Only some of these far-reaching changes can be attributed to deliberate 'policy'. It is important, therefore, to recognise that some of the most powerful forces that have shaped higher education are not the product of higher education 'policy' but other forms of 'policy' and even structural changes that 'policy' has struggled to reflect, often belatedly.

Setting the scene

The 'Robbins settlement', named, of course, after the report of the 1963 Committee on Higher Education chaired by Lord Robbins, consisted of several ingredients: recognition that higher education in the UK constituted a national (and largely publicly funded) system rather than unco-ordinated university, local authority and voluntary college sectors; belief that, within this system, colleges and universities should enjoy the highest degree of autonomy consistent with their status as public (and publicly funded) institutions; attachment to liberal forms of higher education while recognising the claims of professional and vocational education; and, perhaps most significant of all, that the number of student places should be expanded to meet the demand from all those who wished and were qualified by their aptitudes to enter higher education (Robbins, 1963). Almost immediately the 'Robbins settlement' had been modified by the development of the dual or binary system, which distinguished between the 'autonomous sector' comprising universities and the 'public sector' comprising newly established polytechnics and the remaining colleges. Robbins had assumed instead that expansion would be accommodated by establishing more new universities or promoting the leading colleges in the local authority and voluntary sector. However, the extent to which the binary policy was a deviation from, or even repudiation of, the 'Robbins settlement' remains unclear. It has been argued that, in its essentials, it was a reinforcement, endorsing the need for a national system dominated by large multi-faculty institutions, whatever their titles or missions (Scott, 2014a).

However, from the start, it was doubtful whether this 'Robbins settlement' could survive. The rapid expansion of student numbers and the greatly increased public expenditure required to sustain this expansion made it unlikely that the traditional autonomy of the universities, buffered as they were from the political world by the arm's-length 'buffer body' the University Grants Committee (UGC), could be maintained. The moment of truth came in 1981, when the newly elected Conservative Government under Margaret Thatcher imposed deep cuts on university budgets. This was the last time that the UGC was able to take decisions without regard to wider political priorities (or even reference to Ministers). This was never to happen again. Even earlier, politics had intruded on the autonomy of the universities when in the Labour Government of the 1960s the Secretary of State Anthony Crosland – author, of course, of what was perceived to be the 'anti-university' binary policy – required universities to charge higher fees for international students and a little later when Shirley Williams rather delicately proposed her '13 Points' for reform. These were largely spurned at the time but, as it later turned out, proved to be an accurate road map for future policies imposed on the universities as their autonomy began to crumble later.

It was also equally unlikely, once the idea of a national 'system' of higher education had been accepted, that the role of local education authorities could be maintained, nationalisation (however gentle) and localism (except in terms of apolitical delivery of national objectives, the sense in which it is now predominantly interpreted) being incompatible principles. From the start, the new polytechnics were on a trajectory to become national institutions that could no longer be confined within the civic settings in which their antecedent colleges had been developed. Of course, it was not a coincidence that at very much the same time the independence of local government began to be subordinated to the centralising powers of Whitehall, as the independent spirit of the great cities and county councils was curbed.

There was an attempt to square the circle in the 1980s when the National Advisory Body (NAB), a cumbersome national-local agency, was established. But, while NAB enjoyed substantial success in terms of the development of detailed policies (many of which, in fact, have been carried forward), this ungainly experiment had to be quickly abandoned. Again, it is no coincidence that the same legislation – the Education Reform Act of 1987 – abolished both the NAB and the UGC. The traditional autonomy of the universities, with politicians kept at arm's length, and the maintenance of local higher education, independent from and potentially at odds with Whitehall, had both become anachronisms. In a short period during the 1980s, these two pillars of higher education, its guiding principles which had hitherto gone unchallenged, were abruptly abandoned. It is tempting to attribute this abandonment to the particular ideological intentions of the Thatcher government, and certainly its determination to demolish the social-democratic Butskellite post-war settlement played its part (Scott, 1989). But a more sober analysis suggests that this policy trajectory was driven by more fundamental forces, some of which had been unleashed by the very expansion and systematisation that the 'Robbins settlement' had espoused, blind perhaps to their irreversible implications (Shattock, 2012).

Between the mid-1980s and mid-1990s, a new policy environment emerged. It had three major characteristics, all radical departures from past practice:

- The first was a substantial increase in the power of the state to 'steer' the expanding higher education system. It was during this period that the decisive frontier to mass higher education was crossed. The replacement of the NAB and the UGC first in 1988 by two separate funding councils, the Universities Funding Council (UFC) and the Polytechnics and Colleges Funding Council (PCFC), and in 1992 by the Higher Education Funding Council for England (HEFCE), provided the instruments. The new councils lacked the independence of the UGC, although it has been argued that, unlike the UGC, they had statutory foundations. All were subject to the direction of the Secretary of State. During this period, a kaleidoscope of new funding mechanisms was pioneered, with rewards for reducing unit costs in an abortive experiment by the UFC and a long-lasting system of 'core' plus 'margin' funded places developed by the PCFC. HEFCE was obliged to cap overall student numbers to curb the rising curve of public expenditure by imposing so-called maximum aggregate student numbers (MASNs) for each university, while developing yet another funding formula (which was frequently revised). Their details are perhaps less important, certainly three decades later, than the fact that the funding of higher education was now determined by explicit formulas that reflected higher-level political objectives. Funding *systems* and central *steering* were now dominant.

- The second was a proliferation of new pressures to hold higher education to account or instruments designed to preempt such pressures (which, in the end, amounted to much the same). In its dying days, the UGC had introduced a formal system for assessing research, the forerunner of the Research Assessment Exercise (RAE) and now the Research Excellence Framework. Quality assurance of teaching in higher education also now reared its head. A (voluntary) Academic Standards Unit (ASU) was introduced in the universities in a feeble attempt to match the heavy-handed regime of HM Inspectors (now Ofsted) which still prevailed in the polytechnic and college sector. There now occurred a convergence between the two sectors, as the universities were forced to accept that the ASU lacked credibility and the polytechnics (and a few larger colleges) were allowed to award their own degrees (previously their degrees had been awarded through the Council for National Academic Awards [CNAA], although in practice, they had already come close to degree-awarding). With the ending of the binary system, a new body, the Higher Education Quality Council (HEQC) was established, later replaced by the Quality Assurance Agency (QAA). Again, the details of these shifting quality assurance regimes matter less than the establishment of the principle that academic standards – and, by extension, standards of teaching, curriculum design and assessment – should be subject to some form of external scrutiny – even if that scrutiny was exercised, as research assessment was, largely through peer review. The 'quality industry' was launched.
- The third was the creation of a unified higher education system in which the former, and formal, distinction between universities, the so-called 'autonomous sector', and polytechnics and colleges, the 'public sector', was abandoned. This third characteristic was perhaps less far-reaching than the first two, although it appeared to be more dramatic. Technical but important differences in governance remained, with the universities retaining their Royal Charters and the polytechnics being established as statutory corporations. It continues to be argued whether these differences have been reflected in distinctive organisational cultures, notably the balance between collegiality and 'managerialism'. Important status distinctions remained; they may even have been exacerbated because it could no longer be tenably argued that all universities were equal (and the establishment of a unified system coincided with, and maybe stimulated, an explosion in branding and marketing). Separate Scottish and Welsh funding councils were established – before, of course, the reestablishment of the Scottish Parliament and National Assembly of Wales. By these, no doubt unintended, means, a powerful centrifugal momentum was created, leading to the *de facto* splintering of UK higher education into three (or four, if Northern Ireland is counted) sub-systems. Finally, the pattern of institutions remained essentially unchanged when the binary system was abandoned. Indeed, that pattern remains essentially

unchanged today and still reflects the pattern established in the 1960s half a century ago (Oxbridge and the existing civic and red brick universities, the 'new' universities such as Sussex and Warwick, new technological universities based on the former colleges of advanced technology [CATs] such as Bath and Surrey and the former polytechnics, now labelled the 'post-1992' universities).

By the early 1990s, the 'Robbins settlement' had been substantially modified in these and other respects. As has already been suggested, these changes may have flowed inexorably from some of the essential characteristics of that 'settlement'. In retrospect, they seem inevitable. But their cumulative effect was to transform higher education in the UK in ways that were contrary to its spirit. In a very real sense, the 'public sector' won out over the 'autonomous sector' because by the 1990s this distinction had ceased to possess much meaning. All higher education institutions were now treated as if they were part of the 'public sector'. As a result, the policy agendas developed by the NAB and PCFC and the organisational and management cultures of the polytechnics came to predominate in the newly unified system. The state came increasingly to regard colleges and universities as 'delivery' organisations. National policy became more directive and interventionist. The tradition of academic (self) governance atrophied, except perhaps in Oxford and Cambridge. Managerial structures were everywhere strengthened, even in these two universities.

Dearing to Browne

This new policy landscape lasted, in its essentials, from the mid-1990s until the market-oriented reforms initiated by the Conservative–Liberal Democrat Coalition Government in the White Paper of 2011 (BIS, 2011). Indeed, even after these reforms, it has continued to represent the context within which both many national policies and institutional behaviours have been shaped. Whether the Green Paper published in the autumn of 2015 and subsequent White Paper published in May 2016 will initiate more far-reaching reforms that represent a clear and irreversible rupture is not clear at the time of writing (BIS, 2015; BIS 2016). This decade and a half, of course, was the age of New Labour, first with Tony Blair as Prime Minister and then under his successor, Gordon Brown. Policy in higher education, as in most other areas, was deeply marked by the motifs of New Labour rule: a restless search for 'modernisation' (not to reject but to restore the welfare state by reinvigorating the public sector); an enthusiasm for 'improvement' coupled with an emphasis on 'performance' (expressed in – deliberately provocative? – corporate language and powered by new cults and tools of 'measurement'); a distrust of traditional public bureaucracy and a willingness to experiment with quasi-market mechanisms (although without abdicating overall political direction and control); but also a sustained commitment to substantially increasing levels of public expenditure and investment (made possible by the dynamic and less regulated economy which had, it was hoped, relegated the old cycles of 'boom and bust' to the dustbin of history).

In higher education, the New Labour era was book-ended by two reports: the *National Committee of Inquiry into Higher Education* chaired by Lord Dearing, which reported in 1997 and attempted to reproduce the breadth, depth and rigour of the Robbins report more than 30 years before (Dearing, 1997), and the *Independent Review of Higher Education Funding and Student Finance* chaired by Lord Browne, which reported in late 2010 but made no serious attempt to continue this grand Victorian 'blue books' tradition (Browne, 2010). Intriguingly, both reports were commissioned by outgoing governments, Conservative and Labour, respectively, and implemented by their successors, Labour and Coalition. This may suggest that party-political differences have played a more limited role in shaping higher education policy than rhetoric and commentary have suggested.

Dearing made a raft of recommendations, most of which clearly represented 'good practice' within higher education and (mostly) were not regarded as hostile – or particularly challenging – to the values and beliefs of most people in colleges and universities. The report was a masterful exercise in consensus and compromise. However, it did propose a move away from funding higher education almost entirely from general taxation and towards some form of cost-sharing between taxpayers and students/graduates. The new New Labour Government seized on this to (re)introduce tuition fees, initially set at £1,000 a year, although on a different basis to that envisaged by Dearing. However, this apparently radical departure from the principle of 'free' higher education appears to have been largely motivated by the urgent need to increase the funding of higher education which had languished during the dog days of John Major's Conservative Government (Scott, 1994). This motivation remained uppermost five years later, when fees were increased to a maximum of £3,000, a move which revealingly produced the biggest back-bench revolt during the New Labour period (on a larger scale than the revolt against the Iraq war).

As a result, the resources available to higher education increased more rapidly than in any post-war decade apart from the 1960s, when of course the sums involved were very much smaller. This investment not only paid for a substantial rise in student numbers (even if Tony Blair's 50 per cent participation was never quite achieved), but also an equally impressive increase in UK higher education's research base (on which its current high rankings in global league tables is largely based) and also the buildings that characterise contemporary campus-scapes (and replaced the ageing physical infrastructure of the 1960s and 1970s). New Labour largely delivered the publicly funded modernisation of higher education it had promised.

New Labour had other policy preoccupations, although many of these can be traced to the decision to reintroduce fees. One was an emphasis on 'widening participation' by ensuring that under-represented and under-privileged social groups had readier access to higher education. Some, generally critics, attributed this to a traditional Labour desire to engage in 'social engineering'. More plausible interpretations emphasised instead strong links to the skills agenda, the drive to produce a more highly skilled (and, in particular, technologically savvy) workforce to meet the challenges of a global and increasingly knowledge-based economy and also the need to make fees politically acceptable by addressing perceptions that poorer students might be discouraged. To combat any such disincentive, a (state-owned) Student Loans Company (SLC) was established and all full-time students were entitled to receive affordable loans to pay their fees, reproducing the subsidy to middle-class students about which critics of a tax-funded higher education system had frequently complained. The Office for Fair Access (OFFA) was established after fees were increased to £3,000, and institutions charging these higher fees were required to demonstrate their commitment to widening participation through a formal access agreement with OFFA, for similar reasons.

It is probably fair to say that this laudable objective was frustrated in the sense that the gap between the most and the least privileged social groups in terms of access to higher education remained essentially unchanged. But in the face of increasing inequality of income, a feature characteristic of all advanced free-market societies over the past 40 years, and shifting class structures, it is difficult to envisage a different outcome. Perhaps without New Labour's drive for 'widening participation', things would have been even worse.

A second preoccupation was to make higher education more accountable. In general terms this reflected New Labour's focus on 'modernisation', 'improvement' and 'performance'. But it also had more specific objectives:

- One was a desire to improve the information available to students. Although students were not yet regarded as full-blown 'customers', as they were to be after 2010, there was a heightened sensitivity about their reaction to paying fees. As a result, it was believed they were entitled to better information about what to expect – the germs of the contemporary focus on the 'student experience' – and also the likely benefits – to enable them to make better informed choices about courses and subjects and also to assess the 'value for money' of a higher education. Key to this was an emphasis on better teaching, then and now regarded as the poor relation of research in higher education. An early experiment to boost teaching was to establish Centres of Excellence in Teaching and Learning (CETLs). A later, more overtly consumerist, policy initiative was to introduce the annual National Student Survey (NSS) as part of an overhaul of the rather opaque and inward-looking quality assurance systems that had grown up since the 1990s (and remains very much work-in-progress).

• But also important was the drive to make higher education accountable to the state for the very large sums of public, and quasi-public, money that New Labour had made available. The general approach came to be characterised by the principle of 'something for something', in other words, the benefits of this large-scale investment had to be demonstrated (not least to secure further investment). A less beneficial side effect was the proliferation of earmarked funding initiatives for which institutions had to bid; these came to be stigmatised as 'jam-jar funding' and tended to erode the capacity of institutions to make their own strategic choices.

A third preoccupation, which has already been mentioned, was to make higher education more relevant. The focus on linking higher education more closely with the world of work, of course, was not new. The Robbins Report, despite its wider educational vision, had acknowledged its importance. The line of policy initiatives stretches back to the Enterprise in Higher Education (EHE) programme in the 1990s, and even earlier – and forwards, of course, to the contemporary emphasis on 'employability'. But, although lip service (and perhaps more) was always paid to the wider social benefits and civilising effects of a higher education, the focus on its economic outcomes tightened with every passing decade whichever party was in power – whether meeting national skills shortages or improving the rates-of-return for individuals. Tony Blair's 50 per cent participation target, often but perhaps wrongly interpreted exclusively in terms of a drive for social equity, was really based on hard-headed projections of the demand for graduate skills in the future work force. A decade and a half later, that demand remains unmet in key sectors, despite suggestions that many graduates are now employed in 'non-graduate' jobs.

Certainly, the focus on the utility of research in higher education was intensified. Gordon Brown, then still Chancellor of the Exchequer, gazumped a low-key reform of the existing Research Assessment Exercise and announced that the RAE would be replaced by a Research Excellence Framework (REF), although this was not strictly a decision for the Treasury or even the government, but the funding councils. The key change was that, for the first time, 'impact' would be measured – and rewarded. The detailed implementation of this new requirement by the funding councils may have muted its effects; certainly, there was no pronounced trend towards rewarding applied and translational research as a genre. But, in the longer term, 'impact' has been absorbed into the lexicon of higher education policy.

Labour went down to defeat in the election of May 2010, to be replaced by a Conservative–Liberal Democrat Coalition. But much of the architecture of the market-oriented reforms with which the latter has been associated, and many of its instruments, such as the SLC, OFFA and NSS, had already been put in place by New Labour. New Labour had also established the Committee on Student Fees and Funding under Lord Browne, which when it reported in October 2010 was regarded as the catalyst for these wide-reaching reforms. As a result, claims that these reforms represented a 'paradigm shift', the phrase used by Lord Browne at the press conference introducing his committee's report, need to be treated with some caution.

White Paper to Green Paper

Nevertheless, the Browne Report and the White Paper of the following summer were widely perceived to mark a new beginning in higher education policy. Their effect may well have been exaggerated because they appeared to confirm, in stark and even ideological terms, the overall direction of travel of earlier reforms. How much they added to these reforms is a matter for debate. Not as much, perhaps, as both their sponsors and detractors claimed. Although hardly a bolt from the blue, they succeeded in raising the consciousness of the wider higher education community. Reforms, which previously had been regarded as essential (if sometimes uncongenial) adjustments to shifting political realities, coalesced after Browne and the White Paper into a coherent, and threatening, policy discourse. Many people in higher education, ironically in particular from the elite universities least affected by these reforms, suddenly saw the future – and they did not like what they saw.

It is important, therefore, to separate the detailed proposals made in the Browne Report, as modified in the subsequent White Paper, from their shock-and-awe effect (Callender and Scott, 2013). It is also important to recognise that many of Browne's key recommendations were rejected by the incoming government. Browne had recommended that there should be no cap on the fees institutions could charge, but suggested the income generated by fees above £9,000 a year should be 'taxed' at an increasingly onerous (and, above £15,000, at a near-confiscatory) rate to fund national scholarships. This was rejected by the government, which imposed instead an absolute cap of £9,000. This has generally been attributed to the influence of the Liberal Democrats who had promised in their manifesto for the General Election to abolish fees entirely. But it also reflected a general nervousness across the whole government, which was all too aware that £9,000 fees would be the highest charged in any public system of higher education in the world. Ministers also clung to the hope that the £9,000 cap would be a maximum with many institutions charging less.

Browne also recommended that HEFCE, OFFA, QAA and the Office of the Independent Adjudicator (OIA) should be replaced by a single Higher Education Council (HEC). This too was rejected. The main reason appears to have been this change would have required primary legislation, an unattractive prospect for a government with divided political loyalties (intensified by the widespread perception that higher education legislation, especially if it was associated with increased fees, was likely to produce more complications than benefits). But another factor was that, the more attention was paid to the details of establishing an HEC, the more complexities appeared, including conflicts of interest that would have to be resolved. In the end, the game did not seem worthwhile.

The White Paper, therefore, was both a fudge and a compromise (BIS, 2011). It did increase fees to £9,000. But they were capped at that amount. Also, to sweeten the pill, the repayment terms on the loans taken out by students to pay these higher fees were eased and, for the first time, a minority of part-time students were made eligible for loans to pay their tuition. But these compromises had serious, if unintended, consequences. First, the easing of repayment terms reduced any market pressure exercised by students to encourage institutions to charge less than the maximum allowed; the small number of institutions that initially charged less than £9,000 secured no market advantage – and, almost certainly, suffered instead market oppro-brium because their decision to charge less was regarded as evidence of lack of confidence in the quality of the higher education they offered. The second consequence, a direct effect of the first, was that the cost of student loans, still derived from public resources even if 'off-balance sheet', increased sub-stantially and, because the repayment terms had been eased, the proportion that was likely to be recovered from graduates, the Resource and Accounting Budgeting (RAB) charge, fell from more than two-thirds to barely half (Thompson and Bekhradnia, 2013). For a government committed to curbing public expenditure to reduce overall public debt, this was a serious matter. The alarming prospect of graduate debt ballooning to consumer-debt pro-portions, as has already occurred in the United States, opened up. When a majority Conservative Government came to power after the 2015 election, this issue was – partially – addressed by freezing the threshold above which graduates begin to pay back their loans.

The third, and perhaps most serious, unintended consequence was that the increase in fees has dealt a devastating blow to part-time students, which their partial eligibility for loans has been unable to mitigate. In most cases, fees for part-time students were increased in line with full-time student fees. Even when institutions aimed to support part-time courses, upward market pres-sures were strong. The only way to protect part-time courses by keeping fees (relatively) low was to cross-subsidise from the higher income generated by fees paid by full-time students, now of course more sensitive than ever about the quality of their courses and the resources allocated to support them. As a result institutions had limited room for manoeuvre, and overall the number of part-time students in English higher education declined by 35 per cent, from 823,000 in 2010–11 to 536,000 in 2013–14. At first sight, the impact of £9,000 fees on demand from full-time students was limited, a fact seized on by Ministers to accuse their critics of scare-mongering. But it was far from negligible. The total number of students in English higher education, despite the demographic tail-wind of increasing numbers of 18-year-olds, also fell, although less precipitately, from 2.1 million to 1.9 over the same period. To put this in historical perspective, this was the first significant decline in the number of students since the middle of the last century.

The 2011 White Paper introduced other market-oriented reforms. Institutions were now required to publish more detailed data about entry standards, progression and employment rates – so-called Key Information Sets (KIS). The intention was to make students, faced with paying much higher fees, better-informed 'consumers'. The effect, however, appears to have been to provide additional data for media-generated league tables. As a result, the additional 'information' available to students, their parents, advisers and subsequent employers was heavily filtered through these league tables – an outcome that more enthusiastic supporters of a higher education 'market' did not regret.

Efforts were also made to encourage more 'alternative' providers to the existing public higher education institutions. The entry threshold was lowered, but many of the obstacles, in particular to securing degree-awarding powers where a 'track record' of successful graduation was still required, were retained. As a result, only a small number of 'alternative', generally for-profit, providers entered the market. Notable among them were BPP University College (latterly University), a subsidiary of the American Apollo Group, which also owned Phoenix University, the renowned but also notorious leader of the pack of US for-profit providers; and the University (formerly the College) of Law, now owned by a hedge fund. Both, in common with most 'alternative' providers, have focused on high-level training in vocational and professional fields. More traditional 'alternative' providers have been in shorter supply, although Regents College (now University) is a not-for-profit institution on the American model, and the New College for the Humanities has been an interesting experiment in establishing an elite high-fee liberal arts college. A third group of 'alternative' providers has been composed of for-profit colleges teaching mainly non-degree courses such as Higher National Diplomas (HNDs), an example of which is the Greenwich School of Management (also owned by a hedge fund). However, the development of such 'alternative' providers has been inhibited by two concerns. The first is that many recruit a large number of overseas students, which has run up against the government's determination to reduce immigration (in the total of which, unwisely, international students are included) and its increasingly tough attitude to visas for these students and also to institutions that appear as a conduit for immigration. The second concern is that some private colleges have allowed students to access SLC finances without adequate scrutiny of their attendance or completion rates, which has attracted the attention of the House of Commons' Public Accounts Committee, as the guardian of the proper expenditure of public money.

Frustrated by the meagre results of the White Paper's attempt to stimulate the development of a 'market' in higher education, and in particular of variation in fee levels, in 2013 the government decided to loosen controls on the total number of students that could be enrolled and the de facto allocations that had been made to individual institutions. Initially, institutions were allowed to recruit students with 'good' entry qualifications (A grades at

A-level subsequently extended to As and Bs) without limit. From 2015–16, student number controls, on all students, regardless of their entry grades, were removed. On the one hand, this was a radical move, because student numbers have been controlled since at least the 1990s at the behest of the Treasury, concerned about the overall cost of higher education, and in practice for much longer because the original universities were only prepared to increase student numbers if they received equivalent funding in order to protect the unit-of-resource per student, and student numbers in the polytechnics and colleges had been controlled by a variety of mechanisms. On the other hand, the fact that since 2010 overall student numbers have been in the doldrums has left little scope for substantial variation in growth rates between different types of institution, which was the government's plain intention, to reward success (and reputation) and punish failure (although almost certainly the Treasury acquiesced in the removal of student numbers because overall demand for places has been weak). If student numbers had been growing as rapidly as they did between the mid-1990s and 2010, the effect of removing the student number cap would probably have been much greater.

The 2015 General Election has ushered in a new phase, in which the now majority Conservative Government is attempting to remedy some of the deficiencies in the design and implementation of the 2011 White Paper. In the autumn of 2015, the new Minister, Jo Johnson, published a Green Paper (BIS, 2015) and eight months later a White Paper (BIS, 2016). After the 2011 White Paper, because of the vagaries of coalition government, legislation was avoided. Second time round the new Conservative Government was in a stronger position and did not duck the legislative challenge.

Three features of the Green and White Papers stand out:

1   The first is the proposal to establish a Teaching Excellence Framework (TEF). The desire to create some instrument that would oblige higher education institutions to afford the same recognition to teaching that they give to research has been a long-standing political objective, regardless of the paucity of evidence to support the primary allegation. Nor are the proposals for the – initial – implementation of the TEF especially radical or threatening. TEF gradings will depend at first on the broad judgments made by the QAA in institutional audits, although at a later stage more developed metrics will be used. But, even then, the metrics will cover familiar territory, such as entry grades, completion rates, employment data and the like; it is far from clear that it will be possible to develop more sophisticated measures of 'value-added' or 'learning-gain'. However, in two respects the TEF has more radical implications. First, it will represent the first sustained attempt by politicians to get 'inside' the higher education curriculum – three decades after similar intervention in the school curriculum. The 'measurement' to which Ministers aspire will not be possible without some form of

standardisation of the curriculum. This represents a radical departure – and, some would argue, an unacceptable intervention in the freedom of universities (and also a doomed one, because unlike in schools, the higher education curriculum is necessarily open, indeterminate and evolving to keep pace with advances in scientific knowledge and human understanding).

2   The second is the decision to abolish HEFCE, OFFA and OIA and replace them by an Office for Students (OfS). In one sense, this goes back to the Browne committee's recommendation to establish an HEC, although the latter was clearly intended to be a successor-body to HEFCE (unlike the OfS, which has very different functions). But in two other senses it marks a rupture with the past:

- First, with the abolition of HEFCE the OfS will take over its learning and teaching responsibilities, the most important of which is the direct funding for high-cost subjects, notably science, technology, engineering and medicine (STEM) subjects and strategic and vulnerable subjects. There is no precedent in the UK for government departments being directly involved in such detailed allocations. Another consequence is that Quality Research (QR) funding, previously allocated by HEFCE according to the results of the REF, will now be distributed by the newly established body UK Research and Innovation (UKRI). This raises two awkward issues. The first is that it will create further divisions between the higher education systems in the national components of the UK. The UKRI will act as an umbrella group for the research councils, which operate on a UK-wide basis. However, its direct funding of research will only apply to English universities because Scotland and Wales will retain their existing funding councils. The second is that the principle of dual-support funding under which institutions receive core budgets and then bid for research projects, which has always been regarded as a guarantee of institutional autonomy and also a reflection of the need to fund curiosity-driven research (and scholarship) will potentially be undermined. Although the legislation contains an explicit guarantee that dual-support funding will continue, the fact remains that a single body – the UKRI – will now be responsible for funding both elements in England.
- Second, the abolition of HEFCE represents the death of the so-called arm's-length principle, the idea that institutions can be largely dependent on public funding (or, under the new regime, resources either generated from public sources or heavily regulated by political authorities) yet enjoy a high degree of not simply operational but normative freedom. The scope for such arm's-length arrangements was almost inevitably limited in a society addicted to 'measurement', 'performance' and 'accountability' and reluctant to take anything

'on trust'. They also appeared to be profoundly antithetical to the project of establishing a 'market' in higher education. However, in most respects, it is difficult to escape the conclusion that the proposals made in the White Paper would cross some 'red lines' which earlier reform projects have respected, however reluctantly. The OfS is not intended to be in any way a 'buffer body' between higher education and the State. Its explicit purpose is to serve the needs of higher education 'customers', in other words students, and to act as a regulator, its remit inevitably set by government.

3   The third is the decision radically to lower the threshold for new alternative, and often for-profit, providers of higher education, now generally labelled 'challenger institutions' to indicate the role ministers expect them to play. The student number threshold (and subject range) institutions must meet before they can be awarded degree awarding powers or 'university' titles will be substantially reduced. Also institutions will no longer have to demonstrate a 'track record', in effect the successful graduation of a group of students, before they can apply for these powers or seek such a title. Instead they can be granted them from the outset, on a provisional basis. A severe, and perhaps unintended, consequence of this 'liberalisation' is that the new legislation confers on the Secretary of State draconian new powers to withdraw degree-awarding powers, even from universities with Royal Charters.

With the government's decision to proceed with legislation, the die may appear to have been cast. However, important policy choices will remain. Ministers have signalled that they are willing to be flexible and pragmatic with the introduction of the TEF (which has the advantage of helping to win the reluctant acceptance of higher education's key management class). In the short run the transition from HEFCE to the OfS and the UKRI may produce comparatively muted effects, if only because HEFCE staff will transfer to these new bodies. At what stage 'business as usual' will be replaced by disruptive change remains unclear. Also unclear is the appetite for alternative, or 'challenger', providers to enter the higher education market place even now that the bar has been dramatically lowered. The general expectation is still that they will target particular market niches rather than mount a wholesale challenge to 'public' higher education. The point at which a 'tipping point' is reached when an irreversible shift takes place between a policy of 'modernisation' (within which market-like mechanisms play a role) is displaced by a policy of root-and-branch 'marketisation' remains clouded – an issue which will be discussed in the concluding section of this chapter.

However, it is important to recognise that the UK is more than England. Except for the research councils which remain UK-wide institutions, higher education policy has radically diverged between the component nations of the UK. Scotland, in particular, has resisted the advance of fees and maintained 'free' higher education largely supported out of general taxation, a policy which has been criticised on the grounds that more privileged (and higher-income) social groups have benefited most (although, as has been pointed out, the same criticism can be levelled at the new high-fee and universal-loan system adopted in England). Scottish higher education policy has also encouraged collaboration between institutions and mitigated competitive pressures. Above all, the Scottish government has attempted to reinforce the idea that there should be a national system, which has led it to impose more standardised governance arrangements on all institutions (despite the opposition of the traditional universities). Wales has had more limited room for manoeuvre because of the very substantial cross-border student flows (and the National Assembly Government's more limited powers and resource base). However, fees for Welsh domiciled students have been pegged at the £3,000 level set by New Labour, regardless of where they study in the UK. The government has also pursued a more active policy of restructuring, including institutional mergers, than anything attempted in either England or Scotland. Although these Scottish and Welsh policies have inevitably been overshadowed by the reforms undertaken by the UK government in England, they should not be ignored. At the very least, they demonstrate the pluralism of higher education policy making within the UK.

Conclusions and reflections

Interpreting the longer-term significance of the reforms of higher education now being undertaken by the Conservative Government in England is not straightforward. The first issue that must be addressed is the extent to which these reforms represent a radical break with the past. The second is, regardless of whether they should be characterised as revolutionary or evolutionary, what they portend for the long-term direction and character of higher education in England.

On the first issue, there has been a variety of views expressed. At one end of the spectrum was Lord Browne's statement that the recommendations in his report represented a 'paradigm shift', an interpretation that has also been adopted by many of the critics of his report (and especially of high fees) who bemoan the 'marketisation' of English higher education (Brown and Carasso, 2013; McGettigan, 2013).

At the other end of the spectrum is the minimalist view espoused (hopefully perhaps) by many higher education leaders, that against a background of austerity and forced limits on public expenditure, fees represented the only viable alternative if higher education was not to be starved of resources. Evidence can be found to support both interpretations. The claim that these reforms represent a 'paradigm shift' can be justified by the fact that the fees now charged in England are the highest charged by any public system of higher education in the world. The principle of cost-sharing has been firmly, and perhaps irrevocably, established. Even many supporters of 'free' higher education have reluctantly accepted that there is no way back, no alternative to fees (if only because, even if public expenditure is increased, higher education will have lost its place in the queue to public services with greater and more urgent needs, especially in health and social care). Although there are examples of fees being abolished, in Chile and those German *Länder* that had previously charged them, there seems to be little confidence that either the political will or political circumstances will ever allow a similar reversal in England.

The claim that fees, although second best to direct public funding, have become inevitable to protect the resource base of English higher education (and for severely logistical rather than ideological reasons), can be justified because fees have delivered additional resources and (at any rate, full-time) students do not seem to be have been particularly put off by the prospect of much higher levels of future debt when they graduate.

More plausible than either perhaps is a middle-way interpretation, that the current reforms are the culmination of a longer-term policy process that can be dated back to the years of New Labour rule and probably go back much earlier. It can be argued that the direction of travel in higher education policy has been consistent since the mid-1980s, or even that contemporary changes have their roots far back in the initial decision to support the expansion of higher education (and, by default, the establishment of a mass system). It has already been pointed out that much of the architecture and instruments of the current policy regime – the SLC, OFFA, NSS – were established by the New Labour Government before 2010. The emphasis on the need for colleges and universities to produce skilled and employable graduates and also to undertake relevant research with an impact on social wellbeing and (especially) economic growth is also deep rooted and can be traced back many decades. However, successive New Labour, Coalition and now Conservative Government policies have built up a forward momentum. As a result, the emphasis may have switched from essentially technocratic policies designed to 'modernise' colleges and universities still conceived of as constituting a 'public' system of higher education to a more overtly ideological project aimed at establishing a functioning 'market'. However, there may be dangers in exaggerating the degree, or importance, of this switch. The extent to which a functioning 'market' can ever be established in a higher education system still predominately funded by public, quasi-public and publicly regulated income is limited. Also, even the Conservative Government is constrained by political realities (for example, the need to prevent unruly and disruptive market failures) and has shown little enthusiasm for relinquishing its levers of control, which are likely to be as vigorously exercised by means of regulation in the future as they ever were through funding in the past.

The second issue is perhaps more interesting. Even if, as seems sensible, continuities of policy are given greater emphasis than ruptures, it does not follow that radical changes in the character of higher education in England can thereby be avoided. The most powerful drivers of change are to be found not so much in the policy domain, but rather in the structural changes in society, the economy and culture (which are then reflected – prematurely or belatedly, enthusiastically or reluctantly – by policy makers). The forces that are shaping higher education, not only in England or the UK at large but in the wider world, include:

- The reshaping of labour markets and occupation structures (which determine the conditions for graduate employment) (Brown and Lauder, 2012);
- Growing social and economic inequality (at home, which shapes the possibilities for more equitable access, and internationally, which influences the pattern of internationalisation in all higher education systems) (Picketty, 2014);
- The development of new knowledge and technologies (which determines, and is determined by, research in higher education, and also re-engineers universities as organisations);
- The evolution of new social and cultural habits (leading to the creation of so-called 'clever cities' but also fundamentally influencing the pattern of learning and refashioning social and individual identities).

Although consideration of these forces lies outside the scope of this chapter, it is important to recognise that policy-making plays an essentially subordinate role in shaping the future of students, institutions and systems.

However, it would be wrong to end without indicating, if only in outline, some of the more likely consequences of the current reforms in higher education in England. One is clearly the fragmentation of the present system, as new providers enter the market and new types of tertiary courses and qualifications (such as graduate apprenticeships) are developed. Secondly, the habits of solidarity and commonality characteristic of a public system of higher education may also decay as notions of 'publicness' are eroded by the enthusiasms for the 'market'. This is dependent not so much on the development of a functioning market, but on the spread of 'market' behaviours. A third, and related, consequence is that the organic character of individual institutions may also be lost. The delicate balance between higher education, of a liberal or scientific character, and professional training, a traditional characteristic of the university which (perhaps surprisingly) has been maintained through the long years of expansion, could be upset. The integration of teaching, and student learning, with research and scholarship (although in different proportions in different types of institution), already threatened by heightened degrees of specialisation, could be eroded beyond effective recall. Fourthly, the managerial revolution within higher education, in some respects necessary and desirable but always potentially antithetical to older notions of 'community', is bound to accelerate. Fifthly, an extension of political control over higher education appears to be more inevitable, more inevitable perhaps than the establishment of a properly functioning market. The lust to measure achievement, drive up standards, promote transparency is insatiable. Finally, the subtle links between expansion and equity, between the establishment of a mass system of higher education with much more open forms of access and the promotion of social justice, the silent driver of higher education for more than half a century, may be lost and forgotten.

This, for many dystopian, future is not inevitable – and, to the extent it is realised, it can be attributed as much to deeper structural forces as to the deliberate effects of policy. The actual future is more likely perhaps to be characterised by fuzzy compromises and shifting accommodations. It is far from clear that there has been a parallel revolution in attitudes, habits and values among students, teachers, researchers and administrators in colleges and universities to match the policy revolution that, it is claimed, is re-engineering higher education. The opposite is more likely to be true, that there is a growing dissonance between normative and organisational structures, with unforeseeable consequences. The future of higher education remains open, even if the force of trends in recent policy must be clearly acknowledged and understood. Necessarily so, because learning, enquiry, scholarship and science always have open frontiers which permit no predetermined outcomes.

References

BIS (Department for Business, Innovation and Skills), 2011. *Higher Education: Students at the Heart of the System*. London: HMSO.

BIS (Department for Business, Innovation and Skills), 2015. *Fulfilling our Potential: Teaching Excellence, Social Mobility and Student Choice*. London: HMSO.

BIS (Department for Business, Innovation and Skills), 2016. *Success as a Knowledge Economy: Teaching Excellence, Social Mobility and Student Choice*. London: HMSO.

Brown, P., and Lauder, H., 2012. The Great Transformation in the Global Labour Market in *Soundings: A Journal of Politics and Culture*. 51, pp. 41–53.

Brown, R., and Carasso, H., 2013. *Everything for Sale? The Marketisation of UK Higher Education*. Abingdon: Routledge (Society for Research into Higher Education).

Browne Report (Independent Review of Higher Education Funding and Student Finance), 2010. *Securing a Sustainable Future for Higher Education*. [online] Available at: www.independent.gov/browne-report. [accessed December 15th 2015].

Callender, C., and Scott, P., eds. 2013. *Browne and Beyond: Modernizing English Higher Education*. London: Institute of Education Press.

Dearing Report (National Committee of Enquiry into Higher Education), 1997. Higher Education in the Learning Society. London: HMSO.

Engwall, L., and Scott, P., eds. 2013. *Trust in Universities*. Wenner-Gren Volume 86, London: Portland Press.

HESA (Higher Education Statistics Agency), 2015. *Students in Higher Education 2013–14*. Cheltenham: HESA.

McGettigan, A., 2013. *The Great University Gamble: Money, Markets and the Future of Higher Education*. London: Pluto Press.

Picketty, T., 2014. *Capital in the Twenty-First Century*. Cambridge, MA and London: Belknap Press of the Harvard University Press.

Power, M., 1997. *The Audit Society: Rituals of Verification*. Oxford: Oxford University Press.

Robbins Report (Committee on Higher Education), 1963. *Higher Education: A Report by the Committee Appointed by the Prime Minister under the Chairmanship of Lord Robbins, 1961–63*. London: HMSO.

Scott, P., 1989. Higher Education in Kavanagh, D., and Seldon, A., eds. *The Thatcher Effect*. pp. 198–212. Oxford: Oxford University Press.

Scott, P., 1994. Education Policy in Kavanagh, D., and Seldon, A., eds. *The Major Effect*. pp. 332–350. London: Macmillan.

Scott, P., 2014a. Robbins, the Binary Policy and Mass Higher Education in *Higher Education Quarterly*. 68 (2), pp. 147–163.

Scott, P., 2014b. The Reform of English Higher Education: Universities in Global, National and Regional Context' in *Cambridge Journal of Regions, Economy and Policy*. 7 (2), pp. 217–231.

Shattock, M., 2012. *Making Policy in British Higher Education 1945–2011*. Maidenhead: McGraw-Hill and Open University Press.

Thompson, J., and Bekhradnia, B., 2013. *The Cost of the Government's Reforms of the Financing of Higher Education – An Update*. Oxford: Higher Education Policy Institute (HEPI).

3 Education and citizenship

Rowan Williams

Over the centuries, there have been many different ways of understanding what is expected of an institution in which young adults are educated. I use this clumsy form of words because the word 'university', although it has been applied to most or all of these institutions, is a European term with a special history, and it does no harm to be aware of the non-European experience as well, even though much of what follows will be based on the more familiar European history. Thus it is significant to recognise that an imperial academy for 'the sons of the nation' was established in China over a century before the Christian era and an imperial medical college in the fifth Christian century. A good deal of what I have to say about the European experience will have such echoes in non-European contexts. But whatever the precise terminology used, the focus of this discussion will be institutions that educate beyond a certain basic level, that deal with people in their late teens and twenties for the most part, and that have close relationships, but not complete identity, with the processes of training for certain kinds of public life.

In the Greek and Roman world, the focus on public life was crucially important – and it is something whose significance we can easily forget, unfortunately. The young man whose future was likely to be in law and administration, or whose family position at least meant that he would have some sort of authoritative role in society, would spend a number of years, probably in more than one centre, absorbing skills that would seem to us a curious mixture of the literary, the legal and the logical. How much of each of these elements was to be studied was not controlled by an overall curriculum – though if you decided to stay for some years with one main teacher, you would follow what he prescribed. You would learn how to read certain classic texts of your civilisation – to ask questions about the text so that you could understand it better and apply its content to understanding other settings and situations. You would learn about the rules of argument, but you would also learn how to speak in such a way that people would take you seriously, how to build up metaphors and appeal to the feelings, how to suggest indirectly what you did not want to say directly. If you had a certain temperament, you might want also to pursue all this beyond the basic and practical level and reflect on how you could know the truth of the universe and the right way to live. Education in the Western classical world was therefore, unsurprisingly, always subject to disagreement over what mattered more – finding out the truth or winning arguments and persuading people. It is the conflict – so it was often described – between rhetoric and philosophy, with philosophy in that context being understood not as an intellectual discipline alone, but as a method of learning how to grow in virtue.

The product of a classical education would normally emerge as a trained *performer* – someone who could count on being taken seriously in public life because he (the masculine pronoun is deliberate; women were not expected to be active in the public sphere of the classical world) knew the rules of good conversation and persuasive argument. He *might* also emerge as someone with some knowledge of the techniques by which a human mind could penetrate behind appearances and discover the patterns of the universe, physical and moral. What we understand by research was not part of the expectation, and there was little or no sense of the value of being 'original'; on the whole, originality was bound to look like foolish rebellion against well-established wisdom. At worst, the man who had been through this process would be a smooth manipulator of the opinions and emotions of others and would be quite capable of using these skills for selfish ambition. At best, he would be someone who could play a significant part in controlling irrational, excessive and divisive behaviour or talk, and so in preserving justice and stability in the social order.

Naturally, as the order of the old Roman Empire collapsed, in the fifth and sixth centuries after Christ, the ideals of this kind of education largely disappeared – at least in the terms that would have been recognised by earlier generations. Some of it indeed survived in the eastern Mediterranean world, where the Greek-speaking Empire continued for some centuries to need educated public servants. But in Western Europe, the only people left with any of the skills to run society in an age of huge political instability were the priests of the Christian Church. Aspects and portions of the old system were used in the schools that grew up around the great monasteries and cathedrals of the West to train priests and other clergy. Now they were the ones who had to know how to read texts, to construct arguments and to speak convincingly – both so that they could teach in the churches and so that they could manage the business of the new kingdoms that were developing.

As early as the late fourth century, the greatest Christian thinker of the period, Augustine of Hippo in Africa, had argued (especially in his work *de doctrina Christiana, On Christian Teaching*) that Christians needed to learn how to read their Bible with the same sort of skill and attention and literary sophistication that others brought to the classics. So the interpretation of the Bible became, in a sense, the crown and climax of the process of 'higher education'. You would learn what a pagan Roman might have learned about logic and music and mathematics, about good and bad arguments and about the nature of proportion and harmony in different contexts; but then you would move on not only to philosophy but to theology, in which you were shown how to trace the connections and harmonies in the text of the Bible so as to defend the consistency and rationality of doctrines taught by the Church. Not everyone would go on to that level, but the whole system was constructed on the assumption that theology would give you the key to how it all hung together. The word 'university' dates from the Middle Ages, and it originally meant a universal course of studies recognised throughout the Christian world, so that anyone emerging from the courses of a 'university' institution was regarded as competent to teach in any other similar institution.

Just as the fall of the Roman Empire destroyed the old pattern, so the upheavals in the Christian Church in the sixteenth century and the great political changes that came with the newly centralised states of Europe gradually changed the universities of the Christian Middle Ages beyond recognition. Although they still retained the character of training grounds for the clergy and for at least some of the legal professions, there was first of all a widening of the scope of the university to include once more the young men of 'good family' who were likely to play a significant role in public life, and then, especially on the continent of Europe, many new universities were established, often by local rulers, initially to train public officials, bureaucrats, in a common culture, though there was an increasing interest in pure research. While continental Europe developed along these lines, however, English universities experienced remarkably little structural change: they preserved a narrow focus on mathematics and the Greek and Roman classics until the latter part of the nineteenth century. But their role in shaping the ethos of a governing class was no less important. And of course as the political and social atmosphere of Western societies altered with the greater public role of women, it was inevitable that for the first time, women should be included (initially with great reluctance) in the processes of higher education.

Both in Britain and on the Continent of Europe, the significance of research in science and humanities was more and more recognised, and the structures of the university changed to respond to this. It was only in the latter part of the twentieth century that government began to restrict the liberties of the universities in some degree by insisting on measurable production in terms of research (thus putting at a disadvantage some traditional disciplines where quantity of publication was always smaller and the rate of advance in research slower) and by making funding more and more conditional on this measurable production. The extension of the title of university to what had been more strictly technical institutions led to an increasing blurring of boundaries between university study as a goal in itself, with its own measures of quality, and the processes of training in certain skills. The most difficult challenge in the Western university world today is how the university avoids being completely dominated by this external pressure to produce and to offer functional training. It is instructive to note that this is not entirely a modern problem: the twelfth aphorism in Book VIII of the *Analects of Confucius* seems to speak of not dissimilar pressures. 'The Master said, "It is not easy to find a man who can study for three years without thinking about earning a salary"'.

But this immediately raises the basic question of whether the essential purpose of the university today can still be the pursuit of what the Master regarded as the studies appropriate for public wisdom. This brief and super-ficial survey of what European universities have been will have suggested some of the underlying aims of all the very different sorts of institutions mentioned, and before proceeding it may be of interest to try and summarise them. First – and perhaps surprisingly – there is a profoundly *political* ele-ment in the university. It is taken for granted that those who exercise power in a society need to be formed in a particular culture. They need to learn how to reflect on the social interactions around them; they need to learn how to evaluate the reasons that people give for actions and policies. Part of that training in how to evaluate reasons and arguments – and also ideals and aims – has always involved reference to the basic texts of a culture, sacred or not, which are regarded as setting out patterns of human life in society that continue to serve as an orientation. Whether in Europe or in other cul-tures, there is a recognition that knowledge of 'classic' texts is a necessary aspect of what is needed for leadership in public life. But the fact that all this exposure to a tradition takes place in the context of relationships between teacher and student which – in principle at least – are sustained over some significant period of time means that some element of dialogue and interac-tion is recognised as part of the process – even if at many periods this has been formal and almost impersonal.

Then there is research. So far, the definition of the university seems to be completely dominated by the ideal of training in what in Europe we call 'humanistic' study and to leave little room for what we tend to think of now as the most characteristic feature of university life at its best: original research, the discovery of new perspectives and new facts. Historically, what happened was this: as European society became more curious about its phys-ical environment and its history in the period following the Renaissance and Reformation, it was increasingly part of the educated person's expectation that exchanges and conversations about these matters should be possible. At first, the universities were not at the forefront of such development, either in science or in historical and literary studies, but it was impossible that they should remain forever indifferent. If they were to serve a political class and if that political class was increasingly interested in such questioning, there was a natural movement to incorporate opportunity for original exploration and experiment into the routine of the university. But it is worth remember-ing that initially this is not about the universities being seen – or seeing themselves – as laboratories for the material needs of the state. It has to do with the way in which, throughout the seventeenth and eighteenth centuries, it became a mark of the educated man to be able to question traditional authority in every sphere, and so to be familiar with methods of assessing evidence, historical and scientific.

The modern university is the result of these two factors coming together, but there are other important elements to note. We have observed the significance of the need to create a common frame of reference for those who will take responsibility for a society. We have noted the developing 'early modern' interest in asking subversive questions of tradition and seeking to extend the frontiers of what can be known and understood. But the relatively new fact of the twentieth century is that, as democracy spreads, it is harder to speak of a settled 'governing class'; every student becomes potentially someone with significant political views and capacities in the democratic system, someone with responsibilities to vote and to participate in whatever way is appropriate in the governing of his or her society. And so the expectation of more or less universal access to higher education spreads, and issues around access become vitally important to universities in marketing or promoting themselves in a competitive environment.

Each of these elements on its own brings risks. A university that is concerned only with training a settled governing class in its accepted classics will not equip people for a world in which varied cultures exist together in lively and often challenging proximity. To refer again to the Chinese context, it is all too easy for a tradition of government in which education in the classics is all-important to produce a political elite whose capacity to respond to social and international change is seriously limited; reformers in China from the late nineteenth century onwards recognised the problem.

Equally, a university focused only on research runs two different kinds of risk. It may become an institution almost completely forgetful of its inescapable function in forming a *general* critical awareness, forming what might be called 'intellectual virtues' which play a part in public life. A recent British writer (Fryer, 2005, p. 74ff) has referred to the connection between universities and citizenship as 'the forgotten dimension' of higher education, and argues, along with some other influential commentators, that universities should devote serious resource and energy to encouraging public debate on the shared values of their society. This does not mean that a university as such should be a nursery of simple activism and criticism; it does mean, though, that a good university is always looking for ways of opening up general intellectual debate about common hopes and values to the community around it. It does not exist only to refine the work of the specialist.

But there is an opposite risk involved in certain attitudes to research. If research in universities is always driven primarily by where the funding comes from, the danger is that university departments become tools for either government or private business to pursue their strategic or commercial interests. This has more than once become a matter of controversy in Europe when contracts are given to universities for research related to defence matters, for example. The commitment to maintain research that is dictated by independent intellectual concern rather than public or commercial policy is, for most academics, an essential feature of a healthy university life, even if there are inevitably involvements from outside that may affect the balance of effort and resource. It is only when universities are free to pose their own questions that they fulfil their function of enabling people to ask about the foundations of what others take for granted.

There is, finally, a risk in the situation where universities simply become the vehicle for mass movements, for popular protest and no more. Student populations are historically volatile and prone to political activism – a trend visible especially in nineteenth-century Russia and in the France and America of the 1960s and 1970s. To say that students in a university within a democratic society are discovering themselves as what I earlier called 'political agents' should not be taken to mean that their primary role ought to be political agitation or the espousing of popular causes. What is distinctive about the university, as we have already seen, is that it seeks to nurture the ability to *understand* political processes and to weigh political arguments rather than giving uncritical loyalty to any programme.

The student who is in this sense discovering what it is to be a 'political agent' is discovering what it is to exercise thoughtful responsibility in the life of a society. And this is where a narrow definition of what the social and the political might mean has to be balanced by some historical perspective; it is in fact where (in a very broad sense) the 'classics' of a society are relevant, so that a good university allows space for students to test their ideals and concepts against a historical tradition expressed not only in opportunities for discussion but also in the university's public ceremony and its standards and protocols for intellectual exchange. By its very existence, the good university expresses certain philosophical commitments – to civil discourse, to liberty of expression, to careful and honest self-questioning and to the possibility of creating trust through the processes of fair argument and exploration of evidence. This cannot be reduced to the narrow atmosphere of pressure groups.

Ideally, then, the elements of awareness of history and tradition, openness to intellectual innovation and concern for the widest possible engagement with public life should come together in the university to help nurture adult and responsible citizens. But for us in Europe, there are, of course, two major factors which complicate still further the position of the university. One of these has already been hinted at: it is a political and economic climate in which the expectation of short-term and practical results has affected attitudes to 'free' intellectual endeavour in some very adverse ways. A proper concern for accountability has produced a real anxiety about the volume of work produced by universities, and an increasingly sharp competitive spirit between institutions. Every university has to promote itself in two directions – towards the public, to keep up recruitment, and towards funding bodies, which in Britain and much of continental Europe will be under government direction, to persuade them of its profitability. This is not a climate that will disappear overnight; it is part of the way in which 'market' models have come to dominate so many areas of social and institutional life in our context.

The second of these challenges is the sheer diversity of the cultural scene in the modern West; not only has British culture, for example, lost a degree of contact with and confidence in a history or identity shared by British citizens, it is now inclusive of active and often lively immigrant cultures, whose relation with the majority may be, in various ways, strained. Against such a background, what would it mean to see the university as offering an induction into some kind of culture appropriate to people who will grow into public responsibility? Isn't this bound to be hopelessly compromised by the existing dominance of one culture or class or ethnic group (as has been the case in Britain)? And in more complex and less stable political environments, what role has the university in promoting social and political stability in contexts where much rests upon the ability of government to sustain national cohesion and a universal pattern of law, welfare and equity?

Any university now attempting to promote the advantage of one racial or class interest would forfeit its credibility and authority. But the alternative is not an acceptance of pure 'postmodern' diversity, a chaos of non-communicating discourses for mutually isolated communities. Once again, the actual discipline of historic university life imposes a certain ethical attitude. Universities are organised in a way that accepts diversity of discourses; what constitutes a good question in economics is different from what constitutes a good question in physics; what counts as a solution to a problem in mathematics is different from what counts as a solution in literary criticism – or even theology. In other words, the nature of the university is such that anyone involved in it must expect to learn that his or her questions are not the only ones that could be asked and that his or her solutions are unlikely to offer global salvation.

A university then ought to produce a measure of intellectual humility in its practitioners as regards the supreme importance of their own discipline (it must be said that this is not always abundantly evident in practice, since scholars are as frail and human as the rest of us . . .). But a truly functioning university will also, through the encounters of diverse disciplines, model ways in which cultural traditions, religious loyalties and ethnic identities can co-exist, not in mutual indifference, but in a climate of mutual and honest questioning, in which the various commitments are not automatically opposed but can enrich one another. A simple postmodernist assumption that diversity is just a fact of life that needs no exploring and exchange would be a recipe for a depressingly tribal and static intellectual life.

The university sustains a culture of its own, a culture of conversation and mutual criticism and appreciation, in the context of which people may grow into a deeper understanding of what characterises human beings as such in their social interaction. That understanding has to do with seeing human beings as essentially engaged in *learning* – in enlarging their mental and imaginative worlds and approaching one another with curiosity, patience and welcome, being free to imagine how others ask different questions of the world around them. Within that common culture of a 'learning humanity', a university may as a matter of historical fact have a visibly dominant cultural presence – perhaps religious, as often in Europe, perhaps deeply bound up with national identity and independence. But if it is to function as a university, this historical legacy will need to be, not neutralised or denied, but understood precisely as a legacy to be used as the soil on which debate can grow. Its tradition, religious, national or whatever, is not an orthodoxy to be insisted upon (as was the case in English universities until the early nineteenth century), but a secure space in which other voices are welcome and respected and where the interaction of different voices and perspectives within the institution is not seen as any sort of contest for dominance. In many circumstances, an intellectual institution that is clear about its history and tradition can be a more, rather than a less, hospitable place because of this lack of any need to fight for a dominant voice.

So the university plays an essential role in the public life of its society. The fundamental character of this role is not to do with the university's success in meeting the material targets of the society, in the scale and size of its industrial or defence contracts, nor is it to do with the university's unquestioning promotion of a single religious, philosophical or political ideology. Instead, it is about the university's capacity to help create mature citizens, persons who are free from certain sorts of prejudice and fear. A recent book on the *Philosophy of the Teacher* (Tubbs, 2005, p. 79) summarises superbly the proper aim of any teacher – but the words are perhaps specially appropriate to the university teacher: 'The teacher who believes in freedom seeks to be neither master over the students nor surrogate master on behalf of God or nature. Rather, the *critical* teacher aims to be *servant* to the emancipation of students from all forms of tutelage, self-incurred or externally imposed, and to their free and un-coerced development'. But this does not mean that the teacher teaches nothing in particular or teaches only to ask negative and disruptive questions. In managing the tensions and contradictions in the teacher's role, the balance of inevitable power and the call to service, teacher and student both discover something about the nature of learning itself and about the truth that is never to become the possession of any individual or faction or class because it always escapes a single and final definition. It is always discovered in the difficult process of the teaching *relationship*, which is never just the transfer of a body of knowledge from one container to another (Tubbs, 2005, pp. 102–107).

The 'product' of the university, then, is not simply the person who has acquired skills – technical skills, even research skills; it is the person who has acquired the habit and virtue of learning, and who sees the social world as a place not primarily of struggle and conflict over control but as a context where conversation may be pursued with patience. And this is a deeply political matter, in the fullest sense of the much-abused word 'political'. It alters what we think we can expect of each other; it challenges any assumption that conflict is the natural position for human beings. When there are clashes of interest, it tells us how to question what we have taken for granted about our own best interests and encourages us to seek for something new that is not just the property of one individual or faction. The university nourishes 'civility' – in the narrow sense of patience and courtesy in dispute, and in the much larger sense of concern for proper and open public life in the *civitas*, the city, the community of citizens.

Universities certainly educate people according to a doctrine about human-ity, even when they proclaim themselves liberal, pluralist or secular, because they all have, somewhere in their purpose, the aim of showing students the nature of learning and so encouraging them to see the truth as both demand-ing or uncompromising and elusive, impossible to possess. Such a philosophy may threaten some kinds of political society, where control is all-important and open dispute is regarded as always being subversive. But the stronger a society, the clearer its legitimacy, its commitment to law and its concern for universal welfare and dignity, the more it will be able to cope with what, in broad terms, the West has come to speak of as the 'liberal' vision, the idea of conversation, learning and mutual stimulus. If the university is a critical presence in a society, that does not make it a negative and disruptive one. On the contrary, it models ways of negotiating differences and uncertainties and tells us that open conflict is not the natural state of human life together.

In this respect, the religious origins of the European university are not irrelevant. The presence of the churches and other recognised religious bod-ies within society today can often be seen as that of a 'critical friend' – to use a favourite term – witnessing to different standards and expectations about human beings and so opening up a further dimension to human experience. They are not, of course, the same, and it would be wrong to say that all universities should somehow have a religious basis. But both challenge any idea that conflict is natural. Both speak of a reality around us that is at once ordered and mysterious, that enables both confidence and humility. Both therefore help to create what I have been calling the mature citizen. Both should be welcome elements in a society that is seeking to be democratically accountable, non-corrupt, legitimate because it allows its citizens a free voice and is concerned to nourish their intelligence.

The university is a place where 'liberal studies' can be pursued. This rather old-fashioned term originally meant a literary and philosophical education, but it can be applied to scientific research as well, and, most importantly, to the whole climate of the university. It is nothing to do with promoting what some people see as *liberalism*, as a religious or political or moral principle involving what are supposed to be 'modern' values about moral behaviour and so on. But it is about the overarching value of understanding that to be human is to learn and that to learn is a lifetime's work, nourished by all sorts of diverse intellectual and imaginative practices. There are probably periods in the history of any society when this ideal feels like a luxury, when the pri-orities are to consolidate a nation or deal with acute poverty and economic stagnation or defend people against violent attack. Yet what is surprising in modern history especially is the fact that 'liberal studies' survive: intellectual and artistic life keeps going during times of war, desperately poor countries struggle to establish credible institutions of higher education (I recall visiting the University in Bujumbura in Burundi, invited by them to reflect on the role of the university in post-conflict situations), and neighbouring societies riven by terrible conflict maintain some kind of civic protocols about the exchange of intellectual material and even discussion (for example, Israeli and Palestinian universities). The sheer fact of a community declaring that the last word in human relations is not unmanageable conflict turns out not to be in any way a luxury. And in times of stress and shortage, a surprising number of societies seem to recognise this. Whatever the urgencies of the moment, there is some acknowledgement that no solution to these urgencies will last without the broader context offered by the 'liberal' university.

And the Christian believer engaged in this discussion will want to add a further refinement of the argument. If the truth about our human situation demands something of us and is also impossible to possess once and for all, this suggests a picture of us as human agents, human knowers, who can fully exercise their humanity only in a sustained discipline of looking away from or at least bracketing the pressures of the surface self. My agenda as an individual is not the key to learning the truth, from the most mundane state of affairs that can be mapped by simple measurements to the most complex deliverances of astrophysics. Effective learning has about it, in other words, some of the characteristics of *love*: absorbed attention to the givenness of what is before me, relative indifference to my individual comfort or wellbeing while I am pursuing the relation with what is before me, even joy in this curious and (from an outside perspective) uncomfortable process. In other words, one of our most typical human activities, the simultaneously self-aware and self-forgetting exploration of our environment in order to make communicable sense of it, entails what the Greek theologians call an element of *ekstasis*, 'standing outside' our individuality, in a way closely parallel to that other distinctive aspect of our humanity, the exploration of relations between persons.

This convergence of knowledge and love is historically a focal element in what Christian theology has to say about the image of God in humanity and about the mode in which we encounter and explore the reality of God. To say that we are made in the divine image is to say that our personal being is not centred in an enclosed selfhood but realised in relatedness; we are always already in relation, always involved in what is other, and there is no mental or 'spiritual' life that is not generated by this fact of being in the other and the other's being in us. In doctrinal terms, this is why we claim that we are created in the image of God as Trinity, as a life in which identity and otherness are eternally implicated in each other. And while it may seem a long journey from the intricacies of orthodox dogmatics to the business of higher education, the connection is a vital one for any Christian believer trying to make sense of the world of the university. That commitment to 'liberal studies' which we have been exploring is grounded for the believer in the conviction that study – in humanities or sciences – is an ethical and political matter, because study is one of those settings in which we learn how to learn, how to absorb and be absorbed by otherness without this being reduced to the imperialism of a solitary mind and ego; it is thus indirectly about learning love, and if so, it is also about learning citizenship – the liberty to negotiate the relations of self and other, neighbour or stranger, within a moral framework in which *all* are learning, all are receiving. When we face a cultural environment in which the uncriticised dominance of a group or a class or a race blocks off mutuality, or where fear of the other paralyses reasoned negotiation, where – in the memorable phrase used by Jesus in Matthew's gospel – 'love grows cold', we urgently need to retrieve this perspective. A theological vision of the convergence of intelligence and love offers the ground for understanding better why the wellbeing of higher education can be morally and politically good news.

But to return briefly to Confucius: he defines what is necessary for someone to be called 'benevolent' as 'respectfulness, tolerance, trustworthiness in word, quickness and generosity' (*Analects*. XVII.6). What we have been discussing in relation to the vocation of a university seems in retrospect to be the question of how 'benevolent' citizens can be formed – people whose good will towards the common life, whose capacity to question their own selfish instincts is properly developed. Perhaps some educational theorists in Europe or the USA would be surprised to hear a university being defined as a context for learning benevolence; the famous quarrelsomeness of scholars does not seem to promise well. Yet, I have been arguing throughout that the very fact of an institution such as the university – giving space for research, exposure to past as well as present and variety of intellectual disciplines – sends a certain message to the society around it. It suggests what the context is within which genuine politics can go forward – not a politics of control or of naked competition, but a 'civil' argument about the goods we can only discover in co-operation and mutual sympathy.

References

Fryer, R.H., 2005. Universities and Citizenship: The Forgotten Dimension? in Robinson, S., and Katulushi, C., eds. *Values in Higher Education*. pp. 74–106. Leeds: Aureus.

Tubbs, N., 2005. *Philosophy of the Teacher*. Oxford: Blackwell.

4 Education and the common good

Suzy Harris

Section I

In its 1996 White Paper, *Teaching and Learning: Towards the Learning Society*, the European Commission stated quite unequivocally that the purpose of higher education was to serve the needs of the economy (European Commission, 1996). In 2008, European governments were sent reeling by the global financial crisis, which threatened not only the Eurozone and the financial system, but also the neoliberal status quo. Austerity measures were introduced across Europe as some economies (Greece most seriously) struggled to survive and remain in the European Union. In the case of the UK, the crisis was the major factor in the Labour Government's defeat in the 2010 general election. The Conservative success was mitigated by failing to win a majority and having to form a Coalition Government with the Liberal Democrats. The new government's priority was deficit budget reduction, and severe cuts were made across the public sector. Numerous demonstrations and public sector strikes took place the following year in protest against not only government austerity measures, but also what was seen as corrupt free-market capitalism. The year 2012 opened with both Conservative and Labour parties desperate to win over public support for their 'vision' of how to address the problems of capitalism and how to restore confidence in the system. There was a brief period in which leaders of the main parties spoke of the need for a 'fairer' version of capitalism, appealing to notions of a 'moral capitalism', a 'responsible capitalism' and a 'popular capitalism'; this soon petered out as political attention returned to economic recovery. After five years of deep cuts, and to the surprise of the Conservatives and most public commentators, the Conservatives won an outright, albeit small, majority in the 2015 general election. The new administration continued with further cuts and the goal of eliminating the budget deficit.

Although political debate remains focused on economic concerns the financial crisis and its aftermath raise fundamental questions about the kind of society we want and the kind of education desirable in a modern democratic society. Given the urgency of securing economic recovery, such questions may be regarded as irrelevant or indeed as a diversion. It is important, however, that questions to do with deeper moral and ethical matters about the nature and purposes of education are not overshadowed. Serving the needs of the economy is not necessarily the same as serving the needs of democracy or the needs of the common good. This chapter considers the notion of the common and takes John Henry Newman and Alasdair MacIntyre's ideas concerning notions of community, tradition and judgement as a fruitful starting point from which to think about the kind of university that would meet the needs of a pluralistic and democratic society. Although separated by a century, Newman and MacIntyre share a reputation as independent thinkers within the Catholic tradition. The chapter will also consider the conceptualisation of community that underpins their work, arguing that, ultimately, it is too restrictive and that what we need instead is to recognise what is *uncommon*. This idea is found in the work of Henry David Thoreau, a contemporary of Newman's whose writing derives from a non-conformist Protestant background. The idea of the uncommon may offer greater opportunities for keeping alive the kinds of questions that confront us within and beyond our communities.

Section II

For Newman, the university is an intellectual community, where the student is exposed to traditions of thought and the teacher nurtures an enquiring intellect. The ideal university is, in his words, a place

> in which the intellect may safely range and speculate, sure to find its equal in some antagonistic activity, and its judge in the tribunal of truth . . . where the professor becomes eloquent, and a missionary and a preacher of science, displaying it in its most complete and most winning form, pouring it forth with the zeal of enthusiasm, and lightening up his own love of it in the breasts of his hearers.
>
> (Newman, 1856, p. 11)

His views are premised on the view that the university is a place reserved for a male elite; the university teaches universal knowledge and its students become gentlemen, 'made through their learning of the universe' (Newman, 1886, p. 6). There may be a strong temptation at this point to dismiss out of hand Newman's ideas as outdated, but, as we shall see below, there is reason to resist the urge.

According to Newman, all branches of science are interconnected, and theology, which is of a different order than other sciences, is a distinct body of knowledge and therefore must be part of the curriculum. The university is a place of truth and wisdom.

> In order to have possession of truth at all, we must have the whole truth; and no one science, no two sciences, no one family of sciences,

nay not even all secular science, is the whole truth; that revealed truth enters to a very great extent into the province of science, philosophy, and literature, and that to put it on one side, in compliment to secular science, is simply under colour of a compliment, to do science a great damage.

(Newman, 1996, p. 58)

It is important to remember that Newman's lectures about university education were written at a time when the traditional Oxford curriculum was coming under attack: his specific target here was utilitarianism. He stresses the importance of intellectual development and the cultivation of the mind, drawing a distinction between 'liberal' and 'illiberal', or between non-instrumentalist and instrumentalist activities. Joseph Dunne (2006) usefully elaborates this distinction: 'liberal' can be contrasted with 'servile', the latter in the sense of the Greek *banausic*, tied to the needs of the body and without the mind's freedom of thought. A liberal activity is not pursued for any external end whereas an illiberal one is pursued for external ends. Although Newman believed in knowledge for its own sake, a good liberal education would inevitably be of practical importance because it would result in cultivating the public mind.

His thoughts on a liberal education, however, are not as clear-cut as the above distinction may suggest. In Newman's other work, such as *University Sketches* (1961) and *An Essay In Aid of A Grammar of Assent* (1870), it is clear that a liberal education is not seen as constituting the whole of education. A university education is not just about academic formation or intellectual excellence.[1] Newman claims that knowledge by itself does not make a person virtuous; a university education does not necessarily lead to good moral character. But, at the same time, he also argues that a liberal education instils tolerance and patience. Personal, interpersonal, emotional and spiritual dimensions are seen as equally significant and in this sense, perhaps, there are similarities between religious teaching and university teaching; a university must be an emotional and spiritual place as well as an intellectual space.

A well-trained mind is not enough: what is needed, according to Newman, is the capacity of 'arranging things according to their real value' (Cited in Ker, 1991, p. 17). An enquiring intellect or mental cultivation does not equate to getting students through their examinations. The following is a particularly telling remark by Newman that leaves the reader in no doubt about the difference in his mind between a 'so-called university' and a university:

. . . if I had to choose between a so-called University, which dispensed with residence and tutorial superintendence, and gave its degrees to any person who passed an examination in a wide range of subjects, and a University which had no professors or examinations at all, but merely brought a number of young men together for three of four years and

then sent them away again . . . I have no hesitation in giving the preference to that University which did nothing, over that which exacted of its
members an acquaintance with every science under the sun.

(Newman, 1996, p. 105)

In *Discourse VII*, Newman (1996, p. 125) describes the art of the university as 'the art of social life, and its end is fitness for the world'; learning is
a social practice. Real learning arises not from an encounter with a book
but in the encounter with others. The university is more than an intellectual community; it is a 'living community', which comprises emotional and
spiritual, as well as intellectual dimensions. The idea of community runs
through Newman's thoughts about education. It follows from this that the
university must be caring and compassionate. Drawing on his experience of
the Oxford college system, he makes a clear distinction between the college
and the university: whereas the college is concerned with the student and
their emotional and spiritual wellbeing, the concern of the university is with
the intellect, or in other words, the college nurtures virtue and the university
nurtures the intellect. He concedes that the college does have a role in the
moral and religious formation of students but this does not apply to the university: it is separate from the intellectual development of students. The
integrity of the university as an institution is ensured through the college's
role in the moral and religious formation of students; in Newman's words,
the college 'is all, and does all, which is implied in the name of home' (1961,
pp. 207 and 282, cited in Mulcahy, 2008, p. 224).

Newman did not, however, think that a university education, by itself,
makes a person a moral or virtuous person. Although he did not hold the
view that a university education should be religious, his religious views, not
surprisingly, have a strong bearing on his ideas about education. The university is likened to the Church – a living community with a living tradition.[2]

The relationship between Newman's educational and religious thinking is
well articulated in Gerald Loughlin's (2011) article in which he considers the
place of wonder in Newman's account of the university and the importance
of this in thinking about the contemporary university and the diversity of
modern society. Newman agreed with Aristotle's views that wonder is a first
step to knowledge; all sciences begin in wonder and all sciences, including
religion, begin in faith. And so for Newman, the university is itself a place
of wonder and the whole of humanity is the only appropriate ultimate context of scholarship. On Newman's account, the university has a definitive
ethical character that can be good or bad, and this is because teachers do not
just instruct students: they also create a sense of community. Study is not a
passive activity – it is necessary actively to enter into and embrace it. The
aim of the university is to transform the minds of students so that each
becomes a different kind of individual, one who has the capacity for judgement. The question of judgement is central to Newman, and we see this most
clearly in his philosophical work. He was critical of the growing technical

rationality that was becoming attractive to many thinkers of his time and a number of his sermons on the nature of faith and reason, and his major work, *An Essay in Aid of A Grammar of Assent,* (Newman, 1870) address this concern. This 'essay' – over 500 pages – provides a searching consideration of different ways of knowing. Newman's ideas here, however, are not confined to matters of religion: they raise broader questions about knowledge and understanding that are, as we shall see, particularly relevant to a university education.

In the *Essay*, Newman is concerned with the question of how he can believe something that he does not understand. He argues that there are different kinds of reasoning, rejecting what he saw as the limited view of reason found in Cartesian rationalism or Lockean empiricism which was prevalent among many of his peers. In Newman's account, there are areas of life such as faith that do not conform to any formal empirical method. Religious belief involves practices, but these cannot be proved either logically or empirically. This does not mean, as many of his peers would argue, that religious belief is not rational.

> Religion has to do with the real, and the real is the particular; theology has to do with what is notional and the notional is the general and systematic. Hence theology has to do with the Dogma of the Holy Trinity as a whole made up of many propositions; but Religion has to do with each of those separate propositions which compose it, and lives and thrives in the contemplation of them. In them it finds the motives for devotion and faithful obedience; while theology on the other hand forms and protects them, not merely one by one, but as a system of truth.
>
> (Newman, 1870, p. 140)

Faith is an intellectual activity, but reason is not dependent solely on the intellect. Judgement is also necessary and is involved in the formation of beliefs; such beliefs are not the results of any logical deduction or empirical analysis. Newman argues that any systematic enquiry necessarily assumes something; in other words, unless we assume something, we are not able to reason. There has to be a starting point before any deduction or analysis can take place. Here Newman uses the idea of the 'illative sense', by which he means the capacity to make judgements. It is an intellectual skill that is shaped by experience.

> [I]n no class of concrete reasonings, whether in experimental science, historical research, or theology, is there any ultimate test of truth and error in our inferences besides the trustworthiness of the Illative Sense that gives them its sanction; just as there is no sufficient test of poetical excellence, heroic action, or gentleman-like conduct, other than the

particular mental sense, be it genius, taste, sense of propriety, or the moral sense, to which those subject-matters are severally committed.

(Newman, 1870, p. 359)

For Newman, validity of proof is determined by a person's illative sense; it cannot be determined by any scientific method. Following Aristotle, he rejected the idea that mathematical rigour should be the standard used in every field of enquiry. It is not possible, as argued by Aristotle in the *Nicomachean Ethics*, that an educated person can come to a judgement using a common measure; there are different degrees of accuracy, depending on the field of enquiry. In Joseph Dunne's impressive work, *Back to the Rough Ground* (1997), he considers the connections between Newman's 'illative sense' and Aristotle's *phronēsis*, a mode of practical knowledge to be distinguished from *epistēmē*, theoretical knowledge. *Phronēsis*, as *technē*, is a form of activity, but they (*phronēsis* and *technē*) are different: the latter is to do with the capacity to make, whilst the former is about the capacity to act. Dunne describes *phronēsis* in the following terms:

> It is acquired not in the making of any product separate from oneself but rather in one's actions with one's fellows. It is personal knowledge in that, in the living of one's life, it characterizes and expresses the kind of person that one is.

(Dunne, 1997, p. 244)

Although, as we saw earlier, Newman's university was a male elite, and the teaching of universal knowledge was Western in conception, it would be wrong to dismiss his work as irrelevant to contemporary society, particularly the importance he attaches to the centrality of judgement. For Newman, judgement is not only important in matters of faith and religion, but in all intellectual enquiry. It is not simply a matter of acquiring theoretical knowledge; it is about how that knowledge is embodied in the learner and in a particular time. The learner is not a solitary figure; she is a member of a community engaged in a social practice, one based on a tradition, open to critique and change, or, as we have seen above, what Newman terms a living tradition. An understanding of the discipline and its intellectual tradition is required. Being part of a learning community is to be committed to something and this requires a kind of humility, a virtue that is most commonly associated with religious practice but is equally appropriate to a university education. It also involves skills of thinking and judgement, but not in the sense of skills as individualised and autonomous lists of competences as found in current political and educational discourse and its emphasis on generalisable and transferable skills. The centrality of judgement has been lost in the preoccupation with assessment and quality assurance systems which can be found across the education sector in the UK and across much of the world. These systems, however, distort conceptions of professional practice. The nature of study is also distorted, as we are held captive by the need to feed the system with more and better data and a never-ending supply of evidence of performance. Learning and knowledge are both individualised and reduced to what can be easily measured and standardised.[3]

Section III

The idea of community is also central in MacIntyre's work and, as with Newman, it is informed by the Aristotelian tradition. In *After Virtue*, MacIntyre (1985) argues that the tradition of the virtues needs to be restored because it is essential for the individual and for the community; without the virtues, no community can flourish, nor can there be an adequate conception of the common good. He suggests that modern society's preoccupation with individual actions has been to the detriment of social practices. It is, he posits, social practices that are essential to our ethical lives. A common tradition and a common endeavour are, therefore, central. These characteristics are found most typically in religious-based communities as well as the medieval university, but are, he laments, absent in modern culture.

MacIntyre's position is radical: it is not enough to try to adapt or change neo-capitalist society; in fact, modern political traditions, from liberalism to Marxism, are exhausted and do not offer any alternative. What is required is a turning away from the ideology of neo-capitalism and away from any modern politics that rejects the tradition of the virtues – a tradition, epitomised by the virtues of truthfulness, courage and justice that can be traced back to Aristotle. It is the morality found in Aristotle's and Aquinas's writings that MacIntyre believes to be both superior to, and hostile to, that of modernity. He identifies three important aspects of the virtues: practices, individuals and community. Virtues are 'those qualities of mind and character without which the goods internal to such human practices as those of the arts, and the sciences and such productive activities as those of farming, fishing, and architecture cannot be achieved' (MacIntyre, 1991, p. 262). He continues, virtues 'are those qualities without which an individual cannot achieve that life, ordered in terms of those goods, which is best for her or him to achieve'; they are 'those qualities without which a community cannot flourish, and there can be no adequate conception of overall human good' (p. 263).

In *Three Rival Versions of Moral Enquiry*, MacIntyre (1990) contrasts the modern age with the medieval: the latter was characterised by a shared understanding about the nature of enquiry. For Aquinas, for example, membership of a moral community and a tradition were a condition for rational, moral and theological enquiry. Following Aristotle, Aquinas believed that the ends of education could only be developed with reference to the final ends of human beings. It is this rejection of Aristotelian teleology that MacIntyre believes is critical; the loss of a shared moral reasoning means that there cannot be any common agreement on what is the common good. In the modern university there is, he argues, no longer a sense of common purpose or commonality; this has profound consequences for the quality of intellectual and political debate and is the reason why the university is unable to contribute significantly. MacIntyre points to the specialisation and expansion of subjects which has led to the disintegration of the curriculum and the fragmentation of enquiry. There is no longer a shared understanding or anything that brings academics together to engage in debate and to discuss different arguments. He argues further that there is no longer any conception of the disciplines as each contributing to a single shared enterprise. This is crucial for him because it is having a shared enterprise that is ultimately tied up with contributing to the understanding of ourselves and of our place in nature.

MacIntyre (2009) claims that the contemporary university is in danger of losing the ability to think about the ends of the university or to be self-critical. Unfortunately, he does not comment on the rise of interdisciplinary activities which have grown as a result of that very specialisation which he criticises. Putting this to one side, however, what is important to consider here is the idea that the university has become a place for *any*thing and not a place for *some*thing. The latter is reflected in a view of the professor, especially a professor in the humanities, as offering not only an account of the way things are, but a profession of belief in *something*. The use, in recent years, of the university mission statement as a marketing tool reflects the priority given to the need to attract potential consumers rather than as an expression of its mission, or indeed, its vocation.

Both MacIntyre and Newman understand the university as a place where fundamental questions are asked, where there is a tradition of questioning and a disciplined asking of questions. As MacIntyre argues in *After Virtue* (1985), one important feature of a living tradition is that it is 'an historically extended, socially embedded argument, and an argument precisely in part about the goods which constitute that tradition' (p. 222). A common tradition and holistic view of enquiry that characterised the medieval world is problematic today where, on the one hand, the university can be found all over the world, and on the other, modern democracies are pluralistic with different traditions and views of the world existing in very close proximity to each other. In relation to the latter, Newman's idea that the university provided universal knowledge is no longer a realistic goal for a university, although, as Jaroslav Pelikan (1992) argues, this does not mean that it could not be a goal for the university community worldwide if we believe that the university has a responsibility to the wider world. It does not follow from what has just been said that continuities of thought that derive from a common tradition lead to conformity or to a closing down of thought. A common tradition is, rather, a condition for agreement and disagreement within and across traditions. And this is essential to a healthy democracy because we need to ask ourselves constantly what kind of society we want. The

human being is faced with her life as a question, although in a world dominated by the culture of performativity and the one-track thinking that it
induces, we can lose sight of the question of being. It is, however, a question
that is ultimately unavoidable and is one that, following Aristotle, has been
central to Newman and MacIntyre; it is a question that a university education must be concerned with.

Today, it is difficult to see how we can foster the kind of community that
Newman and MacIntyre envisaged for a number of reasons. Newman's view
of the collegiate university where students felt at home is unrecognisable
today. In the case of the UK, among the hundred plus institutions of higher
education, only a handful of these are collegiate universities. The student
body is no longer a small, male elite; it is large and extremely diverse, and in
many universities there are significant numbers of students who are the first
in their family to enter university. There is also greater diversity amongst the
staff body and a growing number of temporary and contract staff, and as
such the university community is more transient than in the past. Newman's
view of the university as a living community, one that is concerned with the
intellectual, spiritual and emotional needs of students, bears little resem-
blance to the student-centredness that informs current political or educational discourse. For example, widening participation and the introduction
of fees, both of which were brought in by Labour administrations in the
1990s, have led to more concern for student-centred learning. Universities
cannot afford to turn away students, nor can they ignore their views
expressed through, for example, their representation on university committees, the creation of a student senate in some universities and the National
Union of Students' Student Satisfaction Survey. The character of student
choice, and what is being chosen, has altered. In the past, students were most
likely to seek admission to a university with standards and demands that they
would strive to meet, whereas today it is most likely that their choice would
be made in relation to indicators of value-for-money and student satisfaction.[4] The Coalition Government's 2011 White Paper *Students at the Heart
of the System,* for example, is primarily concerned with greater transparency
and accountability and better systems to ensure quality of teaching and
learning; the intellectual, emotional and spiritual dimensions of the university as a living community, as envisioned by Newman, are nowhere to be
found. The political discourse is driven by the desire to settle things and is
based on the belief in the need to have a common measure. Since the election
of a majority Conservative Government in 2015, there has been no sign of
any significant rethinking in higher education policy.

There are few communities other than religious communities that have the
kind of coherence implied in MacIntyre's conceptualisation of community.
His idea of community is, I would argue, too comprehensive and restrictive,
placing as it does great emphasis on social cohesion. In questioning the mer-
its of such a comprehensive conception of community, I do not wish to
undermine the importance that MacIntyre and Newman attach to the place

of critique in the university. I want to argue for a different way to think about community which may offer more realistic possibilities for ensuring the place of critique in the university and the kind of university needed today.

Section IV

A central characteristic of the university, and other institutions, is that it is performative. Take, for example, the statement, 'the university term will begin on such and such a date', or 'this paper is a Grade B'. These statements are not just descriptive: there is a performative element as well – they bring something into being. It is helpful to look at J. L. Austin's work, in particular, *How to do things with words* (1962). His general purpose was to move away from the tendency to focus on the true/false or value/fact dichotomisation in the assessment of the meaning of statements and to demonstrate the variety of things that we do with words. He initially contrasts performative and constative utterances, but later discovers that there is a far greater variety in statements than his initial contrast established. Moreover, he also came to see that these categories were far from distinct; in fact, he seemed to respond to this breaking down of the distinction not so much with dismay as with a certain glee. What was perhaps of particular importance was the way that he came to see the 'force' identified as characteristic of the performative as a dimension of language more generally. This prompts him to introduce the notion of the commissive force of an utterance which relates to the way that, or the extent to which, it constitutes a promise to attempt to do something. There is a variety of things that we do with words. Religious language is often seen as something distinct and separate from the rest of what we do and say, but Austin shows that the commissive force found in religious language is there too in other forms of language, including the everyday language that people use, whether religious or not.[5] In uttering something, we are at the same time saying something about ourselves, what is important to us, and at some level expressing our assent to something like a worldview. This is a precondition for, or inherent in, having something to say (Harris, 2015). What is at issue here is not primarily, or not solely, a matter of *religious* belief: it is the relation between reason, as characterised by detachment, and faith, as having 'commissive force'.

It is not only institutions like universities that are performative – clubs and families are also performative in a sense. There are rules of how to behave and act, social practices that take place. It involves conversation and this cannot take place without there being trust, or as Newman would say, assent. A social practice or a tradition is sustained by people who, in some sense, give it their assent. Assent is not an extra to these things: it is constitutive of them. As we have seen, Newman's assent goes beyond the religious to the everyday, ordinary, and gets to the importance of trust that must be there in the lives of human beings – down to the very words we use in conversation. For example, if we think of chess, you can say, 'this is the king', 'this is what it can do', 'it moves in this way'. If you do not use the king in this way, then you are not playing chess.

What is the significance of the performative in thinking about the common? The common depends upon promissory institutions – there is a kind of trust. In the medieval world, the idea of the common would not have arisen, for two main reasons: first, where everything was embedded in a stable order, with the unquestioned pinnacle of God, there was no room for the kind of doubt that would be necessary for any self-consciousness about what was common; and second, that society was marked by stable hierarchies in which notions of any more level commonality would be out of place. In later societies, what you are becomes more problematic and more of a question – the idea of personal consciousness is opened up, for example, with Luther and the theological debates during the Reformation and then later with the Enlightenment – the idea of the common is no longer clear or straightforward. Charles Taylor draws attention to this in *A Secular Age* (2007), where he considers the changes in the notion of the secular, one of which is the contrast in conditions of belief between, on the one hand, a pre-modern European society, where belief in God was unchallenged and unproblematic, and, on the other, contemporary Western societies, where Christianity competes with other belief systems. It is important that disbelief is not considered heretical but rather 'optional' – perhaps given a new inflection by the distinctive prominence of 'choice' in a market society. What it means to believe in God cannot be the same as it was in medieval times, where belief was held firm by a stable order or, we might say, taken for granted: that context has largely disappeared. To the extent that that stable order provided an unquestioned commonality, it has disappeared; rather than given, what might be common, what the common might mean, is now provisional.

Section V

Rethinking the university as a living community, to use Newman's phrase, will depend upon some broader rethinking of the community at large. What is the kind of community to which human beings should aspire? This question of community – of how we should live with others and how, through this, we can live best ourselves – is at the heart of the problematic that draws Thoreau to the woods near Concord, Massachusetts, where he lived.[6] His sojourn is not an escape to the countryside; it is not a rural idyll. His sojourn is, rather, an experiment in living, in placing himself in the world and seeing the world differently, designed to wake up his neighbours.

Unlike Newman and MacIntyre, whose writing derives from a Catholic European tradition of thought, Henry David Thoreau is from a non-conformist Protestant background. A contemporary of Newman his writing reflects his disappointment with what has become of the idea of America, taking America as a perfectionist idea, in a way perhaps similar to Israel – that is, not as the name of a particular landmass but as that of a society to be, never to be finally achieved. In *Walden* (1986), Thoreau ponders what living amounts to and the possibility of living differently; he presents a vision of the good society in which learning is realised as part of a mature and healthy civilisation. He is concerned ultimately with the question of meaning and understanding the world, and as we shall in the passage below, the idea of the uncommon holds a central place.

> It is time that we had uncommon schools, that we did not leave off our education when we begin to be men and women. It is time that villages were universities, and their elder inhabitants the fellows of universities, with leisure – if they are indeed so well off – to pursue liberal studies the rest of their lives. Shall the world be confined to one Paris or one Oxford forever? Cannot students be boarded here and get a liberal education under the skies of Concord? Can we not hire some Abelard to lecture to us? Alas! what with foddering the cattle and tending the store, we are kept in school too long, and our education is sadly neglected.
>
> (Thoreau, 1986, p. 99)

What are we to make of this? What does Thoreau mean? We need to take each sentence and consider his words carefully. 'It is time that we had uncommon schools, that we did not leave off our education when we begin to be men and women'. In this first sentence, he alludes to democracy and the surely reasonable desire of the democrat to provide common schools, but Thoreau also exploits the multiple connotations here. He suggests that it is not merely the common or familiar in a human life, or community, that is important but the uncommon, something that reaches towards the exceptional and the excellent – towards perfection. This will not amount to a consolidation or securing of the bonds of community but rather will reach beyond; there is a sense of the transcendent. Thoreau also challenges the commonly held view of the school as a place for socialisation and for shaping children into adults. For Thoreau, this distinction between children and adults will not do because we do not know what an adult is: we must not assume that we have exhausted the possibilities of the human. We cannot go to sleep, but must remain awake to our place in the world.

'It is time that villages were universities, and their elder inhabitants the fellows of universities, with leisure – if they are indeed so well off – to pursue liberal studies the rest of their lives'. In this second sentence, Thoreau's use of the word 'leisure' is particularly significant; in Greek this is expressed as *schole*, the root of 'school'. He again rejects the view of schools as places of socialisation, laying way for the affirmation of liberal studies. Thoreau, however, is not against a training in practical skills, as his living in the woods makes clear, where he builds his hut and hoes his beans. He wants to see the practical or vocational extend into the liberal.

The third sentence, 'Shall the world be confined to one Paris or one Oxford forever?' returns to the theme of egalitarianism but also makes fun of the snobbery that is found in the institutions he names. 'Cannot students be boarded here and get a liberal education under the skies of Concord?' He suggests that the open air (as opposed to the 'ivory tower') of America (as opposed to the great European cities) implies an enquiry that is open, unfettered. This may also be a new kind of community – that is, a new concord, as implied by his local town's name, with the weight of history that lies behind this. The last two sentences contain a deliberate bathos in mentioning the rather unglamorous tasks of 'foddering the cattle and tending the store' in the same breath as Abelard. He is also suggesting here that there is no tension between a liberal education and a vocational education and that both are needed. The bathos lays the way for an implicit contrast between 'school' and 'education'.

As becomes clear when reading this passage, although Thoreau refers to the university, his concern is not with institutionalised learning but with learning throughout a person's life, an education that never ends. This requires that we remain awake and do not go to sleep. We are constantly challenged by questions, and we are continually put into question over our community – over the nature of our allegiances, over the very idea of community, over what 'community' might mean. Although as noted earlier, the provisional nature of the common suggests a loss; it is, however, also the case that it gives society a dynamism, where what the common is, constantly brought into question. How we understand ourselves and relate to others is crucial and is ongoing. The idea of the common or the community can never be finally resolved. In a Wittgensteinian vein, Rowan Williams's *The Edge of Words* (2014) notes how the ordinary is not so ordinary; language itself can be disruptive and open things up in unexpected ways. This is because of the unfinished character of human language. He argues that we must

> regularly and consciously acknowledge together that we live by incompleteness of understanding, that we are not transparent to each other; and that this, so far from being a handicap, is how we begin to get some grasp of the meanings of love, or attention or respect – or whatever we want to say about that hesitation before each other which stops us eating one another up, in one mode of fantasy or another.
>
> (Williams, 2014, p. 93)

In light of the above discussion, I would like to draw out three potential problems which I believe are of particular pertinence to explorations of the university and the common good. In the first place, it is easy to be carried along by the idea that commonality and cohesion are necessarily virtues of the community. As we saw earlier, the idea of community runs through Newman's thoughts about education, focusing on the importance of the emotional, spiritual and intellectual, while in MacIntyre there is an emphasis on the importance of a shared community of beliefs.

In the second, it may be fruitful to seek in community something other than this cohesion. The etymology of the term 'community' can be of some service here. At the heart of community is the *munus*, the debt or gift or duty that the Latin connotes. It is helpful to think in terms of our being, first and foremost, members of a community of language, of our being responsible for our words and what we do with them. As we find in Thoreau, each of us must make judgements in what we say irrespective of whether or not we are part of a coherent community; ultimately, that responsibility is not one that we can escape. The purpose of a university education must be to extend and enrich the languages of enquiry; it must not shrink from acknowledgement and responsibility.

In the third, and in the light of the previous two points, it is worth attending more closely to the importance that an orientation to the other might have, where the other is to be understood as precisely that which breaks into any complacent self-containedness of commonality. It is the necessary disruption of cohesion, without which vices of complacency and hubris can so easily and so surreptitiously take root. Just as within a religious community there is a distinctive way of living and thinking about our place in the world, so too this must be so within the university. Critical awareness, openness to different ways of thinking and readiness for conversation are central, and the realisation of these goods is internal to the wider public world outside the university.

Notes

1 See Mulcahy (2008).
2 Unlike the Archbishop, who had hoped that Newman's lectures on the Idea of a University would encourage people to see that education should be religious, Newman was more interested in the education of Catholics than with the conversion of Anglicans.
3 See also Harris (2011).
4 See, for example Browne (2010), the report of the Independent Review of Higher Education Funding and Student Finance (2010) which informed the government's thinking and the 2011 White Paper (BIS, 2011).
5 Austin begins by distinguishing between performative sentences – utterances that do something – and constative sentences, which are statements. As he explores this further, the neat distinction between the two breaks down; performative utterances can also be descriptive.
6 Concord was at that time at the centre of New England transcendentalism, a half-religious, half-philosophical belief in the spiritual unity of the world. Ralph Waldo Emerson, another key figure, was also a resident and neighbour of Thoreau.

References

Austin, J.L., 1962. *How To Do Things with Words*. Harvard: Harvard University Press.
BIS (Department for Business, Innovation and Skills), 2011. *Higher Education: Students at the Heart of the System*. London: HMSO.

Browne Report (Independent Review of Higher Education Funding and Student Finance), 2010 Securing a Sustainable Future for Higher Education. No publication details given.

Dunne, J., 1997. *Back to the Rough Ground: Practical Judgment and the Lure of Technique*. Notre Dame, IN: University of Notre Dame Press.

Dunne, J., 2006. Newman Now: Re-Examining the Concepts of 'Philosophical' and 'Liberal' in the Idea of a University in *British Journal of Educational Studies*. 54 (4), pp. 412–428.

European Commission, 1996. *Teaching and Learning: Towards the Learning Society*. A White Paper on education and training. Luxembourg: Office for Official Publications of the European Communities.

Harris, S., 2011. *The University in Translation: Internationalizing Higher Education*. London: Continuum.

Harris, S., 2015. Education and the Grammar of Assent in *Ethics and Education*. 10 (2), pp. 241–251.

Ker, I., 1991. *The Achievement of John Henry Newman*. London: HarperCollins Publishers.

Loughlin, G., 2011. The Wonder of Newman's Education in *New Blackfriars*. 92, pp. 224–242.

MacIntyre, A., 1985. *After Virtue*, 2nd edition. London: Duckworth.

MacIntyre, A., 1990. *Three Rival Versions of Moral Enquiry*. Notre Dame, IN: University of Notre Dame Press.

MacIntyre, A., 1991. An Interview with Giovanna Borradori in Knight, K., ed. 1998. *The MacIntyre Reader*. pp. 255–266. Cambridge: Polity Press.

MacIntyre, A., 2009. *God, Philosophy, Universities*. Plymouth: Rowman and Littlefield.

Mulcahy, D.G., 2008. Newman's Theory of a Liberal Education: A Reassessment and Its Implications in *Journal of Philosophy of Education*. 42 (2), pp. 219–231.

Newman, J.H., 1856. *Office and Work of Universities*. London: Longman, Brown, Green and Longmans.

Newman, J.H., 1886. *Historical Sketches* Vol. 3. London: Walter Scott Publishing.

Newman, J.H., 1870. *An Essay in Aid of a Grammar of Assent*. London: Forgotten Books.

Newman, J.H., 1961. *University Sketches*. Ed: Tierney, M., Dublin: Browne and Nolan.

Newman, J.H., 1996; 1852. *The Idea of a University*. Ed: Turner, F.M., New Haven: Yale University Press.

Pelikan, J., 1992. *The Idea of the University: A Reexamination*. New Haven: Yale University Press.

Taylor, C., 2007. *A Secular Age*. Harvard: Belknap Press of Harvard University.

Thoreau, H.D., 1986. *Walden*. London: Penguin.

Williams, R., 2014. *The Edge of Words*. London: Bloomsbury.

5   Education and the virtues

Mike Higton

For universities to be seats of learning, they must be schools of virtue. This is a necessary condition for their work, if they are in any way committed to the exploration of truth for the sake of the common good.

My exploration of this claim will begin with an explicitly theological account of learning, drawn from a passage in the epistle to the Ephesians that connects 'learning Christ' to a set of deep behavioural dispositions – the kind of dispositions that are named elsewhere in scripture as the fruit of the Holy Spirit. This connection between Christian learning and the fruit of the Spirit is, I will suggest, echoed in a relationship already widely acknowledged in discussions of higher education: the relationship between university learning and virtue. I will argue that Christians might therefore have a role to play, alongside others, in defending and promoting the virtues necessary to learning: the virtues that sustain engagement with the world and with other learners. I also argue, however, that we should not imagine that universities have ever achieved a settled embodiment of virtue, nor see Christians simply as defenders or promoters of patterns of virtuous practice already securely understood and possessed. Rather, the virtuous practices needed for good university learning are still in the process of being discovered, and Christian participants in university life need to be teachable participants in the quest for more virtuous learning.

Learning Christ

Now this I affirm and insist on in the Lord: you must no longer live as the Gentiles live, in the futility of their minds. They are darkened in their understanding, alienated from the life of God because of their ignorance and hardness of heart. They have lost all sensitivity and have abandoned themselves to licentiousness, greedy to practise every kind of impurity.

That is not the way you learned Christ! For surely you have heard about him and were taught in him, as truth is in Jesus. You were taught to put away your former way of life, your old self, corrupt and deluded by its lusts, and to be renewed in the spirit of your minds, and to clothe yourselves with the new self, created according to the likeness of God in true righteousness and holiness.

Ephesians 4:17–24 (NRSV)[1]

In this passage from Ephesians, understanding and living go together. The 'Gentiles' live badly because they understand badly; their disordered minds are incapable of guiding well-ordered lives. To live well requires well-ordered understanding, and well-ordered understanding involves a transformation of the self. It demands a purification of disordered desires, a change in pattern of life from impurity to holiness, a taking off of the old self and a putting on of a new.

The old way of life, precisely insofar as it is driven by misdirected desire, is a life bound to misunderstanding. It is a life in which understanding is yoked to gratification and so to delusion – because our responsibilities and opportunities can only appear in distorted form when viewed through the filter of the old self's avarice. The possibilities open to the old self are drastically limited, narrowed down to a blunt calculus of cost and benefit, insensitive to anything that does not tip the balance of that calculation. To live in this way is to live with a darkened mind, a mind almost blind, because it has such a dim light by which to see. It is also to live with a futile mind, a mind left purposeless because it cannot make sense of the world against any horizon more distant than its own passing wishes. This is understanding alienated from God, the 'Father of all, who is above all and through all and in all', the one truly righteous and holy.

True understanding involves the overcoming of this alienation from the life of God. It is inseparable from holiness because it involves purification of vision from gratification's myopia, and learning to see as God sees. It is inseparable from righteousness because it learns to see justly – to do justice to what it sees. It demands everything of those who would learn it, because it demands the painful stripping away of their old habits of mind: dying to the old self and rising to the new. The way to renewal of mind is the way of cross and resurrection, the way of Jesus Christ. It is under his tutelage that Christians are being taught to see afresh, as they are being reunited in him to the life of God. They learn *about* him, and they are taught *in* him; the passage from old self to new, from delusion to the renewal of their minds, takes place as they learn Christ.

The pursuit of understanding in the likeness of God does not, however, lead to a 'God's-eye view', possessed in grand isolation by an individual knower. It is a form of understanding that cannot be pursued alone, as the epistle had indicated a few verses earlier:

> There is one body and one Spirit, just as you were called to the one hope of your calling, one Lord, one faith, one baptism, one God and Father of all, who is above all and through all and in all. But each of us was given grace according to the measure of Christ's gift . . . The gifts he gave were that some would be apostles, some prophets, some evangelists, some pastors and teachers, to equip the saints for the work of ministry, for building up the body of Christ, until all of us come to the unity of the faith and of the knowledge of the Son of God, to maturity, to the

measure of the full stature of Christ. We must no longer be children, tossed to and fro and blown about by every wind of doctrine, by people's trickery, by their craftiness in deceitful scheming. But speaking the truth in love, we must grow up in every way into him who is the head, into Christ, from whom the whole body, joined and knitted together by every ligament with which it is equipped, as each part is working properly, promotes the body's growth in building itself up in love.

Ephesians 4: 4–7, 11–16

Learning Christ – walking on the way of Christ and growing up into the full stature of Christ – involves becoming the *body* of Christ. This learning takes place as each person learns to play a distinctive role within the body. Each person has received a distinctive gift and *becomes* a distinctive gift to the whole. And that does not mean that each person is apportioned one fixed duty, being assigned to a single category in some divine team-building exercise. Rather, each is given a gift 'according to the measure of Christ's gift', and that measure, 'the measure of the full stature of Christ', is one of unstinting abundance, into which the members of the body grow together. Each member learns to understand more and to give more to the body, the more that he or she receives from others in the body.

To come to the full stature of Christ, each person must therefore learn to receive and to go on receiving the gifts of others, which means learning to avoid any teaching (any 'wind of doctrine') that prevents such learning: any teaching that shows us only how this community might grow according to some faction's pre-conceived scheme. Learning to recognise and to receive the gifts of others and to discover together the life that all can share means learning to receive a life that no individual or faction owns, that comes to them all (and keeps coming to them all) as a gift from above: the gift of a steady enlargement of their capacity to live together in love. Growing into God's understanding means unending reception of understanding from others, and through them from Christ, not the possession of a perspective from which to see and judge all.

The body's growth into the life of understanding requires each member to speak the truth in love, where the truth in question is precisely the yield of an undarkened vision, a renewed mind, capable of seeing justly. It requires each member to speak from the mind that is growing in her or him with the putting off of the old self and the putting on of the new. To speak the truth in love is to speak in ways that reveal possibilities of mutual service, of ministration to one another's needs within this body. This does not mean, however, that 'truth' is simply a name for whatever is serviceable to this community, whatever promotes its unity and security over against the 'Gentiles' from which it has separated itself. This body is called to become a body by growing upwards, into Christ, who himself comes down to us from the God and Father of all. The 'all of us' who are called to the unity of the faith and of the knowledge of the Son of God cannot, finally, be smaller in scope than the 'all' who have God as Father. And the truth that the members of the body are called to see and speak is the truth of how this whole family of God might live as one in Christ. The members of Christ's body are therefore called to grow to maturity as members of a family without boundaries: a truly universal community of all the children of God. Christian learning is therefore learning against a horizon of hope: hope of the salvation, the inclusion in this learning community, of the whole of God's family.

'Learning Christ', therefore, includes within it learning to understand each other. It involves an ongoing commitment to learn together, giving and receiving from each other deeper understanding of the possibilities for just, holy and loving life together.

It is because learning has this goal and shape that learners must have a particular character.

> I therefore, the prisoner in the Lord, beg you to lead a life worthy of the calling to which you have been called, with all humility and gentleness, with patience, bearing with one another in love, making every effort to maintain the unity of the Spirit in the bond of peace.
>
> Ephesians 4:1–3

> So then, putting away falsehood, let all of us speak the truth to our neighbours, for we are members of one another. Be angry but do not sin; do not let the sun go down on your anger, and do not make room for the devil . . . Let no evil talk come out of your mouths, but only what is useful for building up, as there is need, so that your words may give grace to those who hear . . . Put away from you all bitterness and wrath and anger and wrangling and slander, together with all malice, and be kind to one another, tender-hearted, forgiving one another, as God in Christ has forgiven you.
>
> Ephesians 4: 25–27, 29, 31–2

Given the nature of the learning to which the members of the Body of Christ are called, these characteristics, the fruit of the Spirit who is leading them into maturity, are necessary features of their life. Without these fruits, there can be no real learning: no reception of the gift of truth from others, no seeing past the filters of one's own desires, no discovery of ways to live together beyond factionalism. They are the characteristics of a learning life: learning demands holiness, the fruit of the Holy Spirit.

Learning Christ and university learning

The gap between this theological vision of learning and learning as the business of universities (including avowedly secular universities) may seem large, but we can narrow it quite quickly.

To narrow the gap from the theological side, we can note that 'learning Christ' as set out in Ephesians must include all kinds of learning. The God of whom Ephesians speaks is the 'one God and Father of all, who is above all and through all and in all'. This God is creator of the heavens and the earth, and so it is not just the whole human family but the whole community of God's creation, the whole community that waits for redemption with eager longing, that is called into flourishing life together. Christians are called to live well with their fellow human beings, with the wider circle of non-human animals, as participants in the ecology of all living things and as parts of God's material creation. The understanding that can be darkened or enlightened, that is transformed on the way of the cross and of resurrection and that is involved in 'learning Christ'. Therefore includes the understanding of any object whatsoever, if understanding that object can affect how the learner lives in the world as God's creature. It includes *any* learning that can shape learners' understanding of the possibilities for or constraints upon their life in the world.

To narrow the gap from the university side, one need simply note that university learning does indeed shape learners' ways of inhabiting the world and their ways of living together, and that at least some of the forms of learning pursued in a university allow for the present projects and expectations of learners to be interrupted, complicated or derailed by what they learn. Where learning like this takes place, there is at least a possibility that learning can undercut gratification. To put it another way: the gap is narrowed just to the extent that universities are institutions concerned not simply with what is useful but with what is true (even if their concern is primarily with what is useful because it is true).

Of course, the name 'university' has always named a variety of kinds of institution, and that variety has increased in recent decades. Universities speak about their learning and pursue it in a wide variety of ways. My claim about the proximity of learning Christ and university learning can cut through much of this diversity, however. It works with any university just insofar as its students are led to engage, alongside staff, in constructing, testing and refining patterns of understanding by engaging with the realities that those patterns purport to describe. And it works just to the extent that they are interested in exploring, by means of this constructing, testing and refining of patterns of understanding, how we might live well with the objects of our inquiries.

University learning that allows this kind of engagement will tend to be characterised by the following features. First, the objects of its learning will seldom be done with. They will become the focuses of ongoing exploration in which new possibilities of response are proposed, tested, refined, abandoned, replaced and supplemented. Learners will go on examining the patterns of language and practice with which they surround these objects and by which they demarcate them as objects of study in the first place, and they will ask what forms of engagement they enable and what forms they obscure.

And at least some of the time, they will ask whose interests are involved in these patterns of language and practice.

The gap will be at its narrowest wherever it is recognised that the possibilities of 'living with' and 'responding to' the objects of our learning are not reducible to consumption or exploitation. University learning that allows the objects of study to question and disrupt existing projects needs to be open to a wider range of possibilities – to relationships with those objects that can include wonder and lament as well as use and that can together take the form of wisdom.[2]

This idea that university learning has to do with exploring the possibilities of life in the world might seem, at first sight, most clearly applicable wherever universities are concerned with objects of study directly ingredient in that life. It is easier to talk this way about investigation of the role of tree planting in the regulation of floodplains or the impact of foreign aid on commodity prices than it is when universities are investigating the properties of gauge bosons, algebraic number theory or the folding of cytoskeletal proteins – but one can still think of all of these forms of learning together as bound up in our inhabitation of the world and exploration of its possibilities, however limited a role might be played within that by specific domains of inquiry.

The gap between my theological account of learning and university learning is likely to look smallest, however, when the 'objects' of our investigation are animals, especially human animals, and the question about how we appropriately live with and respond to them has become the question of how we can live together. The questions asked in universities about the patterns of language and practice by which we navigate our relationships with others can then (at least in principle) become questions about the justice those patterns do to the needs, experience and integrity of other persons. We attend to the ways in which they appear (or have been made to disappear) within the discourses that shape our world, and we experiment with and test ways of making sense that we hope will do more justice.

My claim is that whenever it can plausibly be thought of as involving this kind of labour on the ways in which we live in and with the world, university learning stands on terrain that, from a Christian theological point of view, is included in 'learning Christ'. At its best, the learning that takes place in universities may therefore contribute, in however limited a way, to the task of learning to live together in the world as Christ's body, regardless of whether those involved in it understand their learning in these terms. Of course, that qualifier 'at its best' is necessary, because nothing I have said requires that university learning will automatically lead to holy and righteous possibilities of living. My claim is certainly not that such university learning inherently or pervasively makes a positive contribution to learning Christ. Even if some of the forms of learning pursued in university settings look like they might contribute to flourishing life together, others might promote ways of living with creation or of relating to others that will look distorted to eyes being trained by the gospel, and there may be nothing in the resources of the university itself that can determine which of these possibilities will be realised. And if we ask at the broadest level about the visions of the common good, the political telos that is avowed by university learners or implied in their practice, we might well find it difficult to make positive connections between most universities and a Christian vision of learning and may even be tempted to portray some grand philosophical opposition between them. At a lower level, however, the level at which university learners engage with particular objects of study by means of specific forms of diligence and disciplined attention, the connections between this learning and 'learning Christ' will be more complex, and potentially, more positive.

My claim is not that Christian learning must build on university learning, nor that university learning can prepare for or produce Christian learning. I am not, in fact, claiming that there is any kind of systematic relationship between them. It is simply that, insofar as university learning explores the possibilities of life in the world, it is exploring territory that a Christian will see as relevant to 'learning Christ', and that it therefore makes sense for a Christian learner (a 'disciple') to interrogate university learning in the light of a Christian vision of learning. Learning Christ and university learning are not incommensurable realities.

Virtue in the university

When I set out a theological vision of learning above, I finished by arguing that the fruit of the Spirit are necessary features of learning. Without them, there can be no real learning; they are the characteristics of a learning life. People learn well by becoming those who learn with humility, gentleness, patience, forbearance, honesty, kindness, forgiveness and the moderation of anger.

One simple effect of examining university learning in the light of this theological vision, therefore, is to highlight the role that these fruit might play – *must* play – in university life. In itself, this is not a particularly striking move, despite the fact that references to the fruit of the Spirit are predictably sparse in secular discussions of higher education policy and practice. References to 'virtue', which covers at least some of the same territory, *are* widespread. The term 'virtue' is not, of course, identical to the term 'fruit of the Spirit', but it still directs our attention to the deep dispositions of the learner that enable and shape learning. At its most neutral, of course, the term 'virtue' simply names the internalisation by students and staff of the standards of excellence appropriate to the practices pursued in university: learning, teaching and research. Normally, however, it is given a more decidedly ethical cast: it is used to talk about these internalised standards insofar as they are constituents of a good human life, or insofar as the practices they govern are contributions to the common good.

It is not uncommon, then, to see university learning presented as a matter of virtue, and the university itself as a school of virtue, even if the accounts of virtue involved vary widely (see, for example, Nixon, 2008; Koetzee, 2014). University learning is seen to involve the disciplining of our existing patterns of thinking by engagement with the reality they purport to describe. Such disciplining of our thinking demands attentiveness of us; it demands that we be open to surprise, with a readiness to notice facets of that reality that do not fit our expectations. It involves the patience required to allow those facets to emerge. It requires the honesty to admit the challenges created by these surprises for our existing thinking, the integrity to trace their implications as far as necessary through the whole pattern of that thinking, and the clarity that makes the tracing of those connections possible. It involves the humility involved both in admitting that changes to our thinking are necessary and in the communication of those changes. At times, it requires the courage to admit that one has been wrong. Yet it also involves confidence in what one has learnt and the willingness to trust the findings to which disciplined investigation has led one, even when that means contradicting others.

It is also unexceptional to suggest that learning involves the formation of communities within which these virtues are formed and sustained. University learning involves patterns of relationship within which certain kinds of give and take, certain kinds of mutual affirmation and critique, are enabled and encouraged. Participation in such a community involves taking responsibility for one's contribution, responding to critiques of that contribution and offering criticism in turn. It involves the maintenance of certain patterns of civility: the maintenance of conventions that permit and facilitate exchange.

None of these claims is unusual in the literature on higher education, nor in the language of universities themselves, even where the term 'virtue' does not itself appear. Universities often speak about academic good conduct, where that covers everything from the acknowledgement of sources and the avoidance of misquotation to standards of clarity and proof. Most universities speak about these matters in ethical terms, and many connect them to the inherent nature of learning. Oxford University, for instance, provides the following guidance on plagiarism:

> Plagiarism is a breach of academic integrity. It is a principle of intellectual honesty that all members of the academic community should acknowledge their debt to the originators of the ideas, words, and data which form the basis for their own work. Passing off another's work as your own is not only poor scholarship, but also means that you have failed to complete the learning process.
> . . . You are not necessarily expected to become an original thinker, but you are expected to be an independent one – by learning to assess critically the work of others, weigh up differing arguments and draw your own conclusions. Students who plagiarise undermine the ethos of

academic scholarship while avoiding an essential part of the learning process.

(University of Oxford, 2015)

Similarly, it is not at all unusual to find standards of behaviour in research being overseen by ethics committees or to find research conduct discussed in ethical terms. The Arts and Humanities Research Council, for instance, insists that the 'seven principles of public life' (selflessness, integrity, objectivity, accountability, openness, honesty and leadership) are essential to the work of research assessment and includes discussion of them in training for members of its Peer Review College (AHRC, 2015).[3]

There is, of course, plenty of scope for criticism of the ways in which these ideas are articulated and of the forms of education and of scrutiny by which the virtues named are supposedly inculcated, just as there is plenty of scope for negative judgments about the actual display of these virtues in academic life. There is, nevertheless, much here that can be affirmed from a theological point of view. Christians can broadly agree with many others that the universities we need have to be virtuous universities, because learning demands of learners patient and disciplined engagement with the world and honest and open engagement with one another.

Can virtue be taught?

From a theological point of view, then, there is a certain proximity between university learning and 'learning Christ', and the theologian's interest in the role of the fruit of the Spirit in learning is matched by an interest on the university side in the virtues necessary to learning. Christian observers of and participants in university life should have a particular interest in this dimension of university learning. They should be amongst those taking seriously the description of university learning as a matter of formation in virtue, in ways that go beyond the formalities of 'academic good conduct' and compliance with codes of ethics.

Looking at the university with theological eyes, however, will involve more than a simple affirmation of existing ways of speaking about and pursuing the formation of educational virtues. Within a theological vision, the learning pursued in universities, and the virtues developed in that pursuit, are situated within a broader narrative. They are good to the extent that they can be contributions to the deep transformation of the self from gratification to righteousness, and contributions to the formation of the just and loving community of all God's children.

Because they see the development of the virtues necessary to learning as, potentially, a limited but real contribution to the deep transformation of the self, Christians may be particularly aware of some of the difficulties involved. 'Quarry the granite rock with razors', said John Henry Newman, 'or moor the vessel with a thread of silk; then may you hope with such keen and delicate instruments as human knowledge and human reason to contend against those giants, the passion and the pride of man' (Newman, 1976, p. 111). After all, the possibility of teaching virtue has been called into question since at least the time of Socrates.

In part, this question has to do with the futility of the direct teaching of virtue. After all, teaching *about* virtue does not inculcate it, and there are good reasons to be sceptical about the value of direct attempts to train university students and staff in virtue. A focus on distinct ethics courses or on the provision of ever more comprehensive information about good practice is very unlikely to be the main yield of a serious focus on virtue. Even a cursory glance at the theological and philosophical literature on virtue is enough to suggest that the focus is far more likely to fall on teachers and mentors *modelling*, habitually and attractively, the forms of attentiveness, openness and integrity that their disciplines demand, and drawing – or seeking to draw – their students into the community of those for whom these virtues have become second nature. Virtues are, it seems, best caught by imitation and repetition, by involvement in a community for which they have become second nature. A Christian concern with virtue in universities might, therefore, take the form of a concern with the kinds of apprenticeship in virtuous learning that the university provides and with the dynamics of classrooms and labs as communities of apprenticeship. The universities we need are schools of apprenticeship: contexts for the formation of relationships that allow for imitation of the habits of attentiveness and communication that constitute learning.

There is another aspect to the difficulty of teaching virtue, however, which goes rather deeper. Virtue cannot be taught, the argument goes, because to learn virtue requires that one already recognise and value it, and that in turn requires one to have already internalised the virtue that one is supposed to be learning. In reality, of course, the patterns of learning can be rather more complex than this criticism suggests. One can imagine, for instance, someone motivated by a thoroughly instrumental desire for some of the extrinsic goods made possible by a university education (salary enhancement, say) and diligently pursuing his or her studies only for the sake of those goods – and yet getting caught up in the process of study almost despite themselves and beginning to value it for its own sake. Such a person might well learn the intellectual virtues necessary for their studies and come in time to internalise them so that they became second nature, and properly deserving of the name 'virtue'.

Nevertheless, the claim that virtue cannot be taught to the unvirtuous rightly suggests that universities as putative schools of virtue cannot be considered in isolation from other contexts of virtuous learning. Students arrive at university already formed in many ways (in families, schools, churches, as participants in and consumers of popular culture and so on); they are normally at university for only a short period of time. As Stanley Hauerwas (2007) has argued, a society therefore tends to get the universities that it deserves: the formation provided by a university can only be sustainable and effective if it is one that those in the society surrounding it are able to value. Universities can only provide formation that makes sense within those broader patterns of moral education that shape that society. A Christian concern with virtue in universities might therefore take the form of a concern with the connections between the university and the wider society, and even though there is no good reason to think that the wider society will be unvaryingly inimical to the possibility of true learning, that concern might include a particular focus on the kinds of moral formation outside the university that undermine the possibility of good work within it, and on the possibilities within university life for resisting and undoing them. Just as theologians have asked about the counter-cultural possibilities of Christian liturgies over against the malformation provided by the quasi-liturgies of consumerism (for instance), so a Christian concerned with virtue in a university setting might ask whether here too there might be, in however secondary and limited a sense, liturgies of formation strong enough to keep the space for true learning open. The universities we need will be contexts for the formation of deep habits of attentiveness and communication, and such formation will be a matter of the whole performance, display and ritual of university life.

There can, after all, be a specificity to the education in virtue provided by universities, precisely because virtues can take domain-specific forms. It is possible to be habitually honest in one domain and not in another, habitually attentive in one domain and not in another, habitually to show integrity of one kind but not of another. That is not to say that the various domain-specific forms of honesty, say, are completely independent – and it might therefore be sensible to ask serious questions about the academic honesty of someone who had proved thoroughly dishonest in some other context – but formation in virtue might indeed turn out to be a complex patchwork affair rather than a coherent whole. That should certainly make us wary of any claims that university learning will inherently have some wider moralising effect, beyond forming students in the virtues necessary for that learning itself, but it does also suggest that specific forms of virtuous behaviour may be kept alive in a university, by the momentum of its own particular practices, in ways that are effectively counter-cultural. Academic communities might be communities of virtue in ways that do not reflect, and might even resist, wider societal patterns – even if only in limited ways. A Christian concern with virtue in universities might take the form of an interest in these counter-cultural possibilities that university learning can provide.

Negotiating virtue

All of these suggestions, however, could leave a problematic picture in place. They could reinforce the assumption that the shape of the virtuous practices necessary for university learning to flourish is clear, that Christians have (either uniquely, or alongside others) a secure grasp of that shape and that their task is therefore simply one of the preservation or promotion of something that they possess. Yet, in the theological vision with which I began, the fruits of the Spirit were the dispositions necessary for an ongoing exchange, in which the members of the body keep on giving and receiving from one another new understanding of the possibilities for living together – in which they keep on *learning* the nature of the life to which they are called. The life discovered in these exchanges is, I said, one that no individual or faction owns, and that comes to them all (and keeps coming to them all) as a gift from above. It involves an unending reception of understanding from others and through them from Christ, rather than the possession of a perspective from which to see and judge all. To promote such a life by acting as guardians of a conception of virtue already securely possessed would involve a performative contradiction – and it might be better to think that one of the roles that Christian participants could play in university life would be to be visibly *teachable*.

Rather than thinking of, say, 'openness' as a virtue that is already securely identified, that can be preserved or promoted by means of appropriate vigilance, we should instead think of it as a vague term that is concretely, repeatedly and diversely specified in particular proposals and counter-proposals for patterns of university life. We should think of it as a site for ongoing negotiation and therefore as a site for ongoing learning. We already know something of what it means to be open and to be formed for openness, but we do not yet know all that openness can and should mean. After all, I argued above that the openness proper to learning has as its horizon the whole human family learning together.

This vision of an ongoing mutual adjustment finds its echoes in the life of contemporary universities. They are often locations where the openness or inclusivity of learning is a matter of intense and difficult negotiation. Universities are often depicted in the press and elsewhere as seedbeds of 'political correctness', but that normally means no more than that they are sites for the sometimes awkward, sometimes heated attempt to identify the forms of exclusion prevalent in our society and mirrored in our society's universities, and to track down the roots those forms of exclusion through all our practices and our language. Such negotiation – genuinely difficult, genuinely contested and inherently resistant to resolution by simple appeals to supposed common sense – is not a distraction from the proper business of universities, but an inevitable and proper accompaniment to learning. It is a symptom of the ongoing exploration of the nature of one of the core virtues proper to learning.

One could look, therefore, at recent debates about the 'no platforming' of controversial speakers, the removal from college facades of statues of infamous figures from the colonial past, the proper approach to avoiding offensive stereotypes in student celebrations or the need for trigger warnings before lectures that include sensitive content, and so on. The existence and fierceness of these debates are not signs of some fundamental breakdown in university life, still less of some easily dismissed immaturity on the part of students. They are evidence of the on-going, complex negotiation of the openness of the university learning community. They are new forms of fundamental and perennial questions facing universities, precisely about the kind of moral formation they demand and provide – and those perennial questions can *always* throw up new forms.

Precisely the patterns of virtuous behaviour on which the academic community has collectively settled can turn out, in subsequent negotiations, to be or to have become forms of viciousness that need to be overcome. The forms of civility that permit and facilitate exchange, for instance, can be masks for very uneven distributions of power. They can all too easily serve to mute challenges that ought to be heard. Even the call for clarity as an intellectual virtue can be problematic in some contexts, where the language of learning has evolved as a home for those in power and where those excluded from power are also excluded from the sense of easy familiarity, the sense of being at home in the language, that common forms of clarity demand.

The theological vision of learning that I have outlined certainly encourages a deep concern with universities as schools of virtue, with the forms of apprenticeship that they provide and with their connection with other patterns of moral formation in society. It should not, however, promote a concern that is predominantly conservative, still less nostalgic in tone. The universities that we need will be homes to an ongoing negotiation of patterns of practice and formation, in which participants go on learning from one another and from those not yet included, what virtue can and should look like. For Christian participants, there will certainly be a constant return to the gospel of Jesus Christ to test, challenge and refine what is being learnt – the fundamental form of learning is, after all, 'learning Christ' – but Christians can expect to discover more of that gospel in the light of the understanding they receive as a gift from others.

In other words, participants in the universities we need will recognise that they, their disciplines and their institutions are *not yet* virtuous and that they do not yet know in full what virtuous learning will involve. They will recognise that there are new habits of attentiveness, of openness and of critique to learn, and they will expect to go on learning them from others and to be weaned, in the process, from habits of thought and action that they had hitherto thought to be good.

For universities to be seats of learning, they must be schools of virtue. To be schools of virtue, however, includes being places where our grasp of virtue is explored, challenged and revised. The universities that we need are not reservations in which the virtues of an imagined golden age are preserved, nor clubs within which a well-understood rulebook of virtuous practices is enforced. They are sites for contestation and discovery, for the restless expansion of the community of enquiry and for the ongoing transformation of the habits of engagement and communication that make true learning possible.

Notes

1 New Revised Standard Version
2 See Higton (2013).
3 These are the 'Nolan Principles', published in 1995 by the Committee on Standards in Public Life.

References

AHRC (Arts and Humanities Research Council), 2015. *The Seven Principles of Public Life*. [online] Available at: http://www.ahrc.ac.uk/about/policies/sevenprinciplesofpubliclife/. [accessed January 5th 2016].
Hauerwas, S., 2007. *The State of the University: Academic Knowledges and the Knowledge of God*. Oxford: Blackwell.
Higton, M., 2013. Wisdom and Delight in the University in *Journal of Beliefs and Values*. 34 (3), pp. 300–311.
Koetzee, B., ed., 2014. *Education and the Growth of Knowledge: Perspectives from Social and Virtue Epistemology*. Oxford: Wiley-Blackwell.
Newman, J., 1976. *The Idea of a University Defined and Illustrated*. Ed: Kerr, I., Oxford: Clarendon.
Nixon, J., 2008. *Towards the Virtuous University: The Moral Bases of Academic Practices*. London: Routledge.
University of Oxford, 2015. *Academic Good Practice – A Practical Guide*. [online] Available at: http://www.ox.ac.uk/sites/files/oxford/field/fielddocument/Academicgoodpracticeapracticalguide.pdf. [accessed January 5th 2016].

6 The university as a place of public theology

David Ford

Introduction: a key insight from China

I begin in China, where in the past two decades there has been the most substantial development of universities ever seen in any country. A little-noticed aspect of this has been a considerable expansion of the study of religions. During visits to China, in which I have given lectures and seminars on the study of religions in universities, I have been struck by how Chinese academics and public officials regard this expansion as obviously sensible.

The reasons they have given for this are various: whatever one's personal position, it must be recognized that the religions are of great importance in the twenty-first century world; a wide range of academic disciplines need to come together in order to do justice to this phenomenon, and universities are the best places for that to happen; universities are places where the diverse religious traditions can not only be studied but brought into engagement with each other with a view to a peaceful future; China's history and culture cannot be adequately understood without the study of its religions; China today has growing numbers of people directly involved in religions, with many good and bad possibilities, and universities need to understand what is going on so as to inform public policy; China needs better welfare provision and the government cannot meet all the needs, so the religions are seen as contributors to this, with a need for university involvement in the educational side of it – whatever is thought about its truth, religion can be useful; since China has gone global economically and educationally it has no option but to go global religiously, which includes keeping up with the ways the religions are described, understood, analysed and explained by academic disciplines; India is increasingly recognized as the main Asian economic rival of China, and there is fascination with the religious character of India, that in so many ways contrasts with China – it is a global 'religious power' in ways China is not – but also faces analogous problems of religions in a plural society; there is something of a revival of Confucianism in China at present (with both popular and officially sponsored elements, not always in accord with each other) and universities are seen by some as an instrument for this, and in need themselves of such a tradition of wisdom and ethics. Many of those points, or analogies of them, would be made in the UK too.

But what about theology?

I also begin my answer to that question with a definition: by theology I mean both the various ways in which religious traditions do their thinking, pursuing the questions that are important for them, and also the discourses that engage with this religious thought historically, critically, comparatively or with a view to contributing constructively to current discussions (including those of public life). This broad definition allows for three important elements.

First, it recognizes the very different ways in which religious traditions name their thinking. Not all use the word 'theology', but neither is there any other term all would agree on. A problem with the general term 'religious thought' is that it is usually an 'outsider' designation, and, as will become clearer below, it is an advantage to have a term that particular traditions can identify with as a discourse concerned with their own meaning, truth and practice. So, when I use the term 'theology', I have this definition in mind and mean (when a range of traditions are being referred to) 'theology and its analogues in those traditions that do not use the term'.

Second, this definition also accommodates the range of theological disciplines (or their analogues in relation to traditions that do not use the term 'theology'), such as historical theology, philosophical theology, hermeneutical theology, dogmatic or doctrinal or systematic theology, constructive theology, theological ethics, political theology, comparative theology, practical theology and the ever-expanding number of sub-fields called 'theology and ...' (... the natural and human sciences; prayer and spirituality; gender; the arts and so on).[1]

Third, it allows for practitioners of theology to be members of particular theological traditions or not – for example, contributors to political theology can be Catholic, Muslim, Jewish, Hindu, agnostic, atheist or unwilling to be labeled at all.

To return to China, the obviousness of the study of religions in universities is not paralleled there by that of theology. It is a far more sensitive matter to sponsor normative discourse related to particular religions and to encourage both the pursuit of questions of meaning, truth, practice and beauty and also the offering of answers. The dominant approach might in UK or US terms be called rigorously 'religious studies' within a normatively secular framework. Yet the interest of China for the present chapter is that it also testifies to how, even in that setting, which might seem inhospitable to theology, and most of all to theology that contributes to public discourse, there are signs of opening up to theology. Some Chinese are recognizing that a 'religious studies' (or 'study of religion') approach in universities is necessary but not sufficient, and that society as a whole is impoverished if this is not enriched by theological discourse. I will describe briefly a specific Chinese instance of that, which has illuminated for me the character of the university as a distinctive place of public theology.

The instance I have in mind is the Institute of Comparative Scripture and Interreligious Dialogue in the Faculty of Philosophy and Religious Studies at

Minzu University, Beijing. That was founded in 2011, and two main strands are woven into it. One is Comparative Theology, as developed mainly by Francis Clooney, SJ, in Harvard, who is a member of the Academic Board of the Minzu Institute. Comparative Theology has so far been mainly concerned with relating Buddhist and Hindu to Christian texts, with a strong theological interest. The second is Scriptural Reasoning, which began over twenty years ago, with the Universities of Virginia and Cambridge as its main incubators.[2] It is a practice of studying and discussing scriptural texts of different traditions, its main focus so far having been on the Tanakh, the Bible and the Qur'an.[3]

The Minzu Institute's purpose is 'to conduct comparative research in the classical or scriptural traditions of the great world religions and to engage in interreligious dialogue . . . The Institute not only focuses on a purely academic or scientific comparison of texts, but also allows for a study of one's own scripture as authoritative Scripture in the context of one's faith community as well as of other faith communities'.[4] That is a purpose which allows for theology in my sense. Visiting Minzu and taking part in Scriptural Reasoning there helped me clarify a key insight: for universities that want to fulfil responsibilities towards religiously plural societies, the engagement between religions is a desirable aim that is best fulfilled by a combination of 'religious studies' and 'theology'.

Around the Scriptural Reasoning table in Minzu there have been, in various combinations, Buddhists, Christians, Confucians, Daoists, Jews, Marxists and Muslims, together with atheists and agnostics of diverse sorts. Each has questions in relation to their own tradition or worldview; each also has questions about the other traditions, and the engagement between them requires that each set of questions is in interplay with the other. In other words, this is a setting in which there come together the questions of meaning, truth, practice, beauty and wisdom raised by and within particular traditions (the main concerns of theology), the questions raised through a variety of academic disciplines about a range of traditions (the main concerns of religious studies) and the questions raised between the traditions (these being issues that most clearly require contributions from both theology and religious studies).

In religiously plural societies there is bound to be public theology, in the sense that understandings generated by particular religious communities will be articulated in relation to issues concerning the rest of society. But there is no guarantee that there will be places where those understandings and issues can be thoughtfully considered, where they can be informed by the best available understanding in relevant academic disciplines, where those from different traditions can consider the issues together and where good practice in doing all that can be passed on across the generations. The university is probably the only place where those things can happen together over the long term. The university can therefore play an essential (though by no means exclusive) role in generating and maintaining wise public theology.

In China, there are only the beginnings of this in an environment where even the study of religion (other than in a Marxist framework for polemical purposes) is new since the Cultural Revolution, and one cannot predict how this and other small innovations hospitable to theology will fare. But it is significant that, in the example I have given, the model for what might be called proto-theological discourse has been creatively adapted from universities where religious studies and theology cohabit – Harvard, the University of Virginia and Cambridge.[5] The combination is rather different in each of those cases, reflecting differing histories and contexts, but it is important that each not only combines religious studies with theology but that they simultaneously foster interreligious engagement.

Public theology in UK universities: towards a vision

Cambridge is by no means unique in the UK in combining theology, religious studies and interreligious engagement. There are several variations on this, worked out by particular institutions over decades, and it is striking that this has been a common direction of development for many departments. One obvious explanation is that it responds to religion having become more prominent in both academic and public discourse, nationally and internationally, and to UK society having become more religiously plural. Though it does not by any means always recognize this, such a society benefits from places where there is teaching, research and debate relating to the religions. With regard to theological thinking, writing and teaching, most of it will always happen in the institutions sponsored by particular religious traditions. I would nevertheless argue for a smaller yet essential role for universities.

In what follows, I have UK universities mainly in mind, but I have begun with China in order to underline the international ramifications. My account and recommendations are distilled from a lifetime of personal involvement in the field, including study in Ireland, UK, US and Germany, employment for 15 years in the University of Birmingham and 24 years in Cambridge and specific engagements with universities in Canada, China, Egypt, India, Israel, the Netherlands and Switzerland. The distillation has tried to take seriously the variety of contexts and histories, while also offering guidelines for what I propose as the healthiest 'ecology' to aim at. So it brings together what I consider the main elements of 'best practice' that might lead to lively, intelligent and wise university-based public theology. No single university best exemplifies all the elements, so the guidelines with which this chapter concludes might act as criteria for how any university might assess and improve its performance in contributing to public theology.

This conception of the university as a place of public theology takes for granted assumptions that are discussed at length elsewhere in this volume. Most importantly, it assumes a rich conception of the character of universities as places where a responsibility is recognized towards the common good not only of the society in which the university is located, but also of the rest of the world. This responsibility is to be embodied in forming students in appropriate virtues, in helping to shape wise and responsible citizens, in informed public advocacy, in research that is beneficial to humanity, in national and international partnerships and in other ways explored by fellow contributors.[6]

Within that broad conception, my specific concerns are three: to envision the 'ecology' of a university that might best contribute to public theology; to ask what particular religious communities might require of this university-based ecology; and to sketch a Christian theological rationale for the vision.

1 The 'ecology' of academically-mediated religion in universities

The concept of 'academically-mediated religion' embraces both theology and religious studies as defined above – it can include pursuing and answering questions of truth, practice and beauty, as well as questions of description, analysis, explanation and meaning. I would suggest three main ways in which academically-mediated religion should ideally be present in universities.

(i) Focused in dedicated departments

The first is the most obvious: that there should be departments dedicated to it. If, as in many universities, the only way in which religions are studied is as part of another discipline (see next section), then it is difficult to study them as wholes and hard to bring together the disciplines that are relevant – history, literature, languages, philosophy, theology, social sciences, natural sciences, gender studies, area studies, medicine and more. It is especially important in a plural society such as ours that there is a variety of religions on the curriculum. And if a university is to be a place of public theology in such a society, it needs to have settings where the conversations and debates within, between and about religions can happen.

The main objection which I have found to universities having departments that include both theology and religious studies and that can contribute to normative discourse on public issues is that an 'academic' approach to religion should be neutral as regards its truth, values and ethics. Yet other subjects are not confined in this way. Philosophy is one clear case. Perhaps even more apposite is economics. Besides history of economics, economic theory, econometrics and other 'religious studies'-like fields, it also includes applied economics, economists are found in public debates on different sides of issues, and many universities have business schools where normative discourse is habitual. The crucial point is not that normative discourse is unacademic, but that it should meet the standards of academic argument, use of evidence, acknowledgement of sources and so on. Those standards are, of course, themselves constantly being debated. Academically-mediated theology needs to meet such standards (and take part in the debates about them) too.

I suspect that with regard to theology there is a long hangover from the time when theological orthodoxy was enforced upon some universities in this country, and also a wariness over what happens to academic freedom today in some religiously affiliated universities elsewhere. These are hardly valid arguments in this country now. If anything, the orthodoxies threatening to dominate universities here are economic and political rather than religious. And the universities with religious affiliations here (for example, the Cathedrals Group) do not have problems with academic freedom. The essential point is that the level of public understanding and debate can be enhanced by the contributions of academically-mediated religion, and those contributions require settings where the religions and their theologies are studied, researched, taught and debated.

(ii) Distributed through other departments

Because of the wide range of disciplines that cover some aspect of religion and theology, its study needs to be distributed across many departments. It is a good thing when, for example, sociology of religion is present both within a religion and theology department and also within a sociology department – in practice, this is often through joint appointments or course sharing. There can, however, be considerable resistance to taking religion seriously in some departments, and even more to taking theology seriously. This is partly a challenge to theology to do 'theology and . . .' better, but it can also be a symptom of a secularist mindset that simply cannot conceive the possibility that theology could be about truth.[7]

(iii) Embodied in a religiously literate institution

The third way is through the university itself in all its aspects being religiously literate. In this country, a major impetus has been given by the Religious Literacy Leadership in Higher Education Programme (RLLP), funded by the Higher Education Funding Council for England. It is led by Professor Adam Dinham and based in the Faiths and Civil Society Unit in Goldsmiths, University of London. It now embraces over 60 English universities, from all university groupings, with participants including Vice-Chancellors, senior management, chaplains, student services staff and a range of other departments. In a pluralist society, religious literacy is important for peaceful diversity. Universities are more pluralist than most parts of this society, but they vary greatly in how they relate to the religions and their members. RLLP has a revealing typology of five differing ways universities handle the religions, from the secular or neutral university at one end to the 'formative-collegial university' at the other. It would be to the advantage of high-quality public theology if more universities could move towards the formative-collegial model, which is summarized as follows:

> This university takes into account the widest experience of its students and staff, seeing their learning and work in terms of their overall human growth and development. This might include recognizing religious dimensions of human life. Faith is not seen simply in terms of require-ments or needs which some students have and others do not. Rather, all people's worldviews, both religious and secular, are taken as essen-tial aspects of identity and culture and as potentially enriching dimen-sions of learning and growth. Its strategy for widening participation emphasizes the personal and intellectual benefits of obtaining a univer-sity education alongside people from different traditions and none, in addition to the economic and material benefits. The student experience is not seen as a process of knowledge transfer in pursuit of a "bank-able" academic qualification, but is taken to be a significant component of a broader life-project. Good campus relations are ensured by trying actively to create an environment in which faith is "at home" on cam-pus, with religious events and forms of expression enjoyed alongside others, and religiously-orientated questions and legacies being on the academic agenda in curricula, teaching and learning. There is outreach to surrounding communities, including faith communities, which are seen as enriching the university experience within and beyond the cam-pus walls.
>
> (Dinham, A. and Jones, S., 2010, pp. 19–20)

Analogous developments are desirable in other institutions and spheres of society, and indeed there are many initiatives in this direction. It is, how-ever, no accident that the RLLP began with work on the place of religion in universities and was developed in Goldsmiths' Faiths and Civil Society Unit.[8] This is academically mediated religion being applied in the public realm, and if there is to be a much-needed increase in religious literacy in this country, universities are best placed to lead the way.

2 Academically-mediated religion and religious communities

Religious communities are part of the public life of our country, and they have their own ways of doing public theology. They sometimes corporately take positions on matters of public concern, and their religious profession-als are public figures on a local level, and often beyond. It is tempting to see them as mainly involved with congregations of their own tradition, but that would be to miss two other vital dimensions, each of which makes demands on public theology.

One is education. There are thousands of state-funded schools that are affiliated to one religious tradition or another. The Church of England, the largest group, has over 4,700 schools. Beyond the schools that are directly affiliated, the various religious communities have many other forms of involvement with community schools, free schools, academies and private schools. Education is one of the most sensitive public issues, and theological thinking about it that informs educational engagement by the religions is therefore of considerable importance.

The other is chaplaincy. In education, healthcare, the armed forces, prisons and a range of public and private institutions, many thousands of chaplains serve in various ways. All of these spheres raise issues of public policy, public and private morality and institutional ethos, and chaplains contribute to these.

The religious communities are resourced for their work in public life, education and chaplaincy in many ways, but within the scope of this chapter it is important to note the role of universities. A great many of the religious professionals have university degrees, a good deal of the relevant literature available to those with or without university degrees is generated through universities and religious bodies make extensive use of university-based consultants and advisors. This adds up to a significant role for universities as places of public theology.

It is worth noting also a more general role for academically-mediated religion in relation to the religious communities. Not all want to be involved with universities, but most do, and all the main traditions are represented in the departments of theology and religion around the country. Such departments are therefore places where those of many religious traditions and none come together as students and teachers. The impact of these plural academic communities on the religious traditions is hard to assess, but in my experience, they often encourage mutual understanding and cooperation, and they learn a good deal from each other, particularly on matters of shared public interest. A more daring verdict would be that, in times when there is in evidence much dangerous and foolish faith, universities contribute to more peaceful and wiser faith and so help to shape a healthier civil society.

3 A Christian rationale for university-based public theology[9]

In a multi-faith and 'multi-secular' society, one way of coming together is around joint statements or platforms that are broadly acceptable to all parties.[10] Especially in a democracy where a good deal of university funding comes from taxpayers, we need to seek such commonality, and much of what I have written so far tries to articulate a rationale for the university as a place of public theology with which most stakeholders in the universities of this country today might agree. In other words, I think a strong case can be made for university-based public theology on the basis of arguments that do not appeal directly to my own Christian theology. But that is not sufficient.

The danger of that sort of consensus by itself is that it is a lowest common denominator which suppresses the deep differences involved. It can be a means of ensuring the establishment or continuation of public theology in universities, but the actual doing of public theology requires something more fully theological. This needs to be plural in form: a variety of rich theologies providing thoughtful, religiously inspired rationales for what is happening. Healthily plural public theology requires deep thought coming from each of the traditions involved, followed by deep and thoughtful engagement between them. This inevitably involves radical differences and fundamental, long-term disagreements, and the university is a place where these should be able to cohabit. It should be a complexly multi-faith and multi-secular space in which life is constituted by teaching, research, argument and conversations that do not require agreement. Those of us who have been part of such environments know the array of pressures, motivations, courtesies, traditions, peer-group responses, virtues and much else needed to sustain them year after year – and also how they can go wrong. One way they can go wrong is by failing to draw on the depths of the traditions, thus not bringing them into dialogue with each other.

So I will seek to give a brief answer to what a Christian rationale for university-based public theology might be, intending it to be an invitation to others to give their rationales and then enter into conversation about them.

In the magisterial multi-volume study of the university in Europe edited by Walter Rüegg, there is a striking list of core elements in the ethos of the first universities and an exploration of how they are related to Christian understanding (Rüegg, 1992–2010). He and the other contributors to the volumes make a convincing cumulative case for there being, despite huge changes, some continuity linking the medieval origins of the university with the character of many of its successors today.[11]

The Christian tradition in which these core elements are historically rooted could be affirmed by most twenty-first century Christians, just as it was affirmed by medieval Christians. The teachings about God as creator of a world order accessible to human reason; human imperfection; humanity in the image of God; the appropriateness of public argument and discussion to the absoluteness of scientific truth; scientific and scholarly knowledge as a public good transcending any economic advantage it might bring; the cumulative and self-correcting process of the growth of knowledge; and the equality and solidarity of those committed to the pursuit of knowledge – would be likely to gain the assent of a broad range of Christians in universities: conservative, liberal, radical, postliberal – though not, perhaps, some postmodern. It is particularly noteworthy with regard to the present topic how many of them insist on publicness. If Christians are true to their basic convictions, then they will be open to full public debate of their positions. All truth is God's truth, and potentially for all people, which means that Christians cannot claim theirs is private, protected or invulnerable.

This also means that it makes sense for Christians to seek out the analogues of their own understanding in those of other religious and non-religious traditions. This is perhaps especially important in practical implications, such as: rational investigation of the world; ethical values of honesty, justice and self-criticism; respect for the dignity and freedom of the individual; rigorous public argument appealing to demonstrated knowledge and rules of evidence; the recognition of the pursuit of knowledge as a public good irreducible to economic interest; the need for continual self-criticism in the course of improving our knowledge; and the value of equality. All these can be justified by Christians in their way and by others in theirs, and there are likely to be differences due to various understandings and beliefs, but at least such concepts and practices shape a public sphere within which the disputes can be held.

There is a further striking thing. The three key purposes identified by Rüegg in the first universities – love of knowledge, understanding and truth for their own sake; formation of students in a way of life, its habits and virtues; and usefulness to society – practical use and employment in various spheres of life – are as relevant today as then, and achieving a balance between them is just as difficult. Christian theology has a great deal to say about each of them.[12] In the public realm, each of the issues they pose (acutely summarized by Robert Anderson[13]) demands theological wisdom.

Conclusion: guidelines for wisdom-seeking universities

I have argued elsewhere that, besides being about information, knowledge and know-how, universities should also be about seeking wisdom.[14] We in the UK are fortunate in having in many of our universities departments of theology and religion that are well suited to being places of public theology as I have defined it. This is a small niche in the global ecology of academically-mediated religion. Most niches are focused on a single religious tradition or on a study of religion that excludes or marginalizes theology. Yet the small niche in this country is of increasing importance, and there are signs, even in China, of its growing attractiveness to those who want wiser religion and wiser understanding of religion in plural societies. The multiple depths of wisdom traditions are resources for a healthily plural world.

In conclusion, I suggest some guidelines that might be borne in mind by those who, as they help to shape the field, have institutional responsibility for academically-mediated religion in universities and care for public theology:[15]

- Develop rich descriptions of the field, both historical and contemporary, in many countries, using the field's academic disciplines to do so, and showing the interrelations of universities, theologies and the public sphere.

- Develop rationales for the field, not just in general terms, but also in Jewish, Christian, Muslim, Hindu, secular and other terms. Then bring the rationales into dialogue with each other and build departments and institutions that can be justified and nourished by more than one tradition.
- Whatever the nature of the settlement in one's own university, make the case for it being open in all three directions simultaneously: towards theology, and the questions raised by and within traditions; towards the study of religions, and the questions raised by many disciplines about religions; and towards interreligious study and engagement, and the questions raised between religions.
- Given that a university has a responsibility towards the wider community, and that most such communities are religiously plural, make the case that they will be more healthily plural if the university is a place of academically-mediated religion and public theology.
- Make the case that the religious communities too, insofar as they are concerned for wisdom and truth, will benefit (even if, at times, in uncomfortable ways) from academically-mediated religion that can help to resource them.
- Seek the good of the whole field of theology and the study of religions, and put intellectual and political energy into debates about its future in order to help it become 'mutual ground' (rather than 'neutral ground'), a place where multiple depths engage with each other and learn how to live with long-term disagreement.
- Have a global vision for the field, commensurate with the global presence of the religions, and embody this not only in the curriculum but also, whenever possible, in the teaching and student body, in institutional alliances and in responsibilities undertaken. Public theology cannot be confined to one's own country.

Notes

1 I only name those that are treated in Ford, D. and Muers, R. eds. (2005), which is far from exhaustive.
2 Peter Ochs of the University of Virginia and I are on the academic board of the Minzu Institute.
3 Scriptural Reasoning is now evolving new dimensions. Besides being involved in the Chinese developments (which in recent years have spread far beyond Minzu University, thanks in part to a collaboration with the University of Helsinki led by Professor Miikka Ruokanen), experienced participants in Abrahamic Scriptural Reasoning are now also participating in a nascent initiative in India focusing on Hindu, Muslim and Christian scriptures.
4 *Brochure of the Institute of Comparative Scripture and Interreligious Dialogue.* Minzu is the 'University of the Nationalities/Ethnicities' – the dozens of non-Han ethnic groups (numbered in tens of millions) recognized by the Chinese

government – so its whole ethos is to do with diversity. Since many of the groups also are religious in distinctive ways, it is well suited to practices that try to deepen relationships and understanding across differences.

5 My most recent report from Professor You Bin, the Director of the Institute of Comparative Scripture and Interreligious Dialogue, shows the creativity continuing. For example, many scholars and members of religious traditions have been taking part in workshops on specific types of comparative scripture reading including Buddhist-Christian, Confucian-Christian, Muslim-Christian-Confucian and Daoist-Christian. During 2015, there were also groups meeting monthly to practice Scriptural Reasoning, including one consisting of religious professionals from Islam, Daoism, Protestantism, Catholicism, Confucianism and Buddhism, and another consisting of younger members of each of those traditions. The results of such projects, and reflection on their practice, theory and method, have been published in the Institute's *Journal of Comparative Scripture* and other journals, and in newspapers. The Chinese Academy of Social Sciences has also been involved.

6 For my own, more general discussion of universities, see especially Ford, D. (2007a, pp. 304–349) and Ford, D. (2007b, pp. 91–142).

7 By secularist I mean the 'programmatic secularism' that sees itself as the only norm for truth, in contrast with 'procedural secularism', which is about the minimal set of ground rules needed to ensure fairness, a distinction recently made by Williams, R. (2012, pp. 2–4) and elsewhere.

8 The idea of what became the RLLP was first mooted in Clines, J. (2008, especially pp. 121–122).

9 Some of what follows is adapted from Ford (2011a), my unpublished Third Lord Dearing Memorial Lecture, *Christianity and Universities Today: A Double Manifesto* http://www.ideaofauniversity.com/media/uploads/files/Dearing_Lecture_2011_fff_Ford_Website_.pdf (accessed February 26th 2016).

10 By 'multi-secular' I indicate that those who do not identify with any religion and see themselves as non-religious or secular are at least as diverse as those who are religious. There are also many religious-secular hybrids.

11 The seven 'evaluative propositions' are:

'(1) The belief in a world order, created by God, rational, accessible to human reason, to be explained by human reason and to be mastered by it; this belief underlies scientific and scholarly research as the attempt to understand this rational order of God's creation.

(2) The ancient understanding of man as an imperfect being, and the Judaeo-Christian idea of a creature fallen into sin, and the proposition deriving from these ideas about the limitation of the human intellect, operated in the Middle Ages as driving forces impelling intellectual criticism and collegial cooperation; they served as the foundation for the translation of general ethical values like modesty, reverence, and self-criticism into the image of the ideal scientist and scholar.

(3) Respect for the individual as a reflection of the macrocosm or as having been formed in the image of God, laid the foundation for the gradually realized freedom of scientific and scholarly research and teaching.

(4) The absoluteness of the imperative of scientific truth already led scholasticism to the basic norms of scientific and scholarly research and teaching, such as the prohibition of the rejection of demonstrated knowledge, the subjection of one's own assertions to the generally valid rules of evidence, openness to all possible objections to one's own argument, and the public character of argument and discussion.

(5) The recognition of scientific and scholarly knowledge as a public good which is ultimately a gift of God had not, it is true, even before universities existed, prevented study and teaching for the sake of money. Nevertheless, there has been less interest within the universities in the economic use of scientific knowledge than there has been in the learned professions outside the university. This relatively smaller interest in the economic utilization of scientific knowledge has been an axiomatic value of the university.

(6) *Reformatio*, which regarded one's own scientific efforts as the renewal of previously established knowledge and its further development "in the cause of improvement", laid a disproportionate weight in the medieval university on already established patterns of thought and older authors. Nevertheless, these were not accepted without criticism; they were critically scrutinized to test their veracity as the basis of one's own knowledge. They were a stimulus to new ways of seeing things and to new theories . . . Scientific and scholarly knowledge grows in a cumulative process, by building on earlier knowledge. In this sense, the progress of knowledge is a continuous process of *reformatio*.

(7) The equality and solidarity of scholars in confronting the tasks of science enable the universities to become the institutional centres of the scientific community. The acknowledgement of the scientific achievements of those who think and believe differently from ourselves and of those who are members of social strata different from our own and the readiness to correct one's own errors in the light of persuasive new knowledge, regardless of its source, permitted the rise of science . . . Indeed, the more highly equality was evaluated, and the more it was joined to the common responsibility for the increase of knowledge, the better the university fulfilled its obligations'.

- Walter Rüegg, 'Themes' in *Universities in the Middle Ages* Edited by H. De Ridder-Symoens, Volume 1 of *A History of the University in Europe*, General Editor Walter Rüegg (Cambridge 1992) pp. 32ff. Walter Rüegg 'Themes' in ibid. vol. I, *Universities in the Middle Ages*, ed. H. De Ridder-Symoens (1992) pp. 3–34 (pp. 32 ff.)

12 For my own understanding, see Ford, D. (2007a, pp. 304–349).
13 Anderson writes: 'If we seek guidance from the past, it is better to see the "idea of the university" not as a fixed set of characteristics, but as a set of tensions, permanently present, but resolved differently according to time and place. Tensions between teaching and research, and between autonomy and accountability, most obviously. But also between universities' membership of an international scholarly community, and their role in shaping national cultures and forming national identity; between the transmission of established knowledge, and the search for original truth; between the inevitable connection of universities with the state and the centres of economic and social power, and the need to maintain critical distance; between reproducing the existing occupational structure, and renewing it from below by promoting social mobility; between serving the economy, and providing a space free from immediate utilitarian pressures; between teaching as the encouragement of open and critical attitudes, and society's expectation that universities will impart qualifications and skills. To come down too heavily on one side of these balances will usually mean that the aims of the university are being simplified and distorted'. Anderson, R. *The 'Idea of a University' Today* in *History & Policy* (March 2010) http://www-histpol.hist.cam.ac.uk/papers/policy-paper-98.html (accessed February 24 2016). Most of those tensions can be read in terms of the three medieval elements.
14 See Ford D. (2007a, pp. 341–345).
15 These are developed from those given in Ford, D. (2011b, pp. 166f).

References

Anderson, R., March 2010. The 'Idea of a University' Today in *History & Policy*. [online] Available at: http://www-histpol.hist.cam.ac.uk/papers/policy-paper-98. html. [accessed February 24th 2016].

Clines, J., 2008. *Faiths in Higher Education Chaplaincy*. London: Church of England Board of Education.

Dinham, A., and Jones, S., 2010. *Religious Literacy Leadership in Higher Education: An Analysis of Challenges of Religious Faith, and Resources for Meeting Them, for University Leaders*. York: Religious Literacy Leadership in Higher Education Programme.

Ford, D., 2007a. *Christian Wisdom: Desiring God and Learning in Love*. Cambridge: Cambridge University Press.

Ford, D., 2007b. *Shaping Theology: Engagements in a Religious and Secular World*. Oxford: Blackwell.

Ford, D., 2011a. *Christianity and Universities Today: A Double Manifesto*. The Third Lord Dearing Memorial Lecture. [online] Available at: http://www. ideaofauniversity.com/media/uploads/files/Dearing_Lecture_2011_fff_Ford_ Website_.pdf. [accessed February 26th 2016].

Ford, D., 2011b. *The Future of Christian Theology*. Oxford: Wiley-Blackwell.

Ford, D., and Muers, R., eds. 2005. *The Modern Theologians: An Introduction to Christian Theology Since 1918*. 3rd Edition. Oxford: Blackwell.

Rüegg, W., (General Editor) 1992–2010. *A History of the University in Europe*, Vols. I-IV. Cambridge: Cambridge University Press.

Williams, R., 2012. *Faith in the Public Square*. London: Bloomsbury.

7 Insights from Church foundation universities

Elizabeth Stuart and Michael Holman

In this chapter, we present two case studies. Elizabeth Stuart, Deputy Vice-Chancellor at the University of Winchester, and Michael Holman, Principal of Heythrop College, University of London, explain how their respective Anglican and Roman Catholic traditions provide for their students an education that is distinctive and different. Whereas Winchester is faring well in the current climate, Heythrop is facing challenges which require fundamental changes to be made. These challenges arise not from being a Church foundation, since there are other buoyant and thriving Catholic universities in England, but from its small and specialist character and from factors which, as we shall see, are particular to Heythrop.

The University of Winchester

Elizabeth Stuart

Anyone entering the University of Winchester will be struck by the imposing sculpture of an angel by Amy Goodman, which is suspended over the entrance to the original Main Building. The angel itself tells a story about the university's dialogue about its Anglican identity. We wanted to commission a piece of artwork which would confidently celebrate our Christian foundation while also at the same time communicate that we welcome people of all faiths and those of none. We considered a cross of some description, but in the end decided that a cross might be perceived to be too exclusive. Angels, on the other hand, figure in a number of different religions and are also popular among people with no religious allegiance. A cynic might say our approach was a typical Anglican fudge: wanting at the same time both to make a statement but also to not offend anyone, we opted for a cipher. A less cynical mind might conclude that our approach was a typical Anglican triumph, making a confident assertion of our foundation but in such a way as to invite and to open a conversation with others who do not share that belief system. Whichever, our authentic Anglican credentials are established! I have worked for the University of Winchester for the best part of 20 years, and I have never known the institution more confident of its Anglican identity.

When I first joined King Alfred's College, as it was then, as its first Professor of Christian Theology, there were endless fretful discussions and debates about its nature as an Anglican foundation and how this should be expressed. There was a fear at every level of the institution that emphasising the foundation too much might impact negatively on recruitment; the assumption being that reference to any kind of religion is necessarily off-putting to those who do not subscribe to it. The *Engaging the Curriculum* project, which had been launched in the early 1990s by the Council for Church and Associated Colleges to encourage the injection of theological insights into all areas taught in church higher education institutions, while producing some excellent material, was not taken up on the ground and petered out. In 2001, Ron Dearing published his report on Church of England schools, which included a chapter on Church colleges (Dearing, 2001). Dearing sought to identify wherein lay the Anglican identity of these institutions. He pinpointed the following: the appointment and makeup of the governing body (with a substantial proportion of the board being appointed by the diocese); a Genuine Occupational Requirememt for at least the Vice-Chancellor to be a communicant member of the Church of England or a Church in communion with it; a commitment to teacher development; chaplaincies and centres of Christian worship; and service to the Church in contributing to the training of teachers for Church schools and various forms of ministerial training. Dearing worried about the future of these institutions and outlined a framework for distinctiveness which certainly encouraged more discussion of the issue at Winchester, but the focus for us (as for others) at that time frankly lay elsewhere on the attainment of degree-awarding powers and university status. I think it would be true to say that at this point the foundation was focussed only in three areas: senior management (and, in particular, the Genuine Occupational Requirememt for the Vice-Chancellor), the chaplaincy and the theology department, in a way which rather ghettoised it and kept it from impacting upon the majority of students and staff. This all changed with the arrival of a new Vice-Chancellor in 2006.

Professor Joy Carter took the view that the risk for the institution in an age of increased marketisation of higher education lay not in being too different, but in being not distinctive enough. She was also very clear that our distinctiveness was rooted in our Anglican foundation, and therefore she was prepared to take the risk on recruitment. First, though, the foundation had to be rescued from its ghetto and made real and meaningful for the whole of the institution. I do not think one can overestimate the crucial role of leadership in determining both the nature and importance of the foundation in Church universities because certain choices have to be made about how to be Anglican. Anglicanism, like all forms of religious identity, is contested. Indeed, tension lies at the very heart of Anglican identity. Any attempt to make an Anglican identity meaningful is then going to involve some choices around several tensions. For Winchester, our Anglican identity is about inclusivity, hospitality and diversity. It is about, among other things, affirming gay and lesbian people and relationships, it is about providing a safe and supportive environment for transgendered people and it is about honouring people of other religious paths and those who reject any such path. We recognise that these are contestable theological choices, and we are happy to engage in conversation and debate about our choices with those within and beyond Anglicanism who dispute their legitimacy, but we flew the rainbow flag when gay marriage was legalised and we fly it during Pride Week. We are proud to be a Stonewall Diversity Champion. These things, we believe, are not incidental to our Anglican identity or in tension with it, but rather an expression of it, and that is a choice and a choice guided by the Vice-Chancellor and her Senior Management team, which I became a part of eight years ago, and supported by the Board of Governors. Because Anglicanism is broad and disputatious at heart, a different leadership could seek to enact a different kind of expression of our foundation, and this is a matter of some concern and nervousness in the institution. On the other hand, without some sort of Genuine Occupational Requirement for the role of Vice-Chancellor, the foundation itself might well be in peril, particularly as we have noticed that as the foundation becomes more deeply embedded, there is a temptation to be less explicit about it in strategic documents.

The embedding of the foundation took place primarily through a university-wide process to agree a set of institutional values. These values very quickly became the conscience and moral compass of the university, the means by which we hold ourselves accountable to each other and to our history and vision. Our first value is Intellectual Freedom. Whenever I pass underneath the figure of our angel, I am reminded of the fact that angels guarded the open tomb of Christ and that they are prone to ask awkward questions: 'why?' 'who?' Christians forever stand before a great mystery which presents questions to us and demands questions from us as part of an invitation to enter into its dazzling darkness. An open tomb demands an open mind and a willingness to enter into conversation. We strive to be a community of scholars, staff and students together, committed to critical thinking as a praxis essential to any free society, striving not just for knowledge, but also for wisdom (as our motto makes clear, *Wisdom ond Lar*, wisdom and knowledge). For a Christian, wisdom is not merely an attribute, it is a living reality, and the desire for wisdom is the desire for God. What we seek to nurture in our students is the desire for knowledge as part of a broader yearning for truth which may be traced in, but ultimately transcends, all forms of knowledge and can only be approached through a combination of life-long learning and striving to change the world for the better. Minds, hearts and, crucially, souls are our business. Winchester offers our students the opportunity to take optional modules in Values Studies. This is a cross-institutional, interdisciplinary scheme in which students explore fundamental questions about values through conversation. One of the modules on offer focuses on contemporary university education. Students therefore become thoughtful critics of their own experience. Staff are encouraged to engage in conversations about our values through Values Days facilitated by an external consultant. The provision of extracurricular opportunities to engage in reflective conversations about the world and develop wisdom is evident in our King Alfred Award, the initiative of our first Dean of Chapel, which brings together students from across subject disciplines and years to reflect on 'big' questions inspired by engagement in a number of group activities which might include reading a book, attending a film, play or musical performance, engagement with an external speaker, learning meditation or commitment to some sort of voluntary project.

David Ford has noted that at the core of the biblical concept of wisdom is the imperative to listen to the cries of the marginalised and oppressed (Ford, 2007, pp. 14–51). It is therefore appropriate that one of the values that binds our community together is Social Justice. Our business school was the thirteenth business school in the UK to be accepted to join the United Nations initiative – The Principles of Responsible Management Education – and the Business School is characterised by a concern for business impact on sustainability and engagement with ethical issues. Winchester was the first primary initial teacher education provider to sign up to the UNICEF ITE Rights Respect Responsibility initiative. We have been a Fair Trade university since 2007 and recently became accredited as a Living Wage employer by the Living Wage Foundation. Widening Participation is part of our DNA, and we have a particular concern for asylum seekers, care leavers and carers. We want our students to be conscious of social justice issues. We have a volunteering module which students can opt to take as part of their degree. We host a Student Hub which offers our students the opportunity to become involved in various forms of social action and preparation for social impact careers. We want our students to understand themselves as global citizens, aware of their impact on others through the choices they make and the communities to which they belong and interested in engaging with cultures, traditions and religions other than their own. We want them to have an active interest in the pursuit of the eradication of conflict, poverty and ecological destruction. We have links with various projects in the Gambia, Syria and Uganda. As an institution, our concept of social justice embraces the other than human. Some of the clearest ways our values are worked out are through our ethical catering, our concern for animal welfare and our efforts to create an environmentally friendly campus. At the heart of Christian discipleship is the notion of living not for oneself but for others, and it is that desire we endeavour to inspire and nurture in our community of scholars.

The city of Winchester has a long association with the Benedictines. At the heart of Benedictine spirituality is the concept of hospitality, of greeting and treating every stranger as a friend and as Christ. As a university, we strive to be an institution hospitable to people and ideas, creating a welcoming environment for students from different countries, local, national and international organisations and local residents. We seek to create an inclusive learning and living environment for disabled students. And, as noted above, we seek to be a community in which people of all genders and sexualities feel safe and supported. Furthermore, as Parker J. Palmer has noted, hospitality is at the heart of a robust pedagogy because hospitality creates a community in which scholars (whether they be staff or students), can challenge each other and seek to learn together (Palmer, 2010, p. 29). Diversity is an important value to us. We endeavour to honour diversity in religion, too. At the heart of our recent 175th anniversary celebrations was the restoration of our chapel; to it we added a side chapel which we have designated as an inter-faith space of quiet and contemplation available for all. We also have a Muslim prayer room.

As far as we know, we are the only university in the UK to have Spirituality as a value. Of course, this honours our foundation. It also makes an important statement in an age when faith is often represented as anti-intellectual, exclusive and judgemental. We seek to model ways of being people of faith which are reflective, self-critical and hospitable to people of all faiths and those of none. Spirituality, of course, is a term that is loved and hated in equal measure. As our first Dean of Chapel noted shortly after his appointment, the use of the term could be interpreted as a way of both nodding to the foundation while also avoiding any offence to those who would not wish to be identified with a Christian place of work or study (Waddell, 2012, p. 11). In a recent survey of staff, 24% of those who chose to answer the question identified as Christian, 20% as having no religion and only 1.8% identified as 'spiritual'. Recent student data suggests 37% identify as Christian, 53% have no religion and only 1% identify as 'spiritual'. Is the term 'spirituality' being used to excuse us from being more robustly assertive of our Christian foundation in a context where the secular and the Christian exist in an almost balanced tension? Perhaps there is an element of truth in that, but I think the overarching reason to use the term Spirituality is to be genuinely hospitable to people of all faiths and none, to convey that what we hope is to create a community in which people search for meaning beyond themselves. We want to fashion not a narrow, suffocating, religious space but one as open, spacious and quizzical as an open tomb and, this is the paradox, we want to create such a space because that is what being Anglican is about in our view.

We aspire to create a community which encourages its members to transcend themselves and search for wisdom. Of course, the primary means through which people in universities search for that meaning is through their study, their research and their teaching. We seek to ensure that all our academic staff are able to engage in research, whether it is entered into the Research Excellence Framework (REF) or not, and we seek to give students the opportunity to become active researchers in partnership with staff through our research apprenticeship scheme. We regard teaching and research as intricately connected and seek to value both equally as we endeavour to create a community of scholars made up of both staff and students. Delighting in learning for its own sake is unfashionable: the emphasis these days is on the need for a university education to be useful in the sense of preparing a person for a career, but historically universities have managed to combine both a relishing of learning and an interest in training as they sought to prepare people, not just for a career but for life. The University of Winchester began its life 175 years ago as a training college for teachers, but it always combined professional training with academic study and reflection, and all those years later, with teacher development remaining an important part of our provision, we maintain, against a dominant discourse that asserts that teachers are best trained on the job, in schools, that the best teachers are those who have had the chance to reflect in conversation with key thinkers and others upon the nature of the profession and their own practice.

St. Augustine famously believed that the person who sang prayed twice. Making music is one of the means by which people experience a sense of transcendence. At Winchester, Foundation Music co-ordinates a range of ensembles and choirs, none of which audition. It provides a plethora of opportunities for students to make friends, find a sense of community and experience the capacity that music has to feed 'the human desire to go beyond. It is in this that it acts transformatively and so becomes a powerful means of locating oneself within the world and so making sense of it' (Stone-Davis, 2015, p. ix).

One of the clearest expressions of our foundation is our chapel and chaplaincy. Some members of our community may never enter the chapel, but nevertheless, every day, they will walk past a building where a rhythm of prayer is played out and students and staff come together to explore the mystery of life through the lens of the Christian story. There is an open invitation expressed in that chapel, in our series of Foundation Lectures and in other ways to enter into a conversation about that story. The development of the role of the chaplain into a Dean of Chapel was a deliberate attempt to make links between the chaplaincy and the academic search for meaning. The Dean of Chapel is a member of the theology department. It is important that the chaplaincy is neither a refuge from big, difficult questions or critical, reflective thinking nor an escape from diversity or issues of social justice, but rather a keystone of such thinking and action in the institution. The thinking undertaken in the chaplaincy will be a particular type of thinking rooted in prayer, contemplation and the economy of grace worked out in the Eucharist. Our students graduate in the magnificent surroundings of Winchester Cathedral. That act confirms that in some way the story of their learning is caught up in the Christian story as told by Anglicanism in the university.

When we say that as a community we value Spirituality, one of the things we are saying is that we value religious ways of knowing. This means supporting teaching and research in theology and religious studies and providing all our students with the opportunity to engage with religious ways of knowing through Values Studies, the King Alfred Award, the chaplaincy and a variety of extracurricular lectures and seminars. Even before they arrive, students can take an online module in religion (or one on global politics).

In recent years, we have also sought to express our foundation in art. Goodman's Angel is the most obvious and striking example of this, both welcoming and offering the prospect of a journey of difficult questions and wrestling with mystery, and itself representing that mystery. A beautiful sculpture of St. Francis and the Hoopoe by Robert Hunt speaks of our concern for animal welfare and ecology and has quickly become a focus for external gatherings of the community to formally commemorate, remember or celebrate.

In the USA, there is a movement dedicated to encouraging and supporting the use of contemplative practices in higher education. The UK has yet to engage with this agenda to any great extent, but Church universities seem ideally positioned to. At Winchester, we are currently exploring the possibility of establishing a religious community on campus to provide students with the opportunity of spending some time living a life in which study takes place in a context of prayer and contemplation.

We recognise that religion can be both a problem and a solution, and our Centre of Religions for Reconciliation and Peace exists to analyse the part that religion has in conflict and the possibilities it offers for peace building.

Perhaps the value that is quoted most often to senior managers is Individuals Matter. We endeavour to create an environment in which staff and students experience the fact that they matter as individuals and have opportunities to thrive and flourish. However, there are inevitable tensions. Unless we are dealing with gross professional misconduct, we would always seek to give people in trouble a second chance with appropriate support. This does not always go down very well with people having to work alongside or manage those people, and it can sometimes seem that some individuals matter more than others. As a senior management team, we are committed to only implementing compulsory redundancy as an absolute last resort, as it can be devastating for individuals and their families and has a terrible impact upon staff and student morale. Sometimes that means that some parts of the institution have to subsidise others and may have to forgo some resourcing in the process. The decision to value all staff research means that colleagues whose research earns money through the REF have to share some of it with colleagues who do not. This is a lot to ask of colleagues, who are very gracious about it. The marketisation of higher education with its emphasis on competition between institutions, league tables and attempts to construct the student as consumer brings its pressures to bear on a values-driven institution which to survive has to compete. This can place burdens on individuals who may feel conflict between those pressures and our values. I think contemplation on this value makes me realise how often we fall short in living up to our values, particularly as senior managers. We sin. We are often caught up in sinful structures. We may not be very good at acknowledging this or repenting of it but we certainly feel it. There is a lot of soul-searching that goes on among senior managers over decisions, and we will instinctively test those decisions against our values and we are not always sure whether we have been true to them and some of our colleagues would say we have certainly not. We falter, we fail, we are always in the process of becoming a values-driven institution rather than being one.

That emphasis on becoming, which has strong Christian resonances, also underpins our final value, Creativity. Creativity is essential to human flourishing because it is to co-operate in the activity and nature of the Creator. The university offers a number of creative degree programmes. For many years our annual Writers' Festival has drawn aspirant authors from around the world. Our prison project has involved staff, students and local prisoners in the creation of an annual theatrical production. Our Centre for Arts as Wellbeing works with a number of agencies, including hospitals, to explore the psychological and political implications of artistic practice, the interface between artistic practice and people's spiritual experience and to analyse how contextual issues affect the potentially transformative effects of artistic practice. Through student and staff engagement, we seek to be a university constantly creating and renewing itself. We are also a university which honours creation, which recognises what St. John of the Cross called 'the trace' of the creator in all creatures (St. John of the Cross *A Spiritual Canticle* st.3–7). The university attempts to be a place in which its community might experience grace, moments of insight or transcendence which enable us to grow in wisdom and love as a community.

These values and their outworking are the principal means by which we at Winchester endeavour to express our Anglican foundation and identity. It is precarious and contentious, it could be accused of being fuzzy, messy and inclusive beyond meaning, but such accusations are always levelled against Anglicanism. It is not always easy to convince some colleagues that the foundation is about the character of the institution as a whole and where its conversations begin and not part of a covert agenda to convert or impose a belief system. As has already been suggested, perhaps inevitably, there are sometimes tensions between our values and the higher education policy of particular governments. We seek to nurture wisdom in our students, and the wisdom tradition is clear that wisdom is better than gold (Proverbs 8:4–6; 18–21), and so an Anglican foundation may find itself in some ways out of sync with a higher education culture that measures a university's status partly on the percentage of graduates in graduate-level jobs and how much they earn. We seek to encourage our students into ethical careers which may not be designated as graduate level and almost certainly will not be well-paid. We want our students to be satisfied and happy, but the Christian tradition teaches that the path to wisdom involves a dark night of the soul, an experience of disintegration, emptying and entropy, which ultimately leads both to a more open mind and to a greater sense of solidarity with all beings who suffer. It must be the role of a Church university to provide a context and support to enable people to go through a crucifixion of the soul and the excruciating process by which, as FitzGerald puts it, wounds are transformed into wounds of love through which the soul awakens in a profound manner to God and to all life (FitzGerald, 2000, p. 330).

The relationship between Church universities and the Church of England is a bit odd. Whereas the Church has always been proud of and interested in its schools, it has given every impression of not being quite sure what to do with its institutions of higher education, particularly since they diversified beyond teacher training. But perhaps we, the Church universities, expect too much of 'the Church', by which we mean the hierarchy and central offices of the Church of England. We need to have a clearer understanding of ourselves as Church, as part of the body of Christ seeking to do what the body of Christ does, be an expression of Christ in and to the world. It could be argued that Church universities bear the marks of the Church which are to be one, holy, catholic and apostolic. Theologically speaking, unity is not about uniformity, it is about being united with Christ. To be an Anglican university, then, is to be one consciously focused on becoming Christ-shaped through prayer and the celebration of the sacraments in the Anglican tradition, through study and through public service. It is not to pretend to be an impossibly neutral community. It is to have an identity and values rooted in the Christ who demands open hearts, open minds and open doors. The Christian concept of holiness is intrinsically related to self-sacrifice, to the cross, and that means putting others before oneself and to stand alongside the weak and the marginalised. For a university, that will mean a commitment to social justice, but it may also mean being sometimes willing to sacrifice league table position for the sake of being true to one's values and mission. A university is almost by definition a catholic institution, its object being the study of the universe in focused form; through our Values Studies and Modern Liberal Arts degree we offer an integrative, catholic approach to higher education which encourages a sense of interconnectedness of knowledge. A university may claim to be apostolic if it seeks to maintain a real connection to its roots as an Anglican foundation and a living relationship with the wider Church. We are a community which has at its heart prayer and the sacraments according to the Anglican tradition and which seeks to welcome all in a common endeavour to explore the mystery of life and to change the world for the better, recognising that we fail to live up to the values we espouse but constantly renewing our commitment to them, we are Church.

Our confidence in our Anglican identity has not impacted negatively upon recruitment. On the contrary, at a time when many institutions contracted, we were one of the fastest growing. We have excellent rates of student satisfaction and generally find ourselves thriving. Students are attracted to us because of our values and ambiance as well as by our academic excellence. These things are rooted in our foundation. Maintaining that foundation as a living reality in a complex political, social and religious world is not easy. It is not without pain or dispute, but being Church is never easy.

Heythrop College, University of London

Michael Holman

On 21 August 2015, in an article on the website of the International Catholic Weekly, *The Tablet*, Dr. Sarah Coakley, Norris-Hulse Professor of Divinity in the University of Cambridge, was reported as describing Heythrop College as 'a jewel at the heart of Christian academia' (*The Tablet*, 2015). What is Heythrop College, and what might there be about it that led Professor Coakley to describe it in such terms?

Heythrop College traces its history back to its foundation in Leuven by the English Jesuits in exile in 1614. It was established to provide an education in theology and philosophy for Jesuit students for the priesthood, a mission it retains to this day. Ten years later, the College moved to Liège, where it remained until 1794 when, with the French Revolution knocking at their door, the Jesuits took their students and their extensive library over the water to England, which by then had become more tolerant of Catholics. They established themselves firstly in the manor of Stonyhurst in Lancashire, then at St. Beuno's, overlooking the valley of the Clwyd in north Wales, moving in 1926 to a property formerly owned by the Earls of Shrewsbury in the village of Heythrop near Chipping Norton in Oxfordshire from which, henceforth, the College would take its name.

Heythrop, therefore, as well as being one of the longest-established institutions of higher education in England, has also been in continuous existence longer than any other theology college in the worldwide Society of Jesus. In June 2014, an international conference took place at the Senate House of the University of London to mark the 400th anniversary of the founding of the College. The conference explored the Jesuit tradition of Catholic education, of which, for all this time, Heythrop has been a part. Speakers considered the Jesuit contribution not only to the study of theology and philosophy but to science, astronomy, literature and the arts, and paid tribute to some of its notable alumni: the poet Gerard Manley Hopkins, the theologian Bernard Lonergan, the historian of philosophy, Frederick Copleston, and the first Catholic Bishop of the United States of America and founder of Georgetown University, John Carroll.

In terms of Catholic higher education in England and Wales, Heythrop was something of a pioneer. When, in the years following the close of the Second Vatican Council in 1965, the Catholic Church was seeking new ways to engage with wider society, Heythrop was the first Catholic college in those countries to be granted university college status when in 1970 it became a member of the University of London.

The purpose of Heythrop College in this new form would be to provide a university education for those who were training for the priesthood and other ministries in the Catholic Church; to enable many more lay students, women as well as men, to benefit from the education the Jesuits had to offer;

and to provide a platform for the Catholic Church to dialogue with those working in philosophy and theology in other university departments in London and elsewhere. The College was incorporated by a Royal Charter which secured for the Jesuits a prominent role in the executive and on the governing body of the College. Membership of the University of London thus enabled Heythrop both to participate fully in the academic life of a world-class university and to maintain a governance structure which safeguarded its Jesuit and Catholic identity.

In the 45 years since its move to London, Heythrop's achievements have been considerable. It developed a number of specialisms, such as those represented by its six research and impact centres and institutes, and its undergraduate degree in the 'Abrahamic Religions' was the first of its kind in Europe. Heythrop's central London location, firstly in Cavendish Square and then, from 1993, in Kensington Square, enabled it to reach an extensive part-time postgraduate market, and in recent years, as many as 250 students have been enrolled on its MA programmes. In the results of the REF in December 2014, 62% of Heythrop's research was judged internationally excellent or world-leading, with its research environment and impact especially commended. The College's international profile continues to be much enhanced by its bimonthly review of philosophy and theology, *The Heythrop Journal*, published jointly with Wiley Blackwell and now in its 56th year.

A previous Vice Principal of the College, Dr. Peter Vardy, described the College in this way: 'There is no institution similar where there is both serious academic inquiry and deep faith'. He went on, 'Heythrop has been a beacon over the last 40 years as a place of open-minded intellectual inquiry in theology and philosophy and has helped thousands of young people to search seriously for God and meaning'.

Dr. Vardy's remarks, like those of Professor Coakley, were occasioned by the announcement made by the Governors of Heythrop at the end of June 2015 that it would close as a College of the University of London at the end of the academic year 2018, once all its commitments to its students had been fulfilled. Professor Coakley was the first signatory of a letter from 30 leading academics in the fields of theology and philosophy which appeared in *The Times* on 18 August 2015 protesting against that decision:

> For those of us familiar with the intellectual stature and impact of this unique Jesuit institution, the announcement came as a rude shock. Deeper reflection makes it clear that its closure, as currently constituted, would be a serious blow to theological, religious and philosophical teaching and research in the UK. We write to urge reconsideration.

But how is it that this 'jewel at the centre of Christian academia' came to grief, and are there lessons to be learnt by other Catholic or Christian centres of higher education which are looking to make their work sustainable?

In 2006, Heythrop College entered the regime of the Higher Education Funding Council for England (HEFCE), having previously been funded, along with a small number of other specialist institutions, by a direct grant from the Department for Education. As HEFCE membership brought with it increased administrative costs while decreasing the amount the College received per student, Heythrop needed to increase its student population, thereby increasing its income. For the first four years, HEFCE allowed the College's student number control to rise to allow for this. When this policy came to an end, and Heythrop had still not quite increased its student numbers sufficiently, a structural deficit was identified, of approximately 10% of its turnover.

Attempts to cut costs and increase income through fundraising and bidding for grants were only partially successful. Significant savings were made in administration and student services, but as these were already minimally staffed, waiting times at help desks increased. The risk was that student satisfaction would diminish, thereby making recruitment still more of a challenge, and in the end, some administrative posts were reinstated. Finding ways to cut costs in academic staffing was still more complicated owing to Heythrop's particular, even peculiar, staffing structure. One of the ways in which the Society of Jesus, other religious orders and the diocesan church had supported the college was by generously providing it with academic staff at no cost, in the case of Jesuits, or on a 50% salary, in the case of other priests and religious. Consequently, the salary bill was heavily subsidised and already considerably lower than it might otherwise have been.

Meanwhile, changes were taking place in the patterns of undergraduate recruitment. One of the effects of the 'credit crunch' of 2008 and the higher unemployment which came in its wake was a move away from some humanities subjects to those which students and their parents regarded as more useful for employment. Data from the Universities and Colleges Admissions Service shows that over the three years 2010–2013, recruitment to theology and religious studies programmes of various kinds fell by 45%. These prospective students, moreover, were becoming more consumer-minded in their approach to the choice of their university and were increasingly likely to look for state-of-the-art facilities and a wider student experience of a kind that smaller institutions such as ours did not find easy to provide. Heythrop was, therefore, not well-placed competitively to attract the fewer available students in the free market of higher education being introduced by the government from 2010 onwards, and the numbers of first-year undergraduates enrolled fell from a high of 200 in 2011 to around 140 thereafter.

Postgraduate recruitment, on the other hand, held up even after the closure of the College was known, and we remain one of the largest centres of postgraduate theology in the country. But our postgraduate market is not financially lucrative. Our postgraduate students are of limited means, typically just beginning or approaching retirement, and experience has shown that this market can stand a full-time rate of no more than £4,500 per annum.

What Heythrop lacks are economies of scale: the cost of administration and student services accounts for a higher proportion of income than is the norm in the sector. This in turn led us to conclude that we needed to find a partner which would have an approach to mission similar to ours and would be large enough to absorb the administrative work generated by our student numbers into their already existing structures. St. Mary's University, a Catholic university in Twickenham, generously spent the first six months of 2015 examining the possibilities of such a strategic partnership, but by the summer, it was clear that agreement was not possible.

To these shorter-term reasons for the Governors' decision can be added longer-term factors. As time moved on, the conditions which enabled the College to join the University of London fell away. In 1970, the College had a large contingent of subsidised staff, but as the years passed, that number reduced and the salary bill increased. In 1970, the University of London's central administration managed much of the administrative affairs of the colleges, but when the funding was devolved by HEFCE to the colleges in the mid-1990s, so too was more administration with its attendant costs. In 1970, and for many years after, undergraduate student expectations of what a university offered were narrower and were of a kind that a small college could provide: smaller class sizes and one-to-one tuition. When in 1970, the Society of Jesus negotiated Heythrop's entry into the University of London, it did so on the understanding that it would not receive grants from the central university and the conditions were such that it could manage without these. But after 2006, when the College was denied HEFCE's 'small and specialist' funding, it did without grants which, had they been received, would have gone some way to making the College more sustainable.

So there were many factors which led the Governors to make the decision they did in June 2015. Even so, one reason stands out, namely, Heythrop's reliance on staffing subsidies. This has been one of the principal reasons for the demise over the last 50 years of many Catholic schools and colleges run by other religious orders and congregations which could not effectively plan for the time when they were no longer able to rely on their own personnel to staff them. So too at Heythrop, as the numbers of Jesuits, priests and religious reduced, the number of staff who needed to be employed at full cost increased, thus making the consequences of entering the HEFCE funding regime in 2006 that much harder to withstand. Furthermore, the availability of such subsidies meant that the College was to an extent insulated from the market forces impacting on the rest of the sector, with the result, perhaps, that it moved too slowly to adapt its programmes and exploit new international and distance-learning markets to make up for changes taking place in the UK.

One way of compensating for these increased staffing costs, it could be argued, would have been to seek a partnership which provided economies of scale at a time when the College was able to negotiate from a position of strength. Another way, it could also be argued, would have been to increase income to the College, either by fundraising or by diversifying into other more marketable subject areas which could then have cross-subsidised the College's mission-critical commitment to theology and philosophy.

These strategies were considered but were either not taken forward, for what at the time were good reasons, or were taken forward and failed. There was some understandable resistance, at least at first, to the very idea of forming a partnership which would, in all likelihood, have taken Heythrop out of the University of London, thereby threatening to reduce its academic status and the impact of its activities. In addition, preserving the College's autonomy was thought to be a condition of maintaining its denominational identity and Jesuit character. Diversification into other areas was constrained by the terms of the Royal Charter, which specified that only subjects related to theology could be taught. It would, moreover, have required an up-front investment beyond the College's means. Neither could a college specialising in just two disciplines offer programmes in combination with others judged to favour greater 'employability'. Meanwhile, fundraising efforts never took off: donors were reluctant to give to a college sitting on a site of great value in the heart of Kensington.

When in June 2015, the Governors took the decision to close Heythrop as a College of the University of London shortly after the end of the academic year 2017–2018, they also announced that, with the Society of Jesus, they would continue to research ways in which Heythrop's mission and work could continue. It remains to be seen whether we can find a way forward, but it would be a tragedy if, despite all our efforts, a viable future could not be found. Higher education would lose one of those places which provides a form of education for its students which is distinctive and different.

When the news of the closure of the College in its present form broke, comments from present and former students underlined Heythrop's distinctive character. 'Heythrop helps to save the soul of our society . . . absolutely irreplaceable . . . a beacon of light . . . unique . . . whose closure would be a tragedy for higher education in Britain'. All of which was very encouraging. The distinctiveness can, of course, be both an advantage and a disadvantage: what differentiates the College from the rest of the sector may be what threatens its very existence in the sector. How exactly does what we have to offer, and what might be lost, stand out as different?

Colleges and universities like to claim they are distinctive, especially those with a faith foundation. But our claim to distinctiveness needs to be carefully understood. Individual characteristics are usually not unique and are sometimes recognised across the sector generally as 'good practice'. Nonetheless, the emphasis given to particular characteristics, singly or together, may make a particular place distinctive, and it's that kind of distinctiveness I would claim for Heythrop. Having a 'unique selling point' is considered important in the now competitive world of higher education, but our distinctiveness owes more to our Jesuit educational heritage, which has been particularly well articulated today by Jesuit universities in the United States (Association of Jesuit Colleges and Universities, 2012), than to commercial considerations. This distinctiveness is to be seen in who we are, what we do and how we do it.

Heythrop is certainly unique in Britain in this sense: it has a double identity. It is both a College of the University of London and has been established by the Congregation for Catholic Education of the Holy See as ecclesiastical faculties of theology and philosophy, known together as the 'Bellarmine Institute', with the right to award Church degrees. This means that those students enrolled on the Heythrop's University of London 'theology for ministry' programme are awarded both the BD of the University and also the STB of the ecclesiastical faculty of theology. The same applies to those enrolled on ecclesiastical masters or licentiate and doctoral programmes. This facility should make our programmes attractive to those students from countries abroad where the government will not recognise Church degrees and where the Church requires an ecclesiastical qualification for teaching in a seminary or Catholic university. This facility would be lost if Heythrop closed for good.

Is the work we do distinctive as well? We are distinctive in the way we do theology and philosophy, for while respecting the integrity of these disciplines, we also see them as inter-linked – theology is in dialogue with philosophy, and philosophy is in dialogue with theology. As one of our internal curriculum planning documents expressed it in 2015:

> The Jesuit intellectual tradition has always been based on this creative and integrative engagement with philosophy and theology . . . While the distance between the two disciplines has grown rapidly in academia, Heythrop retains a more generous view of their interaction and their potential to provide a distinctive student learning experience. The result is a vitality in the conversation of learning between teachers and students and an imaginative response not just to important developments in society at large but to the ways in which the College's clear sense of identity can turn challenges into opportunities.

The teaching and study of theology at Heythrop also takes place within an active faith community, a believing and praying community, centred around the celebration of the weekly College Mass, and that also makes us distinctive, though not unique. As Cardinal Nichols put it during his homily at the Mass inaugurating the Bellarmine Institute in January 2013, for us, 'wisdom and understanding are given after prayer and entreaty and . . . are indeed rooted in the very life of God' (Nichols, 2013).

A further distinctive feature is the way the Ignatian understanding of the God who is found in all things impacts on our work. It makes us interested in how theology dialogues with contemporary society, in how we can reflect theologically on what is happening in our world. This interest is illustrated by our decades-long commitment to inter-religious dialogue and learning and by the work of the Heythrop Institute for Religion and Society, by the research it undertakes and the seminars and conferences it sponsors. Thus, Heythrop has been one of the principal means by which the British Jesuits have fulfilled the mission given by successive Popes to the whole Society of Jesus, to work on those frontiers where faith and modern culture meet.

Is the way we go about our work distinctive too? The form of education which Heythrop has to offer exhibits many features which are characteristic of Jesuit higher education elsewhere. One of these is *cura personalis*, an attention to each individual student. The College is small, never having had more than 800 full-time equivalent students. Each student has a named personal tutor, and for each assessed paper at both undergraduate and postgraduate levels, a personal tutorial is offered. This means that each student can be known by name, individual talents can be developed and needs met as is evidenced perhaps by the fact that year by year over 80% of undergraduates, whose A level points at entry were not so special, graduate with an upper second degree or better.

Our aim is also to offer an education which is 'personally formative', another characteristic of Jesuit education. Our vision of education is one which sees human life as a unity in which our studies are related to the other aspects of our lives: moral, spiritual, social. It is a vision which has the care of the person and a personal approach to learning at its centre because it understands education to be a formation of that person. As Lord Williams, the former Archbishop of Canterbury, reminded us at the conclusion of our 400th anniversary conference, being faithful to this vision ensures that education remains a work of service, a 'ministry' and does not become a mere 'commodity' (Williams, 2014).

What does this personally formative approach to education mean for our students? In whatever profession our graduates later find themselves, it is our hope that they will bring to their work the creative, critical and reflective skills that our two specialist disciplines teach them together with a capacity for depth and complexity of thought which to an extent overcomes what the present superior general of the Jesuits, Fr Adolfo Nicolás, has called the 'globalisation of superficiality' (2010).

Heythrop also seeks to provide an 'education for service'. Fr. Pedro Arrupe, a predecessor of Fr. Nicolás as superior general, used to say in the years following the Second Vatican Council that Jesuits seek to educate 'men and women for others', people who take as their model of life Jesus who was above all a 'man for others' (Arrupe, 1973). Two or three years ago, a career survey reported that almost two-thirds of leavers pursue further study or enter the 'people professions' – teaching, ministry, health care, social care and third-sector charity work. Our alumni appear to exhibit that 'generosity of spirit' of which our mission statement speaks: this is a proud record for a college such as ours, and it makes our work and all we are doing to sustain it worthwhile.

A great deal is now being done, by the Society of Jesus as well as by Heythrop's governors and senior staff, to ensure that many of these distinctive features are not lost to higher education in the UK. We are researching a model for the future which is academically viable and financially sustainable and which also delivers the mission of the Catholic Church in general and of the Society of Jesus in particular. Happily, at the time of writing, there are options to pursue.

Academic viability and financial sustainability preclude certain models, such as our being an institution which awards ecclesiastical qualifications only. Such a formula would place the College outside the remit of the bodies which regulate quality in higher education and would consign the College to the margins of academic life. If a future model of Heythrop stood outside the framework of the REF, how could the quality of its research be assessed? And if it stood outside the Quality Assurance Agency for Higher Education, how would the quality of its degree programmes be recognised? The numbers of students which such an institution would attract would be small, and so it would be financially fragile.

Academic viability and financial sustainability, on the other hand, argue for continuing the search for a partnership with another institution supported by an endowment from part of the sales proceeds of the present site. Such a partnership would need to provide the economies of scale which we presently lack, an academic environment rich enough to enable Heythrop's research tradition to develop and a commitment to theology and philosophy that would support a range of programmes broad enough to reflect at least some of the College's specialisms as well as its work in the public square. We would hope that any partnership would enable us to reach new markets online and internationally and to take full advantage of the opportunities which our membership of the worldwide network of Jesuit higher education offers.

The particular challenge for Heythrop's leadership in bringing about such a partnership is to ensure that it can also guarantee the denominational identity of Heythrop generally and that of the ecclesiastical faculties, the Bellarmine Institute in particular. The statutes of ecclesiastical faculties require the approval of the Congregation for Catholic Education for the appointment of the director of the Institute and for its teachers and what they teach. So any partner university would need to guarantee these while at the same time honouring its own commitment to academic freedom with respect to what is taught and to equality of opportunity with respect to appointments.

During that conference at the Senate House in June 2014, a number of speakers referred to the capacity which Heythrop has demonstrated during its long history to adapt itself again and again to changing circumstances, as is well illustrated in the History commissioned to mark the 400th anniversary of Heythrop's foundation (Walsh, 2014). And here we are, trying to do that all over again. Mindful that Heythrop has survived rope, rack and revolution, our determination to maintain a college that makes a distinctive contribution from its centuries-old Jesuit tradition to the landscape of higher education in Britain remains as strong as ever it was.

Conclusion

These case studies raise many questions for policy makers in government and for church leaders. Could it be the case that higher education policy, which purports to extend diversity and choice, is in danger of forcing out smaller institutions and therefore limiting choice? Is there an argument for special funding for those subjects which, like theology and religious studies, may not recruit well but which are important for the intellectual and cultural capital of the nation and even its social wellbeing? Will Church institutions inevitably be vulnerable in a policy environment based on commercial principles which they find hard to embrace? Will the churches be able to maintain their presence in higher education at a time when, as they might see it, an increasingly secular society needs their distinctive contribution all the more? We believe that Church universities are precious parts of the body of Christ and the present higher education offer is equally precious but in the current socio-political climate inevitably fragile.

References

Arrupe, Pedro, S.J., 1973. *Men for Others,* Address to World Congress of Jesuit Alumni. [online] Available at: http://onlineministries.creighton.edu/Collaborative Ministry/men-for-others.html. [accessed January 5th 2016].

Association of Jesuit Colleges and Universities (AJCU), 2012. *Some Characteristics of Jesuit Colleges and Universities.* [online] Available at: http://sites.jcu.edu/mission/pages/some-characteristics-of-jesuit-colleges-and-universities/. [accessed January 5th 2016].

Dearing, R., 2001. *The Way Ahead: Church of England Schools in the New Millennium.* London: Church House Publishing.

FitzGerald, C., 2000. Transformation in Wisdom: The Subversive Character and Educative Power of Sophia in Contemplation in Culligan, K., OCD, and Jordan, R., OCD, eds. 2000. *Carmel and Contemplation.* pp. 281–358. Washington DC: ICS Publications.

Ford, D., 2007. *Christian Wisdom: Desiring God and Learning in Love.* Cambridge: Cambridge University Press.

Nichols, Cardinal V., 2013. *Homily at Mass of Thanksgiving for the Reactivation of the Ecclesiastical Faculties at Heythrop College.* [online] Available at: http://rcdow.org.uk/cardinal/homilies/mass-of-thanksgiving-for-the-reactivation-of-the-ecclesiastical-faculties-of-theology-and-philosophy-at-heythrop-college. [accessed January 5th 2016].

Nicolás, A., 2010. *Challenges to Jesuit Higher Education Today.* [online] Available at: http://www.sjweb.info/documents/ansj/100423_Mexico%20City_Higher%20 Education%20Today_ENG.pdf. [accessed February 17th 2016].

Palmer, P.J., 2010. Toward a Philosophy of Integrative Education in Palmer, P.J., and Zajonc, A., eds. 2010. *The Heart of Higher Education: A Call to Renewal.* pp. 19–34. San Francisco: Wiley.

Stone-Davis, F.J., ed., 2015. *Music and Transcendence.* Aldershot: Ashgate.

The Tablet, 2015. [online] Available at: http://www.thetablet.co.uk/news/2369/0/ leading-academics-urge-jesuits-not-to-give-into-fear-over-heythrop-future. [accessed December 27th 2015].

Waddell, P., 2012. *Like Shovelling Fog: Spirituality and the University*, Foundation Lecture, Winchester: University of Winchester.

Walsh, Michael J., 2014. *Heythrop College, 1614–2014.* London: Heythrop College.

Williams, R., 2014. *For the Greater Glory of God and the More Universal Good.* [online] Available at: http://www.heythrop.ac.uk/sites/default/files/docs/about_ us/400years/Rowan%20Williams%20lecture%20400th%20conference.pdf. [accessed January 5th 2016].

8 An Islamic perspective

What does Islam offer to the contemporary debate?

Alison Scott-Baumann and
Sariya Cheruvallil-Contractor

Islam has a long and rich intellectual tradition that is embedded in its religious texts and in its history as a world religion, and which together with confessional approaches to the study of religion encompasses a diverse range of what we today understand as modern academic disciplines, including poetry and literature studies, sociology and lived religion, philosophy and liberal critiques of dogmatic theology and indeed, the physical sciences. As we shall discuss later in this chapter, Islam has made undeniable contributions in the shaping of Western academic thought, the preservation and transmission of Greek and Roman philosophy and has played a foundational role in the development of university campuses as we know them today. Yet, and despite the enduring significance of its *historical* intellectual tradition, contemporary debates about the role of Islam in academia are mired in two antagonistic but also interconnected debates. Firstly, there is a gradual devaluing of 'secular' traditions from within Islamic education and an overemphasis on confessional approaches that has emanated from within diverse Muslim communities, which started around the 18th century. Secondly, there is, the much more recent agenda of 'preventing violent extremism', an anti-terror 'lens' through which much policy discourse seeks to examine Islam in the West. In Britain, this entire discussion is further problematized by rapidly changing understandings of what the function of universities should be – are they institutions of learning that produce scholars, thinkers, conscientious citizens and loyal dissenters, *or* are these institutions that produce efficient but unquestioning employees to staff global conglomerates that satisfy our collective capitalist, materialist demands?

The debate about the role of universities is an important one that this book seeks to advance, with particular emphasis on the ethical and moral contributions that religion can bring to the table. With this in the foreground, in this chapter, we seek to uncover Islamic intellectual tradition for our readers and the ways in which Islam and Muslims contribute to and participate in modern academia. In doing so, we aim to facilitate a discussion about the contemporary relevance of this tradition in British universities, which in the reflection of contemporary Britain, are diverse and plural, and within which understanding and knowledge of the different other is essential. Denying such differences would represent an example of the human tendency towards negation that the French philosopher Paul Ricoeur identified (Scott-Baumann, 2013a, pp. 141–142). We ask and answer the question: how does the study of Islam and the presence of Islam (through students, staff and information) on campus influence how these campuses function? We critically examine whether the campus is enriched by the presence of Islam, or if freedoms that are usually associated with Western academia are impeded by this presence. We also examine the modern othering of Islam and Muslims through the violent use of language in the discourse on 'preventing violent extremism'.

In order to illustrate our proposition that, following Rowan Williams, the faithful voice must be allowed a place at the negotiating table to discuss ethical, moral and practical issues about how to lead a better life, we will address five interlocking phenomena: (1) the history of Islamic intellectual contribution in the wider world and in the UK; (2) the current relationship of Islamic institutions of higher education in the UK with the university sector; (3) the position of Muslim women and all women on campus as an indicator of the state of modern society as reflected in the British university; (4) recent legislation that directly affects campus activity (such as the 2015 Security and Counter Terrorism Act); and (5) finally, the impact these factors may have on the future of university curricula and academic freedoms. We will propose that the presence of Islam can help when there is a need to address such issues – issues that may often otherwise go unchallenged. We go even further to suggest that it is instructive to argue that Islam can help to *identify* difficult issues, in order that they *can* be addressed, for there is much to be challenged on the modern campus that goes unidentified.[1] We will demonstrate that it is a modern imperative to make such a strong addition to the debate about higher education and the language used. Moreover, such an addition will facilitate productive collaboration between non-Muslims and Muslims in order to evaluate and protect what it is that they all hold dear about Western society in university education.

In response to the agenda of 'preventing violent extremism', we will argue that the university must be protected in a democracy as a unique public and safe space for discussion of difficult subject matter and complex issues. We can see a form of democracy in the work of German philosopher Jürgen Habermas. He prizes ways of knowing that develop through critical reflection and engagement or *praxis* (practical action for change) (Habermas in Borradori, 1987). Constitutional patriotism is an idea that Habermas has worked on extensively and public space is crucial to his thinking: people should form a political attachment to the norms and values of a pluralistic liberal democratic constitution, attempting to re-conceptualise group identity, interpreting citizenship as a loyalty that goes beyond individuals' ethnocultural identification and religion in the public sphere. Yet, we will question the current capacity of the British university to provide this, given the pressure upon universities of a hegemonic securitization narrative in Britain that pathologizes Islam. In this context, there is a pressing need to challenge such violent use of language – and we propose that the university is one special place to make this challenge. We will also demonstrate that new security measures, imposed explicitly on schools and universities, and misunderstood by the sector, make this ever more difficult for universities to achieve, not easier. First, we will set the scene with a historical approach to Islam and then contextualize that within Britain.

Islamic intellectual traditions

We began this chapter with reference to a rich and long Islamic intellectual tradition. This tradition can perhaps be traced back to the oft-repeated Quranic description of humankind as 'men and women of understanding' or 'rational thinkers' who learn and understand through the 'signs' that God/Allah has provided on earth, who do not become dogmatic and who reflect on their social and environmental contexts and who seek their own ontological standpoint:

> Indeed, in the creation of the heavens and earth, and the alternation of the night and the day, and the [great] ships which sail through the sea with that which benefits people, and what Allah has sent down from the heavens of rain, giving life thereby to the earth after its lifelessness and dispersing therein every [kind of] moving creature, and [His] directing of the winds and the clouds controlled between the heaven and the earth are signs for a people who use reason.
>
> Holy Quran, Chapter 2, Verse 164.

Such emphasis within the Holy Quran on 'reason' and 'understanding' meant that for the earliest Muslim communities – in Mecca and Medina in the prophetic era – learning and study was a significant aspect of religious life. Memorizing verses of the Quran was a large proportion of this early learning. However, an exploration of the hadith or narratives from the Prophet's (pbuh) life illustrates that there was more to this early version of Islamic Studies.[2] As the early Muslims sought to understand and *live* their new faith, and then subsequently consolidate a nascent Muslim community, they became involved in study that was more nuanced and that reflected their social, historical and political contexts. They began to study what we now recognize as theology, ethics, morality and the social sciences including lived religion, law, citizenship and nation building. According to Sahin, Islamic intellectual traditions include 'a rich heritage of critical education' that it 'shares with Abrahamic faiths' and which comprises 'continuous self-examination, so that the faithful remain balanced in their religious observance'.[3]

After the Prophet's (pbuh) death in 632 CE in Medina, the expansion and diversification of Islamic intellectual traditions continued. These intellectual traditions had their beginnings in the early Muslim communities that formed in and around the Arab cities of Mecca and Medina. As Islam spread beyond these cities and beyond the Arabian Peninsula, there was a need for systems of learning that could cater to the great demand for knowledge about Islam from newly converted peoples and nations: not all of whom knew Arabic but who nevertheless wanted to learn, understand and recite the Quran, who wanted to know the histories of early Muslim communities and who wanted to intimately and, as far as is possible, know the life history of Prophet Muhammad (pbuh). Thus, in the first four centuries of Islam, began the systematization of Islamic knowledge – which drew strongly on the pre-Islamic, quintessential, Arab love of poetry (that is reflected in the melodious recitation of the Quran), grammar (to learn a new language), translations and hermeneutics, history (with particular emphasis on prophetic example and collating the Sunnah) and genealogy (Kennedy, 2001). After this early systematization, the diversification continued as new *madhabs* (schools of thought), denominations, traditions were formed. It is beyond the scope of this chapter to delve any further into this history,[4] but to summarize in the words of Daftary:

> As Islam spread outside the Arabian peninsula, its birthplace, it became enriched by the intellectual contributions of a multitude of individuals, communities and cultures in regions that eventually comprised the Muslim world. Indeed by the 10th century, the Islamic civilization was already characterized by a diversity of literary and intellectual traditions in various fields of learning such as theology, laws, philosophy, literature, mysticism, arts and natural sciences, while Islam as a religion had been elaborated in a plurality of expressions and interpretations.
>
> (Daftary, 2000, p. xi)

The spaces – *madrassas* or schools (*madrassa* is simply the Arabic word for school) – where learning was undertaken were as diverse as the tradition: memorizing the Quran from the Prophet (pbuh) in his mosque in the 7th century to discussions of philosophy in the medieval era and Islamic learning in the modern era, in universities, and also in Muslim institutions, *madrassas, hawzas, jamias* and *darul ulooms*. These diverse Muslim institutions that were spread across different parts of the Muslim world reflected the intellectual traditions that had led to their creation. They functioned in a manner that unlike their modern counterparts was akin to that of modern universities. They were multi-disciplinary and, while they taught Islam, they also imparted what may be described as education in the skills of life. Medicine, astronomy, mathematics, science and philosophy were among the subjects taught, together with poetry and the arts. A case in point could be the Al-Qarawiyyin mosque and madrassa, founded in 859 CE in Fez, Morocco. to provide, in addition to a space for worship, a learning center for the migrant Qayrawaniyyin community that settled there. It gradually developed into a place for religious instruction and political discussion.

Alongside the study of Islam, it provided courses on grammar, rhetoric, logic, medicine, mathematics, astronomy, chemistry, history, geography and music. It was also one of the first institutions of learning to provide a 'diploma in learning'. Like modern universities it offered courses from a variety of disciplines, attracted students from all over the world and had rigorous selection criteria.[5]

It is now well known that when Europe was in what many consider as the 'Dark Ages', Muslim cultures globally, under the Ottomans in the West and the Mughals in the East, were at the peak of intellectual discourse in the arts, humanities and sciences. For example, Winter and others write about how Arab and Muslim thinkers in Spanish Andalusia learned, preserved and subsequently developed the thinking and writing of Greek and Roman philosophers (Gutas, 1998; Winter, 2008). At the end of the European Dark Ages, this knowledge of Greek and European philosophy as preserved and developed by Muslim thinkers was transmitted to European thinkers and philosophers, leading Gutas to conclude that:

> One can justly claim the study of post-classical Greek secular writings can hardly ever proceed without the evidence in Arabic which in this context becomes the second classical language even before Latin.
>
> (Gutas, 1998, p. 2)

While evidence is scant about the roles and contributions of women, it is nevertheless clear that across its history, women were involved in various ways in the development of Islamic intellectual tradition. During the lifetime of the Prophet (pbuh), the hadith indicate that men and women shared the same space, usually in the mosque, to learn the Quran. However, the first indication of what may be understood as a school exclusively for females can be traced back to a hadith stating, 'Some women requested the Prophet to fix a day for them as the men were taking all his time. On that he promised them one day for religious lessons and commandments'.[6] Women acted as patrons founding new schools – indeed the Al-Qarawiyyin mosque and madrassa were funded by a woman Fatimah bint Muhḥammad al-Fihri (d. 880 CE). Islamic education for women continued to develop, often under the patronage of female scholars and or female members of various royal families.[7]

Yet today, the intellectual contributions of Islam to European and 'Western' thought are almost invisible and are subverted firstly by a gradual focus within Muslim religious institutions on religious learning alone – in many Muslim institutions, religious learning became the sole focus – and secondly, by the more recent and widespread entrenched positioning of Islam and Muslims as the different other. Geaves (2008), for example, notes how the Darse-Nizami curriculum (a form of study that is used in Sunni South Asian institutions) developed partly as a response to colonialism on the Indian sub-continent and a resulting defensive desire to protect Islamic traditions and values. Such attitudes caused communities and traditions that were open to become more inward looking. On one level, this led to educational syllabi in Muslim institutions that only examined classical Islam theology. On another level, a desire to protect women led to reduced social roles for them. Criticisms of modern religious education provision for Muslim women is that these further patriarchal agendas indoctrinate women to lead sheltered lives and that they offer education to females that is less prestigious than that provided to males. Pickthall (1926, pp. 41–42) bemoans this loss of critical- ity, openness and multi-disciplinarity from Islamic education. Islamic univer- sities, he says, no longer taught the diverse sciences that they were once at the forefront of. Instead they taught 'the hair-splitting niceties of *fiqh* – religious jurisprudence – a science of great use to every Muslim, but taught in such a way as to imprison the intelligence'.

The modern western university campus

The modern Western university campus has changed too and reflects the wider society in which it finds itself. In his *The Idea of a University*, New- man (1852) describes the university as 'the office of intellectual education' that is steadied by the Church 'in the performance of that office'. Today, most British universities are 'secular' institutions with only limited connec- tions with religious offices, perhaps extending only as far as providing reli- gious chaplaincy and other 'reasonable accommodation' to students and staff who are religious. This is an expression of two worrying and significant societal features that are being reflected in universities – neoliberalism and a form of non-religiosity that is assertive in its devaluing of religion. Neo- liberal tendencies show themselves in the need that universities now have to function as profit making businesses, and assertive secularism shows itself as an increase in attitudes that seem anti-religious, such as campus promiscu- ity cultures as testified in Phipps's work (2012). Secularism can debate well with religious thematics, yet each may seem crowded out of the other's con- versation. These tendencies go against the understanding of British universi- ties that obtained, until recently, a higher education that protected academic freedoms so that staff and students could safely discuss controversial issues in a rich curriculum without fear of censure. In the *new* campus environ- ments, social relations become less important than economic success, and this subordinates moral and intellectual obligations to conformity.

The modern university now provides for the educational needs of diverse students – different ethnicities, cultures, class and religions. With regard to this discussion about faith on campus, this diversity is reflected within Islam, for example, in chaplaincy and pastoral provisions on campuses and to a lesser extent in provision of prayer spaces and other 'reasonable accommo- dations', such as the availability of halal food on some UK campuses. Yet Islam and Muslims are also marginalized and viewed with suspicion, and Ricoeur demonstrates how dangerous the hermeneutics of suspicion can be

(Scott-Baumann, 2009). This suspicion is partly because of terrorism and the discourse on 'preventing violent extremism' and partly because of the enduring influence of historic orientalist constructions of Muslims and Islam as the 'barbaric' aliens who do not have a place in 'civilized' Western culture. There is also the growth of non-religious voices that seek to challenge the privileging of the Christian religious influence in British public affairs, and which in their criticisms of religion also devalue religious knowledge of all forms, including knowledge that is seen to have developed in Islamic contexts.

An introduction to the history of Islamic education in Britain

The history of Islamic intellectual history in Britain can be traced back to Abdullah Quilliam, who converted to Islam and established the first mosque in Britain in 1889. This mosque became a place both for religious worship and for religious learning. The first British purpose-built mosque built in Woking in 1889 also had provision for Islamic education. Mohammed Marmaduke Pickthall's and Yusuf Ali's translations of the Quran into English (completed in 1930 and 1938, respectively) and their various writings add to the beginnings of a British Muslim intellectual history. Finally, we must consider the contributions of the British-Yemeni communities who have lived in Britain since the middle of the eighteenth century (Seddon, 2014). The *zawiyas* established by the Yemenis and the first two British mosques were the earliest places where Islamic education took place in Britain.

The wider development of Islamic educational institutions took place much later when Muslim communities who arrived in Britain in the 1960s and '70s began to establish themselves. These communities came from the Indian sub-continent, and also from the East coast of Africa and other erstwhile British colonies, bringing with them their own cultural traditions and 'versions' of Islam. They set up institutions for the study of Islam – initially developing *madrassas and maktabs* that were attached to mosques and which provided basic Islamic teachings to children, and then, more gradually, *hawzas, darul ulooms* and *jamias,* where more detailed study could take place leading to the formation of faith leaders. For more details on the discussions in this section, please see Chapters 1 and 2 of our book on *Islamic Education in Britain: New Pluralist Paradigms* (Scott-Baumann and Cheruvallil-Contractor, 2015).

Relationships between Muslim colleges and British universities

The subject discipline of Islamic studies is taught in two different ways in Britain: in the Muslim seminaries (*madrassas, darul ulooms, jamias and hawzas*), it is taught confessionally.[8] In the universities, it is taught as a combination of humanities (usually history, geography, sociology and politics). Siddiqui critiqued this model in 2007, yet it is still largely unmodified (Siddiqui, 2007). For some time, there has been a movement to bring together the strengths and limitations of both sectors (Scott-Baumann, 2003; Scott-Baumann and Cheruvallil-Contractor, 2015, chapter 6). Seminary students themselves have often suggested that they could benefit from adding secular and (other) religious components to their study (Mukadam et al., 2010). This is possible because all UK universities have structures in place that permit collaborations with non-university institutions, set out in the Quality Code for Higher Education.[9] However, Muslim institutions find it difficult to find a partner university. Recent legislation under the Prevent agenda will probably accentuate this difficulty. There are two existing successful partnerships: between Markfield College of Higher Education and Newman University, and between Islamic College for Advanced Studies and Middlesex University. Thus, the majority of these seminaries (over 50 in Britain) do not have validation for the higher levels of their courses (although their students are successful in GCSEs and A levels). Without 'mainstream' recognition for such courses, seminary students do not have the employment and further education opportunities that university students have.

Partnerships between universities and Muslim colleges make possible the important debate between secular and religious epistemic approaches. This will create opportunities to shape the future of young British Muslim citizens as they study at university, live, work and contribute to pluralist Britain and have as much influence upon young non-Muslim Britons who wish to explore alternative approaches. We also demonstrate next the urgency for considering the needs of all students on campus, to which end broader-based discussions of identity and spiritual need are required.

Muslim students (women and men) on campus

The position of all women on campus is a test of the state of modern society as reflected in the British university; Muslim women who wear headscarves are often seen as out of step with modern society and with so-called 'fundamental British values' and may even be accused of 'non-violent extremism', this term used by the British government. They may be thought to be even harboring terrorist sympathies: in any event, they would not be seen as able to contribute to the debate we are framing in this discussion about women on campus. Phipps shows two ways in which this can work: the neoconservative view of the Muslim woman is as a victim and the neoliberal politics of recognition has a homogenizing effect so that Muslim women are seen as fundamentally different from any one else. Therefore, their views are seen as irrelevant to other students on campus (Phipps, 2014, p. 133).

Yet, Muslim students form the most numerically significant religious minority on campus and in British life, and we suggest that it is necessary to think about the university specifically from the point of view of the student, and especially the woman student, although our concern also affects men as does everything that affects women. British Muslim women are caught between the patriarchy of their home culture and the secularism of their adopted home (Cheruvallil-Contractor, 2012). They are viewed by their communities as being in need of restraint and by their adopted country as being in need of liberation into Western democracy. Like 'Western/secular' students, many Muslim women students dislike the aggressive 'laddism' of the campus and can avoid university by having access to Islamic theology through different avenues, including attendance at Muslim institutions such as *darul ul looms, jamias* and *hawzas,* study circles and less traditional routes such as internet-based resources (Barazangi, 2004). Research consistently demonstrates these women's desires for peaceful conflict resolution, dialogue and cohesion, when they are invited to have their own voice.

Spiritual needs are also expressed more clearly in the Muslim communities than among the general non-religious population, and this can raise issues for those who may seek some sort of spiritual, moral guidance and nourishment from their university. Yet, Muslim concerns about the secular world are dismissed as puritanical and even bordering on an attack on Western values, as we saw in the Trojan Horse episode, signalled by the demand by then Secretary of State for Education, Michael Gove, that schools must promote British values.[10]

What are British values? The findings of Phipps and Young's (2012) *That's what she said* research show that, when asked by researchers, female university students, who happened not to be Muslim, express considerable worries about their lives on campus and the implied value systems. Interviewees defined 'lad culture' as a group or 'pack' mentality framed in activities such as sports and heavy alcohol consumption, accompanied by 'banter' that was often perceived as sexist, misogynist and homophobic. Most reported that they saw sexual harassment and violence as closely related to 'lad culture', which included verbal harassment, physical harassment and sexual molestation. They felt pressured to engage in frequently changing sexual relationships. When asked about university teaching, they described university education as 'gendered', and they cited issues such as the descriptions and status of particular subjects and classroom interactions. They also identified negative attitudes towards feminism and gender-related topics in the university curriculum.

With these findings Phipps and Young's research suggests that important issues are not being understood, not being dealt with in university life and not being covered in the curriculum: how to behave on campus, how to deal with what Le Doeuff (2003) calls gendered knowledge (the 'sex of knowing'), how to identify and challenge implicit bias, how to recognise stereotype threat and how to manage one's body and desires. These sexualities are true for men and women of all faiths and of none: such issues belong together, male and female, yet they need to be differentiated as well as accepted as similar. The Islamic approach to being a woman can make a valuable contribution towards creating discussions that are simply not taking place on campus. There are several reasons why the religious voice can make a unique contribution. There is also the opportunity to see a situation differently, to break away from the perceived hegemony of the majority, as demonstrated by Phipps and Young. Specifically with regard to Muslims, we can also consider Kundnani's point in his book *The Muslims Are Coming*, that 'a transformative politics is more likely to emerge from racialized sections of society' (Kundnani, 2014, p. 284). We propose that this is relevant to a group that is singled out, as Muslims are, and of course there are historical precedents, such as the emancipatory actions of those in the civil rights movement in the USA in the 1950s and '60s. Moreover, in general terms, established religious traditions provide the language and concepts for discussing ethical and moral issues. We can see this exemplified in the religiously inspired writings of Prudence Allen.

Sister Prudence Allen, a philosopher nun, incorporates the 'woman question' into an existential debate about human beings, male and female, and an epistemological debate about the university curriculum. Also, at an ontological level, she argues that the human is comprised of four major and different factors: rationality, materiality, individuality and spirituality, and that Aristotelian thought separated these areas and thereby dispersed modern Western thought and being, whereas Allen believes that they must be combined in order that each individual can be a complete person. This division is also reflected at the institutional level. She describes how the Faculty of Arts (rationality), the Faculties of Medicine and Law (materiality of body and of society respectively) and the Faculty of Theology (spirituality) created an institutional fragmentation of thought about the nature of humanity (Allen, 1985, vol. 1, chapter 4). We can see starkly the need for Christian, Jewish, Muslim and others of faith as well as those of no faiths to have a curriculum that combines, unites and also differentiates the four characteristics of a fully developed human: the individual, the rational, the material and the spiritual. Yet, this is not easy because Western philosophy has taken two steps that are only now being reversed: the first step is that since Aristotle the Western philosophical tradition has excluded woman from education because her body is different from that of men. The second step is that this exclusion, based upon physical differences, is seen as irrelevant because metaphysical traditions avoid the physical (Scott-Baumann, 2016). Thus, the exclusion of woman cannot easily be discussed in mainstream philosophy.

It is thought provoking to consider that the Muslim woman on campus is considered by many to have nothing relevant to say about how to live a good life on campus because she is assumed to be completely different from the majority of female students. Yet, all women face similar issues to each other. Even worse, the Muslim woman on campus, if she dresses conservatively, may even be considered to be potentially dangerous, partly due to the new criterion of 'non-violent extremism', which we consider next.

Recent legislation that affects campus activity

The UK university sector is currently in a state of unprecedented flux, uncertainty and economic insecurity that, arguably, makes it vulnerable to outside pressures. There are accusations from the government about allowing radical preachers onsite and failing to stem on-campus recruitment to extremist Muslim causes. There is very little evidence of such activities, and there is no real resistance from the sector over these accusations, although individual universities are responding to specific accusations in order to refute them with fact (*The Independent,* 18th September, 2015). Since 2007, the government has been developing a counter terrorism strategy called Contest. Part of this is a programme called Prevent, and within Prevent lies an initiative called Channel, which is designed to intervene when an individual is thought to be at risk of radicalization. Children and young people can be referred to Channel for treatment if their views and/or behavior are thought to be extremist. All these terms can be contested. In 2015, major legislation was passed, in the form of the 2015 Counter Terror and Security Act (CTSA) with attached Guidance. Legal guidance demonstrates that there is a difference between an Act, which is mandatory and Guidance, which is guidance. Currently, there is a discrepancy between the requirements of the CTSA and the Prevent Duty Guidance. Section 26.1 of the CTSA describes a duty 'to have due regard to the need to prevent people from being drawn into terrorism'. Section 31(2) of the CTSA on universities also emphasises freedom of academic expression:

When carrying out the duty imposed by section 26(1), a specified authority to which this section applies:

(a) must have particular regard to the duty to ensure freedom of speech, if it is subject to that duty;
(b) must have particular regard to the importance of academic freedom, if it is the proprietor or governing body of a qualifying institution
(Counter Terror and Security Act, 2015, p. 20).

Yet, a particular sort of very assertive language has grown in use around the legislation: such language is extreme and suggests a different understanding of those requirements in the university sector. In many public and media discussions, this 'having due regard to' is understood to mean monitoring. It is mandatory upon universities to have policies in place which can be scored against the new Higher Education Funding Council for England (HEFCE) Monitoring framework to demonstrate having due regard and strengthening existing policies where necessary. The Prevent Duty Guidance instructs the sector of the legally binding need for monitoring staff and students even though this is not explicitly required by the Act. This sense of urgency has caught on. As an example, the HEFCE Monitoring framework writes of the 'Prevent duty obligation' (HEFCE, 2015, p. 6), which sounds legally binding when the guidance is not, and seems more onerous than it is. The HEFCE Monitoring framework also normalises the abnormal, e.g., it describes 'business as usual (for example straightforward Channel referrals)' (HEFCE, 2015, p. 12). On the contrary we hope it is reasonable to believe that Channel referrals are never either 'business as usual' or straightforward. This violent use of language enacts Agamben's (2005) 'state of exception', in which the law is transgressed by lawmakers because we are supposed to be in great danger. Huysmans calls this the jargon of exception (Huysmans, 2008). In Section 1(7) of the Channel duty guidance, Channel is described as 'a multi-agency approach to identify and provide support to individuals who are at risk of being drawn into terrorism'. Such accusations demonstrate the violence in language, the unfounded assumption that the risk of terrorism in the school and university population is high. The British university sector has a superb track record for facilitating conversations about complex and controversial issues. Yet, concern about the new legislation effectively renders the sector fearful of encouraging, fostering and hosting critical debate – even to challenge the violent language used in the new legislation. What do we mean by violent language? In his essay *Violence and Language*, Paul Ricoeur demonstrates how violently language can be used: 'A violence that speaks is already a violence trying to be right; it is a violence that places itself in the orbit of reason and that is already beginning to negate itself as violence' (Ricoeur, 1976, pp. 88–101).

Ricoeur analyses the way in which language can be used to express violence that is as far away from language as it could possibly be. This distance between violence and words is real, of course, because words themselves do no physical injury – and yet, through Ricoeur, we see how each human has subjugated their own private violence to the rule of law. Thereby, the rule of law can become a great force of willpower that may do damage and is 'an enormous violence which elbows its way through our private violences and speaks the language of value and honour' (Ricoeur, 1976, p. 94; Scott-Baumann, 2013b, pp. 81–84). Compliance with the duty will also require the institution to demonstrate that it is willing to undertake Prevent awareness training and other training that could help the relevant staff prevent people from being drawn into terrorism and challenge extremist ideas which risk drawing people into terrorism (Revised Prevent Duty Guidance, 2015, p. 22).

Every university already clearly asserts a duty of care to take action if evidence emerges of possible danger to any member of the university. This duty of care is now believed by some sections of government to be inadequate, inserting through legislation a need for compliance in policing another unclear aspect of the new legislation, namely the identification of 'non-violent extremism', which may be seen in an increase in conservative dress or a growth of beard and is, in effect, a form of religious and often racial profiling. We propose that the legal constraints now placed upon universities may in fact increase the likelihood of non-violent 'pretenders' or 'drifters' becoming violent extremists: there is a risk that this will be a self-fulfilling prophecy, because it is based upon the assumption that non-violent opinions influence non-violent extremists who are likely to transform into violent extremists. Under the 2015 CTSA legislation there will be even less opportunity to discuss difficult issues that are a burden for Muslim communities. These are considered to be 'dangerous' topics and may involve British foreign policy or the condition of Palestine, for example. Ideas, when driven underground, can appear to become more desperately important, more potent and less susceptible to moderation because less visible. As Lakhani argued in 2013, 'It may be that the government needs to soften their stance to find an agreeable way to work with these groups who fall under the non-violent extremism category' (Lakhani, 2013, p. 244). Even more seriously, we see here a direct assault being made upon the capacity of the university to address such violent use of language by means of discussion, expert input and the teaching and exercising of debating skills. Thus we can extend Lakhani's assertion beyond a plea for a softening of stance towards non-violent extremists, to plead for the softening of the government's stance towards universities, instead of them being treated by government as a source of extremist ideas.

Britain has more anti-terror legislation than most countries in the developed world, and lawmakers are concerned that citizens' rights are breached in the pursuit of terror suspects. The 2000 Terrorism Act permits police to seize property if they believe it will lead to terrorist arrests. We are told that the security services have foiled several terror attacks and for this we must be grateful, so that we can preserve the way of life that is based upon democracy, human rights and freedom of speech. Indeed, recent legislation pays tribute to the importance that these ideas play in modern British culture and especially as they are practiced/exercised in the British university sector. Yet increasingly, over the last 20 years, Islam and secular university campuses are being linked together in governmental narratives as sources of risk, even danger. More and more the expression of Islam on university campuses is associated with a subversive form of religion and a dangerous 'radicalisation' among students. Our work endeavors to 'analyse the polarization that appears to have been effected between secularism and Islamism' (Scott-Baumann and Cheruvallil-Contractor, 2015, p. 82). Clearly, current security perspectives on university life sit uncomfortably alongside long-standing ideals of intellectual freedom and the Western image of the university as a safe context for experimentation, free thinking and social protest. What is at stake here is the status of universities within Western democracies and whether limiting academic freedom and freedom of speech can ever be justified.

What impact will these factors have on university curricula and academic freedoms?

At the time of writing, there is debate about whether universities can allow freedom of speech, and if so, how this should be best achieved. Islam is seen in some circles as one of the issues being used to constrain the university sector, to accuse it of permitting too much free speech, and thereby permitting dangerous thoughts to develop. In 2011, anticipating publication of the government's anti-terrorism strategy, UK Home Secretary Theresa May accused universities of 'complacency', suggesting they had not been 'sufficiently willing to recognise what can be happening on their campuses and the radicalisation that can take place'.[11] In 2013, as a result of the murder of Fusilier Lee Rigby by Muslim radicals who had connections with the University of Greenwich, Theresa May made a commitment to investigate Muslim activities on university campuses, and this process led to the 2015 Counter Terror and Security Act. This is not to deny that there are issues on campus that need to be addressed, and yet we can also argue that such issues can be addressed by education. We can see this in the doctoral research undertaken by Suraj Lakhani and entitled *Radicalisation, a moral career. A qualitative study of how people become radicalized in the UK*. One of Lakhani's interviewees was exposed to 'extremism' at university:

> At university he attended a study circle which he found to hold distinct extreme views. His depth of Islamic knowledge, he felt, ensured he did not internalise the extreme ideologies they were espousing. However, it is important to note that as a result of these social bonds he continued to attend these groups for some time; something akin to Lofland and Stark's (1965) account of cults. He explained how these individuals were:
> "... people who have grievances but not a great deal of knowledge about Islam. So I sit there and it was like these guys don't have a great deal of knowledge. In fact I felt like I knew more than them ..."
> (Lakhani, 2013, pp. 159–160)

Here we see how a well-educated young Muslim can critique arguments because of his superior knowledge of Islam. Kashyap and Lewis (2013, p. 2135) compared British Muslim youth with Christians and the non-religious of the same generation, finding 'higher levels of education and employment are related to lower religiosity and more liberal social attitudes', suggesting the need to revisit generalizing claims connecting 'radical' Islam with the university experience. However, now that this issue has become a security matter, we worry that it will no longer be possible for staff and students to discuss such matters in an open, democratic way. We can see a form of democracy in the work of Jürgen Habermas. He prizes ways of knowing that develop through critical reflection and engagement or *praxis* (practical action for change) and asserts that eruptions of violence can provide understanding of what has been damaged in human relations and what needs to be repaired by painstaking process (Habermas in Borradori, 2003, p. 35).

We believe these processes can and should have their roots in knowledge developed in educational establishments; schools and universities. Yet we have to ask whether the school and the university form part of the public space that Habermas sees as central to the development of constitutional patriotism – society engaged in critical public debate – or whether universities have been taken over by a form of free market fundamentalism that inhibits the exploration of ideas unless they are commodities. Information that appears to be about counter-terrorism may be more marketable than peace. Lyotard in the *Postmodern Condition* tells us that:

> Knowledge is and will be produced in order to be sold; it is and will be consumed in order to be valorised in a new production: in both cases, the goal is exchange. Knowledge ceases to be an end in itself, it loses its "use value".
> (Lyotard, 1984, pp. 4–5)

We suggest that a neoliberal approach (in which the state is shrunk, government becomes a business not a service and knowledge is commodified) creates the conditions in which it becomes increasingly difficult to be clear about the accuracy of what we are told by the media and even by certain groups within government. In such a setting, it is of paramount importance to challenge constructs like 'radicalisation' through working with and including Islamic discourses within the wider tapestry of British campus life. It is also imperative to avoid radicalization becoming the starting point of discussions about Islam on campus – we have demonstrated that there are other matters to talk about, to address and to challenge. We propose that Islam is an integral part of British life, as we have shown with the history of Islam in Britain and the shared traditions that bind us together. We also suggest that Islam is a moderating force and we have shown this with our discussion of the lives of modern British Muslim women, who can make a precious contribution to British university life if they are accepted as sharing the same goals, hopes and fears as their fellow students. There is therefore a pressing need to appreciate that we can even understand ourselves better through attempting to understand those whom we may perceive as very different from us. Paul Ricoeur goes even further by arguing that it is only through trying to understand other people that we can come to a better, although still imperfect, self-understanding. The university is indeed one of the few safe places left where, in trying to think of oneself as another, we may learn together about how to improve the world we share.

Conclusions

> Islam has for too long been studied from "outside in" while there is a need for and much to gain from looking "inside out".
> (Siddiqui, 2007)[12]

At the time of writing, there is debate about whether universities are protecting academic freedom and freedom of speech, and how this should be best achieved (Furedi, 2015). In this context, Islam is seen in some circles as an issue that is being used to constrain the university sector, to accuse student societies of permitting too much or too little free speech, and of thereby permitting controversial thoughts to develop or to be suppressed. We propose that if this issue is perceived as a security matter, it will no longer be possible for staff and students to discuss such matters in an open, democratic way (Habermas, 1962). Like Sahin, we believe these processes can and should have their roots in knowledge developed in educational establishments: schools and universities.

> Islamic extremism can be defeated by robust and competent internal Islamic intervention. The struggle against extremism needs to include a measured, long-term educational response where Muslim communities, without being stigmatised, can join wider civil and educational efforts to counter it.
>
> (Sahin, 2016)

The provision of Islamic studies in a balanced and well-informed curriculum could support those who wish to understand Islam in the modern world. Yet we have to ask whether the school and the university form part of the public space that Habermas sees as central to the development of constitutional patriotism . . . or whether they have been taken over by a form of free-market fundamentalism that inhibits the exploration of ideas unless they are commodities.

We also need to question the vested interests and politics that have positioned Islam as the different other. Both orientalist and post-colonialist thinkers have demonstrated how Western academia gave preference to Western ontologies and political interests – Islam was studied as the different other that was exotic and distant. Yet, Siddiqui insists that Islam must be studied as an inherent part of British social fabric. This approach will allow us to recognize the historical inter-linkages between Islamic and Western intellectual traditions and the potential for these to work together now and in the future:

> Those who promote enmity and convey information based on the knowledge that we inhabit a world of rivalry only reveal severe ignorance when it comes to the divergences and continuities between Islamic and Western civilizations. We need to interrogate the terms of the differences promoted by those ideologies so that a more productive dialogue may take place.
>
> (Salama, 2011, p. 212)

Notes

1 Christianity, Judaism and other world religions and belief systems, including humanism, must have a voice too: in this chapter, we focus on Islam.

2 (pbuh): Peace be upon him.
3 http://www.theguardian.com/education/2016/jan/12/islam-education-extremism-
   schools-muslim-prevent?CMP=share_btn_tw (accessed January 27th, 2016).
4 A good first reading on this subject is Daftary's *Intellectual Traditions in Islam*
   (Daftary, 2000).
5 http://www.muslimheritage.com/article/al-qarawiyyin-mosque-and-university
   (accessed January 27th, 2016).
6 Ṣaḥīḥ Bukhārī, Vol. 1, Book 3, No. 101 http://sunnah.com/bukhari/3/43 (accessed
   January 27th, 2016).
7 A number of examples of such courses may be accessed in Cheruvallil-Contractor,
   S., 2013. *Qur'anic Schools for Girls* in *Oxford Encyclopaedia of Islam and
   Women*. ed. Delong-Bas N.J., New York, Oxford University Press.
8 Literally, a house of knowledge, but by extension this refers to a school that provides an in-depth course on Islamic sciences, popularly known as the *alimiyyah*
   syllabus. *Deobandis* usually use the term *darul uloom* and *Barelvis jami'ah* for
   this type of institution. *Shias* use the term *Hawza*.
9 www.qaa.ac.uk (accessed January 27th, 2016).
10 http://www.telegraph.co.uk/education/educationnews/10887976/Trojan-Horse-
   schools-must-promote-British-values-says-Gove.html (accessed January 27th, 2016).
11 See Daily Telegraph: http://www.telegraph.co.uk/news/uknews/terrorism-in-the-
   uk/8558499/Universities-complacent-over-Islamic-radicals-Theresa-May-warns.
   html (accessed January 27th, 2016).
12 http://www.mihe.org.uk/sites/default/files/upload/Documents/siddiqui_report2007.
   pdf (accessed January 27th, 2016).

References

Agamben, G., 2005. *State of Exception*. Translated by Attell, K. Chicago and Lon-
   don: University of Chicago Press.
Allen, P., 1985. *The Concept of Woman*. Vol. 1. Grand Rapids, MI and Cambridge
   UK: Eerdmans.
Barazangi, N.H., 2004. *Woman's Identity and the Quran – A New Reading*. Florida:
   University Press of Florida.
Borradori, G., ed. 2003. *Philosophy in a Time of Terror: Dialogues with Jürgen
   Habermas and Jacques Derrida*. Chicago: University of Chicago Press.
Channel Duty Guidance, 2015. [online] Available at: https://www.gov.uk/government/
   uploads/system/uploads/attachment_data/file/425189/Channel_Duty_Guidance_
   April_2015.pdf. [accessed November 10th 2015].
Cheruvallil-Contractor, S., 2012. *Muslim Women in Britain: Demystifying the Mus-
   limah*. London and New York: Routledge.
Cheruvallil-Contractor, S., 2013. Qur'anic Schools for Girls in Delong-Bas, N. J.', ed.
   Oxford Encyclopaedia of Islam and Women. New York: Oxford University Press.
   http://www.oxfordreference.com/view/10.1093/acref:oiso/9780199764464.001.0001/
   acref-9780199764464-e-0330?rskey=LCSLua&result=267 (accessed 10th July 2016)
Daftary, F., 2000. Preface in Daftary, F., ed. *Intellectual Traditions in Islam*. London:
   I B Tauris. pp. xi-xii.
Furedi, F., 2015. [online] Available at: http://www.telegraph.co.uk/education/
   educationnews/12059161/Politically-correct-universities-are-killing-free-speech.
   html. [accessed January 4th 2016]
Geaves, R., 2008. Drawing on the Past to Transform the Present: Contemporary
   Challenges for Training and Preparing British Imams in *Journal of Muslim Minor-
   ity Affairs*. 28 (1), pp. 99–112. April 2008.

Gutas, D., 1998. *Greek Thought, Arabic Culture: The Graeco-Arabic Translation Movement in Baghdad and Early 'Abbasaid Society (2nd-4th/5th-10th c.) (Arabic Thought and Culture)*. London and New York: Routledge.

Habermas, J., 1962. *The Structural Translation of the Public Sphere*. Cambridge, MA: MIT Press.

HEFCE (Higher Education Funding Council for England), 2015. *The Prevent Duty: Monitoring Framework for the Higher Education Sector*. [online] Available at: www.hefce.ac.uk › Regulation and assurance. [accessed January 27th 2016].

Home Office, 2000. *Terrorism Act*. London: HMSO.

Home Office, 2011. *Prevent Strategy*. London: HMSO.

Home Office, 2015. *Counter-Terrorism and Security Act*. London: HMSO.

Home Office, 2015. *Revised Prevent Duty Guidance*. London: HMSO.

Huysmans, J., 2008. The Jargon of Exception – On Schmitt, Agamben and the Absence of Political Society in *International Political Sociology*. 2 (2), pp. 165–183.

Independent 18th September 2015 [online] Available at: http://www.pressreader.com/uk/theindependent/20150918/281870117229967/TextView. [accessed September 20th 2015].

Kashyap, R., and Lewis, V.A., 2013. British Muslim Youth and Religious Fundamentalism: A Quantitative Investigation in *Ethnic and Racial Studies*. 36 (12), pp. 2117–2140.

Kennedy, H., 2000. Intellectual Life in the First Four Centuries of Islam in Daftary, F., ed. *Intellectual Traditions in Islam*. pp. 17–39. London: J.B. Taurus.

Kundnani, A., 2014. *The Muslims are Coming*. London and New York: Verso.

Lakhani, S., 2013. *Radicalisation, a Moral Career: A Qualitative Study of How People become Radicalized in the UK*. Cardiff University PhD [online] Available at: http://orca.cf.ac.uk/59779/. [accessed October 12th 2015].

Le Doeuff, M., 2003. *The Sex of Knowing*. Translated by Kathryn Hammer and Lorraine Code. London: Routledge.

Lyotard, J., 1984. *The Postmodern Condition*. Manchester: Manchester University Press.

Mukadam, M., Scott-Baumann, A., Chaudhary, A., and Contractor, S., 2010. *Muslim Faith Leader Training Review*. Department for Communities and Local Government [online] Available at: http://www.communities.gov.uk/publications/communities/trainingmuslimleaderspractice. [accessed January 27th 2016].

Newman, J., 1852. *The Idea of a University*. [online] Available at: http://www.newmanreader.org/works/idea/. [accessed January 27th 2016].

Phipps, A., 2014. *The Politics of the Body: Gender in a Neoliberal and Neoconservative Age*. Cambridge: Polity.

Phipps, A., and Young, I., 2012. *That's What She Said*. [online] Available at: http://www.nus.org.uk/. [accessed January 15th 2014].

Pickthall, M., 1926. *The Cultural Side of Islam*. Chennai: S Muhammad Ashraf.

Ricoeur, P., 1976. Violence and Language in Stewart, D., and Bien, J., eds. *Violence and Language in Political and Social Essays*. pp. 88–101. Athens: Ohio.

Sahin, A., 2013. *New Directions in Islamic Education*. Markfield: Kube Publishing.

Sahin, A., 2016. *Let's Tap into Islam's Heritage of Critical Education to Defeat Extremism in Schools*. [online] Available at: http://www.theguardian.com/education/2016/jan/12/islam-education-extremism-schools-muslim-prevent?CMP=share_btn_tw. [accessed January 27th 2016].

Salama, M.R., 2011. *Islam, Orientalism and Intellectual History: Modernity and the Politics of Exclusion Since Ibn Khaldun.* London: I B Tauris.

Scott-Baumann, A., 2003. Teacher Education for Muslim Women: Intercultural Relationships, Method and Philosophy in *Ethnicities.* 3 (2), pp. 243–261.

Scott-Baumann, A., 2009. *Ricoeur and the Hermeneutics of Suspicion.* London and New York: Continuum.

Scott-Baumann, A., 2013a. *Ricoeur and the Negation of Happiness.* London and New York: Bloomsbury.

Scott-Baumann, A., 2013b. *Ricoeur and Counter-Terror Rhetoric: A Calculus of Negation in LoSguardo.* Rivista di filosofia. ISSN 2036–6558. No. 12, 2013 (II) Paul Ricoeur Intersezzioni pp. 81–93 [online] Available at: http://www.losguardo.net/. [accessed January 27th 2016].

Scott-Baumann, A., 2016. Speak to Silence and Identify Absence on Campus: Sister Prudence and Paul Ricoeur on the Negated Woman Question in Henriques, F., and Halsema, A., eds. *Feminist Explorations of Paul Ricoeur's Philosophy.* pp. 37–61. Lexington: Rowman & Littlefield.

Scott-Baumann, A., and Cheruvallil-Contractor, S., 2015. *Islamic Education in Britain: Pluralist Paradigms.* London and New York: Bloomsbury.

Seddon, M., 2014. *The Last of the Lascars: Yemeni Muslims in Britain, 1836–2012.* Markfield: Kube Publishing.

Siddiqui, A., 2007. *Islam at Universities in England: Meeting the Needs and Investing in the Future.* [online] Available at: http://www.mihe.org.uk/the-siddiqui-report. [accessed January 27th 2016].

Winter, T.J., 2008. *The Cambridge Companion to Classical Islamic Theology.* Cambridge: Cambridge University Press.

9   The global melting pot of universities

John Wood

The world of global universities is facing an unprecedented time of change. The quiet hum of learning in the cloister is being replaced in many countries by the rise of the multinational university operating in real time 24/7. When I was head of engineering at Imperial College London, the Rector told me to treat my faculty as a subsidiary company with financial targets contributing to the overall success of the College. The faculty was swamped with outstanding applicants for undergraduate places, especially from overseas, mainly from Asia, who outshone many of their EU counterparts. Limiting the undergraduate intake meant that the financial targets had to be met by high-priced postgraduate taught degrees, research and industrial income. There were almost daily meetings with heads of global companies, international charities, policy makers and ministers from a wide variety of countries. Imperial was and does see itself as a truly global university with tentacles that reach around the world. That the then Chief Operating Officer had been an investment banker further emphasised the focus of the senior management team.

Compare that with a university in a developing country, provided by a faith community to aid development, where the power supply is a lottery, academics are only one step ahead of the student, students are exhausted from lack of food and having to earn a wage to support themselves and their families, there is a constant threat of terrorism (sometimes in the name of religion), yet all business meetings are conducted in an atmosphere of prayer.

The Association of Commonwealth Universities (ACU), which I lead, covers this complete spectrum.[1] Do they have anything in common? Has the university that is entirely focused on size and league tables sacrificed its soul in the globally competitive environment that is the lot of higher education? Are faith-based universities relevant to what is required for the modern era? As an organisation, ACU cannot judge. We rely on national recognition of an institution by a government agency, at least two cohorts of graduating students and audited accounts before accepting an institution as a member.

It is estimated that there are around 18,000 universities in the world, 4,000 in the European Union, about 750 and growing in India; in Kenya, there are 30 new universities being planned. Never before has there been such growth. What is driving this rush to create universities? What is expected of them? The largest rise is in those that are privately funded, both for profit and not for profit. Many are linked with one world religion or another. Does the faith-base influence the running and approach to teaching and research of the university? A further issue is whether a mono-subject university is really a 'university' in the truest sense of bringing people with different ideas and values into a melting pot where ideas can flourish and differences can be tolerated. In India there are 'Law' and 'Business' universities, in parts of Africa, 'Agricultural' universities, while in former Soviet bloc countries, there are universities of 'Medicine', Civil Engineering', and others emphasising a hothouse atmosphere around a single discipline.

In addition, the impact of current and future internet access (the UK university broadband spine will soon be operating at 400 gbits/sec, whereas less than a decade ago, it was operating at 10 gbits/sec), with huge collections of information in the cloud, challenges the concept of a university being a single physical entity rather than a network with access to information centres and unable to control what their academics and students are involved in.

Rushing headlong into oblivion

I have the privilege of meeting Vice-Chancellors, Rectors and Presidents of universities from all around the world. Some are faced with direct physical violence, political interference and societies that are based on extortion and bribery, whilst others in developed countries grapple with financial and reputational targets that are short term. In this latter case, the typical tenure can be compared with those of football managers. Professor David Turpin, the Vice-Chancellor of Alberta University in Canada, has done a survey to compare the average tenures of heads of universities in Canada. Some 40 to 50 years ago the average was around 18 years; now it is 3.7 years.[2] A similar story is emerging in the UK today. In many countries, including most of the rest of Europe, the heads are elected by fellow academics. While democratic, it means that the Rector is entirely in the hands of their fellows, who will depose the Rector if they do not like what is happening. This leads to the university being run as it has always been, making it less and less relevant to the world of today. Academics worldwide are inherently conservative. This was emphasised at a meeting of the Vice-Chancellors of the universities in northern India at their annual meeting in 2015 when the head of the country's university admissions agency (responsible for 40 million applications a year) stated that for every one academic wanting to move ahead, there are a thousand who oppose any idea.

Managing or leading a university is not easy in this environment, but good leadership is essential in today's global environment if a university is to move forward. A fun but practical book on university leadership in the modern era is *Herding Cats* by Geoff Garrett and Graeme Davies (2010). Garrett and Davies interviewed 50 ex-leaders of universities and similar establishments from around the world for their advice on how to survive in the hothouse environment of passion, pride, intellect, independence, political extremism and prejudice. This book is about the reality not the theory: 'Command and control approaches do not prosper, time scales to get things done, may be lengthy if not sometimes glacial; disagreement ubiquitous' (Garrett and Davies, 2010, p. 1).

Some ten years ago, I sat in the iconic Berlaymont building of the European Commission, in the room of the Commissioner for Science and Research, Janez Potocnik, who asked me, 'We have about 4,000 universities in the European Union, most of them are dysfunctional, what should we do about them?' We did not discuss the reasons for this but there are many, including weak university governance structures in parts of Europe and a lack of incentives to pursue excellence by academic staff. However, it is acknowledged that not all universities can be world class, and he went on to ask me, 'How many truly international universities can we support in Europe?' I joked that I thought about ten and certainly not 27 (the then number of member states in the Union). He replied, laughing, that his own university where he was professor of economics, Ljubljana, would not be one of them.

What, then, is a university? Is there a common definition? Should all universities aspire to be the same, or distinctive, and to what extent do cultural and religious/philosophical foundations actually matter in the twenty-first century? Into this palette of questions come some searching questions regarding the cost of universities, their responsibility to all stakeholders, their need to challenge convention (to be one of the consciences of society) and to what extent their ethos of teaching is leading the world towards a doomsday scenario. This latter point was highlighted in 2012 when the ACU was celebrating its 100th anniversary. Sir David King was our centenary lecturer and attended many conferences around the Commonwealth that year. His lectures focused on what demands a future population of nine billion would put on the world's ever-decreasing resources (raw materials, energy, food, water) and that this was not sustainable, not to mention the impact of climate change. Professor John Leung (the then Vice-Chancellor of the Hong Kong Open University) asked the pertinent question along the lines 'all our university teaching is based on individual achievement, greed, growth, yet this is impossible if the world is to survive. Just how should we teach and motivate students in the future where their quality of life and aspirations will have to be less than we have?'

The tension between global stewardship and the aspirations of individuals and governments is a crisis point for all citizens of the world. If we are training students one way but realise that in reality we are training for poverty or even global suicide, this presents a moral dilemma for the heads of universities. So just what should the prophetic voice of universities be?

Up until 2015, the ACU ran a campaign called 'Beyond 2015' to highlight the role of universities in developing the United Nations Sustainable

Development Goals. Many of our members, especially those in developing countries, contributed. Their messages were collated and presented to heads of governments via various routes, including the Commonwealth Education Ministers' summit held in the Bahamas just before the United Nations agreed on the 17 overall goals. Below is the cover page that accompanied our evidence:

**The Association
of Commonwealth
Universities**

Progress and potential

Higher education playing its part in the Sustainable Development Goals

September 2015

The Association of Commonwealth Universities (ACU) believes that higher education is uniquely placed to help address global challenges – not least through informing policy with research evidence, and through graduating generations of new leaders and skilled professionals. The Millennium Development Goals (MDGs) did not explicitly reference higher education – either as a development goal or as a potential agent to address development challenges. With the Sustainable Development Goals (SDGs) set to replace the MDG framework this year, a unique opportunity emerged to help advance the role of higher education in development spaces. The ACU's 'The world beyond 2015 – Is higher education ready?' campaign was launched in October 2013 to raise awareness, elicit expert views, gather evidence and advocate for the role of higher education in delivering social and developmental impact.

Key points

- **Higher education underpins all development targets**, from poverty reduction to employability, health to environmental sustainability.

- Higher education institutions are well placed to feed **research evidence** into the design of national development policy and strategy.

- Meeting the MDGs and SDGs depends upon **skilled graduates**.

- Harmonisation of education strategy from **primary through to higher education** can ensure sustainable paths for students and can lay the groundwork for accommodating growth in enrolment at **all education levels**.

- Growing enrolment at primary and secondary levels behoves a comprehensive strategy to ensure **access and quality** at the higher education level.

- The ACU's 'The world beyond 2015 – Is higher education ready?' campaign has published an extensive and open access body of evidence of how higher education can **demonstrate social impact** and influence development policy (www.acu.ac.uk/beyond-2015).

Here at least was one aspect of a global prophetic voice emanating from a cross-section of universities. While it is possible to question how effectively universities responded and contributed to almost all the Sustainable Development Goals, in target four (Quality Education for all), the following are given as specific responsibilities of universities:

4.a By 2030, ensure that all learners acquire the knowledge and skills needed to promote sustainable development, including, among others, through education for sustainable development and sustainable lifestyles, human rights, gender equality, promotion of a culture of peace and non-violence, global citizenship and appreciation of cultural diversity and of cultures' contribution to sustainable development.

4.b By 2020, substantially expand globally the number of scholarships available to developing countries, in particular least developed countries, small island developing states and African countries, for enrolment in higher education, including vocational training and information and communications technology, technical, engineering and scientific programmes, in developed countries and other developing countries.[3]

Yet when talking directly with ministers in various countries, their reasons for funding universities are primarily for the economic growth of their own country. However, in the UK, the funding for research at universities does now contain a component (£1.5b over the period) directed at working on so called 'Global Challenges' research (BIS, 2015). An interesting quadrant study has been published by the Department for Business, Innovation and Skills (BIS) in the UK entitled *The Benefits of Higher Education Participation for Individuals and Society* (BIS, 2013). The summary is given below. The market benefits are entirely devoted to economics, finance and betterment of both society and the individual.

	NON MARKET	MARKET
SOCIETY	Greater social cohesion, trust and tolerance Less crime Political stability Greater social mobility Greater social capital	Increased tax revenues Faster economic growth Greater innovation and labour market flexibility Increased productivity of co-workers Reduced burden on public finances from co-ordination between policy areas such as health and crime prevention

(Continued)

(Continued)

	NON MARKET	MARKET
INDIVIDUAL	Greater propensity to vote	Higher earnings
	Greater propensity to volunteer	Less exposure to
	Greater propensity to trust and	unemployment
	tolerate others	Increased employability and
	Lower propensity to commit	skills development
	(non-violent) crime	Increased entrepreneurial
	Better educational parenting	activity and productivity
	Longer life expectancy	
	Less likely to smoke	
	Less likely to drink excessively	
	Less likely to be obese	
	More likely to engage in	
	preventative care	
	Better mental health	
	Greater life satisfaction	
	Better general health	

Some examples of university missions and values

This approach of assessing the benefits of a university education as perceived by a public funder is not confined just to the developed world. Yet there are wider attributes that individual universities aim to fulfil, as set out in their public statements about vision, values and missions. It is interesting to analyse the mission statements of many of our members as stated on their websites, noting their similarities and differences, which reflect their circumstances and values, and to compare these with those in the table above:

The University of the West Indies (UWI)

UWI expresses its mission as follows:

> Our Mission Statement reflects the primary purpose of our University, that is, the reason for its existence. To advance education and create knowledge through excellence in teaching, research, innovation, public service, intellectual leadership and outreach in order to support the inclusive (social, economic, political, cultural, environmental) development of the Caribbean region and beyond.
> The Mission of the UWI is further explained in the following context:
> To advance education: Provide opportunities to the population of the region and beyond for higher education that fosters creative activity and notions of shared community, enhanced social and interpersonal relations, and critical and creative thinking skills;
> To create knowledge: Engage in research that serves to: (i) create significant new insights, (ii) explore and apply solutions to priority national and regional problems and challenges, (iii) exploit developmental

potential and competitive advantages, (iv) position self and society in a changing world order, and (v) provide a sound basis for public policy formulation and decision making;

To support inclusive development of the Caribbean region and beyond: Maintain a capacity to supply and support a wide range of expert technical, professional and advisory services to meet the needs of national governments, public and private sectors, and regional and international institutions, and to involve all stakeholders in the process; and be a significant contributor to global intellectual growth and human development by producing scholars that harness the creative energies, cultural diversity, social experiences, biodiversity and other assets of the region and beyond.[4]

Sant Gadge Baba Amravati University (India)

This university expresses its vision and mission as follows:

Vision: To emancipate the youth from the darkness of ignorance for elevation of the society by imparting knowledge and fostering wisdom at its most plentiful.

Mission: To contribute to the society through the pursuit of education, learning and research at the highest level of excellence.[5]

University of the South Pacific

Our Vision: Achieving excellence and innovation for sustainable development of the Pacific Island Countries.

Our Mission: To provide Pacific people with a comprehensive range of excellent and relevant tertiary qualifications;

- To deliver the benefits of advanced research and its applications;
- To provide communities and countries in the Pacific region with relevant, cost effective and sustainable solutions, including entrepreneurship, to their main challenges; and
- To be an exemplar of tertiary education for the Pacific Islands in quality, governance, application of technology and collaboration with national tertiary institutions.

Our Values: (a selection)

Protection and nurturing of the environment;

Strong relationships to guide engagement with national governments, Pacific communities, and development partners;

Humility in performance, learn from others, value the trust given, and honour Pacific knowledge, contexts and aspirations.[6]

University of Zimbabwe (unfortunately no longer a member of the ACU)

The University of Zimbabwe gives its mission as:

> Enabling our clients and customers to make meaningful contributions to sustainable development in Zimbabwe. To this end we provide high quality education, training and advisory services on a needs oriented basis. We guarantee the above by maintaining excellence in Teaching, Learning, Research and Service to the Community.
>
> Vision: To be (and be recognised by others as) a leading University working for prosperity, peace and dignity in Zimbabwe and beyond.[7]

Some of our members have a specifically faith-based mission and vision:

Banaras Hindu University (India)

This university says its mission is:

(i)   To promote the study of the Hindu Shastras and of Sanskrit literature generally as a means of preserving and popularizing for the benefit of the Hindus in particular and of the world at large in general, the best thought and culture of the Hindus and all that was good and great in the ancient civilization of India;

(ii) to promote learning and research generally in Arts and Sciences in all branches;

(iii) to advance and diffuse such scientific, technical and professional knowledge, combined with the necessary practical training as is best calculated to help in promoting indigenous industries and in developing the material resources of the country; and

(iv) to promote the building up of character in youth by religion and ethics as an integral part of education.[8]

Strathmore (Kenya)

Strathmore describes its work in the following terms:

> Strathmore University is a Corporate Undertaking of Opus Dei that specializes in teaching Commerce, Information Technology, Humanities, Law, Finance and Applied Sciences. It is a leading not-for profit private university in Kenya. Strathmore holds a peerless reputation for quality in both academic and professional education, and personal formation.
> Opus Dei, an institution erected by St. Pope John Paul II as the first Personal Prelature in the Catholic Church provides spiritual and

doctrinal orientation for the University. It ensures that ethical teachings on human dignity and social justice are instilled in the students by
including courses on ethics in the curricula of all Strathmore training
programs. It also provides Strathmore with a chaplain who gives spiritual counselling to anyone who may wish to receive it.

The involvement of Opus Dei in Strathmore, therefore, is strictly in
the sphere of ethics and does not take part in temporal matters. It leaves
individuals free to express opinions on these matters in a way that con-
curs with their own perception of things.[9]

It should be noted that there are very many Catholic universities around the
world, and it is impossible in this short chapter to capture the full flavour of
their mission tempered by the local cultural traditions.

Hindu University of America

The Hindu University of America describes itself as follows:

Hindu University (HU) of America is an educational institution established to serve mainly people of North America by providing a unique
dimension in learning and growth. It is a broad-based institution providing many thought provoking insights into all aspects that encom-
pass human existence. The unique insights are derived from the age
old accumulated systems of knowledge and practices from what is
popularly known as Sanatan, Vedic thought, tradition and culture. The
word "Hindu" in the name of this university signifies an all inclusive
and acceptable term by which people adhering to the traditions of rich
Bharat, i.e. India, settled anywhere in the world, associate and are called
by others. It is not the intent of the university to promote any one aspect
or any one view or any one practice over the others. HU strives to present all that is authentically available under such broad terms as Hindu,
Vedic, Sanatan, and other similar names or under specific terminology
such as Saivism, Buddhism, Jainism, and Sikhism etc. Thus the words
"Hindu" and "Hinduism" as used in the university's name and its various documents, have the broadest possible connotation.[10]

International Islamic University, Islamabad

The web page of the International Islamic University, Islamabad says:

The foundation of the Islamic University, Islamabad was laid on the
first day of the fifteenth century Hijrah i.e. Muharram 1, 1401 (November 11, 1980). This landmark of the beginning of the new Century
symbolizes the aspirations and hopes of the Muslim Ummah for an
Islamic renaissance. The university was created to produce scholars and

practitioners who are imbued with Islamic ideology, whose character and personality conforms to the teachings of Islam, and who are capable to cater to the economic, social, political, technological and intellectual needs of the Muslim Ummah. Islamic Research Institute and few other units like Iqbal International Institute for Research & Dialogue, Dawah Academy, Shariah Academy and Institute of Professional Development are situated within the premises of majestic Faisal Mosque (spread over an area of 189,705 square meters) which is a symbol of International Islamic brotherhood and unity. In conformance with the Islamic precepts, the university provides academic services to men and women through separate campuses for each segment.[11]

If nothing else, the above (random) sample of universities gives a flavour of the vast diversity of missions and values of universities across the world. Some initially based on religious principles (e.g., Bologna, Oxford etc.) have long since morphed into organisations that largely ignore their religious roots, at least in terms of their day-to-day activities (as universities, not necessarily their constituent colleges). However, others that are specifically faith-based do not impose their faith values on students. One such is the B.S. Abdur Rahman University that is an Islamic university in Chennai, India, specialising in science and technology. I had the honour of receiving an honorary degree there and graduating students in 2014. The teaching and approach was very similar to that which might be experienced in any European university. It was only when I was having dinner with the son of the founder that I understood that it was because of his faith that the founder (and his son who was Chancellor) felt that he had to give back to young people so that they could build a better society. Compare this with the Kwame Nkrumah University of Science and Technology (KNUST) in Ghana which is responsible for training 90% of science and engineering graduates in Ghana. Their vision is:

> To be globally recognised as the Premier Centre of excellence in Africa for teaching in Science and Technology for development; producing high calibre graduates with knowledge and expertise to support the industrial and socio-economic development of Ghana and Africa.
>
> In summary, the vision can be stated as "Advancing knowledge in Science and Technology for sustainable development in Africa".[12]

In 2015 I was invited to give a series of lectures on the future of universities at KNUST. Both before and after each lecture, the university chaplain led the audience in Christian prayer, and I was struck by the fact that he took up some of the themes of my lecture in his closing prayer. Another example is the University of Technology, Jamaica, where every university committee meeting starts with Christian prayer and the chair invites someone at the meeting to lead the prayer without prior warning!

Internationalisation

Students, staff and institutions are on the move. According to the Organisation for Economic Co-operation and Development (OECD), the number of students studying outside their home country in 1990 was 1.3 million, and in 2011 it was 4.3 million. The OECD predicts that by 2020 that number may be nearer 10 million. Currently, the US and the UK are the favoured destinations, with 12.6% coming to the UK in 2011. Europe in total accounted for just under 50%. However, things are about to change, with the East becoming more dominant. By 2020, China expects to admit 500,000 foreign students, Japan 300,000, Korea 200,000, Malaysia 200,000 and Taiwan 120,000. Even within mainland Europe, we find Germany with a target of 350,000. Increasingly, universities from Finland down to central Europe are offering courses taught entirely in English, realising this is the key to attracting international students and students from the UK. Major attractions are the lower fees and wider student experience. For example, the University of Maastricht in the Netherlands has 14 undergraduate programmes taught in English. The Rector Magnificus, Luce Sute, has told me they have 700 UK students studying there now.

Many universities are creating campuses in different countries. Nottingham University, where I was once Dean of Engineering, has campuses in both Malaysia and China. Many US universities have large operations in the Gulf States. Carnegie Mellon University and Texas A&M University have invested heavily in Qatar with a view to attracting students from the Indian sub-continent. In Abu Dhabi, the Masdar Institute of Technology was set up in collaboration with Massachusetts Institute of Technology (MIT) in the US, initially with a view to developing a totally new approach to innovation. Currently, their vision is stated as:

> To be recognized as a regional and global model for research intensive universities of the 21st Century, while underpinning the growth of Abu Dhabi's rapidly developing economy across key sectors. The Institute will redefine learning and discovery in a global context and set new standards in education, research and scholarship that will benefit Abu Dhabi and the world.[13]

MIT has a long history of partnering with other universities, such as Cambridge, National University of Singapore, University of Lisbon with varying success, which highlights the problem of differing cultural attitudes in different regions of the world. Nowhere is this more apparent than in the burgeoning rise of the Massive Open Online Courses (MOOCS). Many of these coming from the West are seen in African countries as having cultural overtones that have been described as a new form of 'Western Imperialism'. However, such courses are contributing to the internationalisation of higher education in an increasing way. According to Coursera (a leading provider of MOOCs internationally), one in eight courses from the US are available as MOOCs, and one out of three US students has taken at least one course online in 2012.[14]

In a major study on *Internationalising Higher Education* conducted by the European Parliament in 2015, the following recommendations are cited:

1 Address the challenges of credit and degree mobility imbalances and institutional cooperation, stemming from substantial differences in higher education systems, procedures and funding.
2 Recognise the growing popularity of work placements and build options to combine them with language and cultural skills training and study abroad.
3 Support the important role of academic and administrative staff in the further development of IoHE.[15]
4 Foster greater higher education and industry collaboration in the context of mobility of students and staff.
5 Pay more attention to the importance of 'Internationalisation at home', integrating international and intercultural learning outcomes into the curriculum for all students.
6 Remove the barriers that impede the development of joint degrees.
7 Develop innovative models of digital and blended learning as an instrument to complement IoHE.
8 Align IoHE with internationalisation at other levels of education (primary, secondary, vocational and adult education).
9 Stimulate bilingual and multilingual learning at the primary and secondary education level[s] as a basis for a language policy based on diversity.
10 Remove barriers between internationalisation of research and education, at all levels, for greater synergy and opportunity (European Parliament, 2015).

In an earlier report undertaken on behalf of the European Parliament entitled *Global Trends 2030 – Citizens in an interconnected and polycentric world*, three major trends that will have an overall impact on citizens are cited:

• The **empowerment of the individual,** which may contribute to a growing sense of belonging to a **single human community;**
• Greater stress on **sustainable development** against a backdrop of greater **resource scarcity** and persistent poverty, compounded by the consequences of climate change;
• The emergence of a more **polycentric world** characterised by a shift of power away from states, and growing **governance gaps** as the mechanisms for inter-state relations fail to respond adequately to global public demands (European Strategy and Policy Analysis System (ESPAS), 2012, p. 6).

The key question is: how can a responsible university operate in this environment when they are funded locally and are locally accountable and where there is intense inter-university competition? What should a university's values be in these circumstances, or is it wishful thinking that global responsibility should overcome stakeholder pressure? There is a clear need to raise this debate at an institutional and international level. Could it be that certain faith-based universities could form a nucleus to address this issue?

Community engagement

The Talloires Network of Universities is one initiative which brings together institutions involved in community engagement. Their website states the following:

Our Mission:

The Talloires Network is an international association of institutions committed to strengthening the civic roles and social responsibilities of higher education. We work together to implement the recommendations of the Talloires Declaration (signed in 2005) and build a global movement of engaged universities.

Our Vision:

We believe that higher education institutions do not exist in isolation from society, nor from the communities in which they are located. The Talloires Network envisions universities around the world as a vibrant and dynamic force in their societies, incorporating civic engagement and community service into their research and teaching mission.[16]

Many of the growing number of members of the Talloires Network incorporate social engagement into both their teaching programmes and in staff development.

A useful compendium of principles and examples of community engagement of higher education institutions can be found in *Higher Education and the World – Knowledge, Engagement and Higher Education Contributing to Social Change* (Global University Network for Innovation, 2014).

The tension between idealism, values and stakeholder pressure

Ford (2007) has suggested a list of six core challenges faced by universities, including how they contribute to society, which he interprets more widely than just community engagement. He suggests it includes the supply of trained (well-formed) people to society and knowledge transfer (which can be interpreted in a number of ways). He goes on to suggest a seventh challenge, that of institutional self-analysis which coincides with the medieval ideas of self-criticism but takes the issue much further to discuss the very *raison d'etre* of the university. Ford goes on to ask whether this is too much to hope for given most academics are familiar with the status quo and are able to survive pragmatically in the current environment.

Is a single idea of what a university is, or should be, wishful thinking in the current era? Is the frontispiece to Barnett (2011) right in saying:

> There is no single idea of the university. Ever since its medieval origin, the concept of the university has continued to change. The metaphysical university gave way successively to the scientific university, and then to the corporate and the entrepreneurial university. But what might lie ahead?

Or are universities buffeted about so much from external forces that they cannot contribute meaningfully to the issues facing their future or their contributions to society? Professor Stephen Toope (ex-President of the University of British Columbia, Canada) has written in *Taking action for Canada – Jobs and Skills for the 21st Century* (2012):

> "I love you, please change" – those two little phrases nobody wants to hear together. In personal relationships, they usually signal that all is not well. The person delivering the message is dissatisfied; the person hearing it feels trapped or inadequate. Universities around the world, including in Canada, are hearing those phrases a lot these days.[17]

Globalisation and polycentrism (a new renaissance)

In the first European Research Area Report *Preparing Europe for a New Renaissance*, Commissioner Janez Potocnik wrote:

> The words "excellence", "openness" and "mobility" are recurrent themes and these virtues need to be firmly held when political expedience and local issues are at stake. We cannot bury our heads in the sand and both researchers and society at large need to be fully engaged with and realise the consequences of the wider challenges facing us. This holistic thinking and approach epitomised the first Renaissance, where scholars and artists moved relatively freely around Europe among centres of learning and culture. While this privilege was the domain of a few at that time, it should be our ambition, in the new Renaissance, that this should be the expectation of all citizens especially in the field of research and innovation.
>
> (European Commission, 2009)

Of course, treating a university as an isolated organisation is to miss entirely the reality in that institutions, individual academics and, increasingly, students, see themselves as part of a global environment and are increasingly mobile both physically and virtually. This is in line with the ESPAS observations above: 'The **empowerment of the individual**, which may contribute to a growing sense of belonging to a **single human community**', and the rise in polycentrism (defined as allegiance to more than one centre of power and influence, leading to a breakdown of governance within an organisation) leading to the loss of control by organisations such as universities on content and activity. (There are many countries where excessive political control is exercised on university governance, leading to universities being shut down and senior academics imprisoned). Examples exist where split-degree programmes occur between universities with widely differing cultures, and where academics feel more loyalty to a global research project than to their own institution or government. Academic freedom is constantly the cry of an academic, but in reality it is neither the case that the academic has much freedom nor that the host institution has much control on individual academics. In the UK the Haldane principle (decisions about what to spend research funds on should be made by researchers rather than politicians) is sometimes pushed to the limit by government. However, despite these attempts to muzzle universities and academics by various countries, globalisation is now a reality, and the implications are causing major disruptions in what a university is all about.

As examples of the impact of polycentrism and the growing governance gap emerging, I cite two recent developments which have brought this concept of polycentrism much more to the fore. One is based on recent developments of the internet, and the other on the rise in what are termed in the UK 'academic analogues', which are independent institutes or national or global research infrastructures. Probably the best-known example of the latter is CERN in Geneva, which is just over 60 years old. Thousands of students and academics are connected with the various experiments there. The independent CERN Council with its Science Board determines the priorities for the work undertaken and the rules of engagement. Within the various experiments, data and information are shared. Many university staff are almost permanently based at such facilities and pay little regard to their home university. With the rise of the internet, these infrastructures are not just large physical facilities, and more and more academics are taking part in global projects, sharing data across the world and breaking down cultural and religious traditions, including in the arts and social sciences. In 2001, the European Strategy Forum for Research Infrastructures was formed to try and co-ordinate activity across Europe and beyond, including working on common legal and governance structures that transcended individual institutions and countries. While physical institutions such as CERN in Geneva, the Institut Laue Langevin (nuclear research reactor) and the European Synchrotron Radiation Facility (both in Grenoble) have involved scientists from several countries, including those outside the European Union, the door is now open for academic researchers (including students) from all disciplines to take part in research. The result is that many academics now feel their allegiance is to the Research Infrastructure and its values and mission more than their own university. In some countries, this is resisted by universities since they feel loss of ownership of the academic and some university funding models discourage collaboration.

It is worth selecting an example in the area of arts and humanities to demonstrate the impact that this global freedom is having on arts and humanities. There is a research infrastructure project called CLARIN. CLA-RIN is concerned with the meaning of words in different languages, taking into account the context of where they are said or written and being aware of the cultural backgrounds of the readers or hearers. It looks to create a common language repository. It is being implemented and constantly improved at leading institutions in a large and growing number of European countries, aiming at improving Europe's multi-linguality competence. CLA-RIN provides several services, such as access to language data and tools to analyse data, and offers to deposit research data, as well as enabling direct access to knowledge about relevant topics in relation to (research on and with) language resources. It is now linked with many other similar projects; there is a group at the University of the North West in South Africa actively involved with CLARIN with a focus on indigenous languages, for example. The initial director of CLARIN was at the University of Utrecht and the co-ordinator was at the Max Plank Institute for Physco-linguistics in Nijmegen. The legal structure is a so-called ERIC (European Research Infrastructure Consortium) which deals with employment conditions, taxation etc. independently from contributor institutions. There is a board of directors who report to a General Assembly.

Perhaps the most exciting project with the most ability to create a global approach between academics and industry which is far outside of the control of any one university is the Square Kilometre Array consisting of radio telescope dishes and antennae spread across Southern Africa and Australia. With over 40 countries and over 100 universities involved as either core partners or affiliates, this project has both scientific and developmental goals. It will push data sharing to the limits. The claim is that the information generated will be ten times the current internet traffic, and that the data from one day would take 2 million years to download on an Ipad.

In a report from the European Commission entitled *Riding the Wave – How Europe can gain from the rising tide of scientific data*, it is stated that data sharing of this magnitude creates 'global collaboratories' (2010, pp. 17–18) helping to solve global challenges facing society.

Driven by the ability to share information freely across the world, in many advanced countries it has been mandated that all publicly funded data must be publicly available. This places huge obligations on universities to create and protect the data from corruption in addition to making sure it is accessible. Yet it removes ultimate control on how the data is used from the individual universities. The nature of what is truth in this environment will reflect on the values of the university and who funds it. In fact, the raw data is seldom useful, and it is the metadata that is important. For example, if the university is holding data that could be interpreted by others in other cultures to discredit the policies of the home government, there could be a move to suppress those data. So we are moving from open access of publications to open access for all of the fundamental results of research. There are huge ethical and policy issues that still need to be resolved, especially at the local level of the university. Interestingly, UNESCO has just started to create a set of policy guidelines to help governments and universities come to terms with the issues involved. This is work in progress and not published as yet.

The following, from the European Commission's report *Riding the Wave*, is an example of how this might work in the future for a research student and an academic (European Commission, 2010, p. 14):

> Roger is working on an international PhD. It's a relatively new programme, in which a student applies to become a member of an international team working on a big problem that affects all people. His group is comparing many forms of nonverbal communications between cultures. It has several hundred members and his university tutor is one of the nodal points contributing expertise in "synergistic communication between biological components". Others in the network are using archaeological evidence to study communications between ancient Mesopotamian and Hellenic cultures; some are studying computer-computer interactions between different systems; yet more are studying communications in refugee camps. Each node contributes to the whole. Results are communicated as they happen, and there are daily, virtual-presence planning sessions. Roger had to sign a contract not to misuse data or contribute anything that is not for the common good – such as externally sourced information that he has not thoroughly checked for provenance.

In *Riding the Wave*, this was seen as a possible scenario for research in 2030. However, elements of this approach are already with us, and the impact on universities is yet to be realised.

This so-called 'Open Science' is now probably the most urgent topic that could help create a work space for value-led universities to operate in. Commissioner Carlos Moedas, the European Commissioner for Research, Technology and Development refers to the three 'O's' in his speeches: 'Open Science, Open Innovation, Open to the World'.[18] Underpinning this initiative is the global Research Data Alliance consisting after three years of almost 4,000 researchers from over 110 countries realising that sharing is better than hoarding.[19] With its strap line of 'research data, sharing without borders', this has been a phenomenal researcher-led project with groups looking at the details of how to share data across disciplines and cultures to groups applying data sharing to global challenges such as food security and the quality of urban life. Just what role do universities have in this environment? What is the value of place both for teaching and research?

The principle that all publicly supported research data must be openly available has been upheld by the G8 Open Data Charter signed by ministers in 2013 with five key principles:

- Open Data by Default
- Quality and Quantity
- Useable by All
- Releasing Data for Improved Governance
- Releasing Data for Innovation.[20]

To what extent the individual countries have implemented these principles in reality is debateable, but now most public funders in major countries have adopted them, including in Europe and the US. Academics in this environment see that universities with rigid concepts of location and culture are no longer relevant. While the above principles are policy driven, the majority of people working with data have adopted the FAIR principles (Findable, Accessible, Inter-operable and Re-usable).

In some senses, this is a revolutionary movement of (mainly) academics and, increasingly, of institutions deciding to take matters into their own hands. Ultimately, it is based on universal trust. Just how can that trust be earnt? Are there common notions of global trust? Is there a need for a globally agreed set of common values for which universities are accountable? Can an institution give a guarantee that information from that university is trustworthy? What governance models must be in place to ensure academics in this global movement are trustworthy? The implications for universities are huge but largely ignored at present. Universities now need to act as guardians of truth based on their values, and only universities that can enforce their ethical and value base are likely to benefit.

Is this just a storm in a teacup without relevance to the grand challenges facing the world today? Far from it. One working group in the Research Data Alliance is looking to share data on wheat to increase the security of wheat supplies, especially in those regions of the world where crop yields are subject to droughts and climate change:

> The Wheat Data Interoperability Working Group aims to provide a common framework for describing, representing linking and publishing Wheat data with respect to open standards. Such a framework will promote and sustain Wheat data sharing, reusability and operability. Specifying the Wheat linked data framework will come with many questions: which (minimal) metadata to describe which type of data? Which

vocabularies/ontologies/formats? Which good practices? Mainly based on the needs of the Wheat initiative Information System (WheatIS) in terms of functionalities and data types, the working group will identify relevant use cases in order to produce a "cookbook" on how to produce "wheat data" that are easily shareable, reusable and interoperable.[21]

Here is an example of a recent blog post from that group:

Wheat Data Interoperability WG

- Hello, We are pleased to announce the public availability of the INRA Small Grain Cereals Network Phenotypic Trials dataset. This includes observations (agronomic, quality, disease, phenology, . . .) on 11 locations and 15 years for more than 1700 bread wheat germplasms/genotypes. It is available for consultation and download at the following URL: https://urgi.versailles.inra.fr/ephesis/ephesis/viewer.do#dataResults/ tr . . . etIds=5,6,7 Thanks to François-Xavier Oury, Arnaud Gauffreteau and Gilles Charmet. Feel free to forward this email. Best regards The URGI Information System Team INRA.[22]

In many ways, such initiatives are breaking down the concept of a university. Jamil Salmi (2015) has written about the implications of Open Science for how universities will operate both educationally and in terms of research when information is freely available to students, researchers and citizens. He cites data showing the change in the percentage of international co-publications between 2003 and 2013. It indicates more and more academics are choosing to publish with colleagues in different countries. Global research is now transcending individual universities and without regard to the mission and values of the home institutions.

Country	2003	2013
Canada	42%	52%
Finland	46%	61%
Canada	8%	24%
France	44%	57%
Germany	43%	54%
Italy	37%	47%
Japan	21%	29%
Netherlands	48%	60%
South Korea	26%	29%
Sweden	58%	70%
United Kingdom	40%	57%
United States	26%	37%

Source: Mund et al. (2014)

One of the largest growth areas is that of Citizen Cyber-Science, which involves setting problems, sharing and analysing digital data or inviting citizens to make measurements and then contribute their results back to the project. Probably the best known is 'galaxy zoo' whereby the data from the Hubble space telescope is shared online. It is said that about 50% of the galaxies have been identified by non-professional astronomers. A case study quoted by Salmi (2015, pp. 42–43) is given below of how this concept works:

Amateurs solving complex science problems: The foldit experiment

Foldit is a science game designed to tackle the problem of protein folding with the help of ordinary people who enjoy videogames acting as scientists. It was developed by the Center for Game Science at the University of Washington (http://centerforgamescience.org), which creates game-based environments in order to solve important problems that humanity faces today.

Over 100,000 amateur players from all over the world, each with different backgrounds, are engaged in the Foldit game. As the official site of the game states, the best Foldit players have little to no prior exposure to biochemistry.

Playing the game implies folding proteins starting from a set of provided tools and models of proteins. Users receive scores for how good they do the fold and these scores can be seen on a leaderboard, therefore stimulating competition among players.

The game was developed with the premise that humans' pattern-recognition and puzzle-solving abilities are more efficient than the existing computer programs dealing with this kind of tasks. The data gathered can be used to train and improve computers in order to generate more accurate and faster results than they are capable of achieving at present.

So far, Foldit has produced predictions that outperform the best known computational methods. These results have been published in a Nature paper with more than 57,000 authors, most of them being non-experts in biochemistry related fields. This is a great example of how this type of gaming environment can create skilled researchers out of novices (http://fold.it/portal/; Sauermann and Franzoni (2015).

Quoted by Salmi, 2015, pp. 42–43)

We are now faced with the faith or ethical base of individuals who may not be connected with any particular academic institution. For further examples of the phenomenal rise of 'Citizen Cyber-Science', see www.zooniverse.com.[23] Just how will universities cope with this, and to what extent should they try to control it? It certainly is taxing university promotion procedures where many papers have tens or hundreds of authors. Yet Open Science and Citizen Science are now seen as just two aspects of the rapidly evolving 'Open Ecosystem' which has largely developed during the last five years.

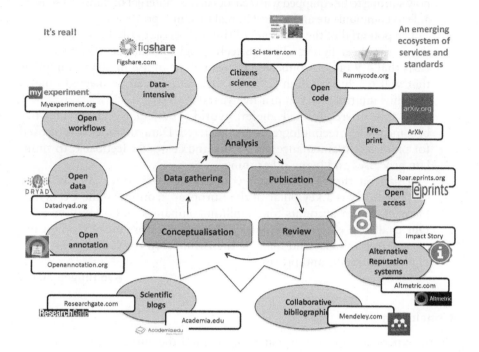

The above diagram produced by Jean-Claude Burgelman (2015) at the European Commission, and used with permission, shows the interactions and apps that facilitate the various components. It may look complex, but it does demonstrate the new environment in which leading universities and academics are playing.

Yet, this is only the beginning. The Commissioner for the Digital Economy, Gunter Oettinger, has gone further in recent speeches:

> We are in the middle of a true revolution – the fourth industrial revolution. It will change our industries, it will change our economy. And it will have a profound impact on our lives.
>
> At the third industrial revolution, sometimes referred to as "the digital revolution", information held on paper turned digital. Data was no longer handled on cardboard files stored in large filing cabinets. IT systems were created for customer relation management, for warehouse management, for accounting. Assembly lines were automated.
>
> But all of this happened separately. Different vendors of software or hardware supplied different solutions, not always compatible. This resulted in a situation where many different IT systems, still in use today, do not talk to one another.
>
> We are now in the midst of the next digital revolution which is precisely based on interconnection and communication: Any object, any machine, are

now starting to be equipped with sensors in this "internet of things" – sensors able to communicate and to feed in real time into processes.

The potential of the "internet of things" becomes obvious when looking at the sheer figures: The US technology consultancy Gartner forecasts that 4.9 billion connected things will be in use in 2015, a number that will reach 25 billion by 2020. The number of connected objects will thus multiply by 5 in just five years!

In this interconnected digital world, particularly data analytics become the key technologies to be mastered. Data analytics can be used for predictive maintenance, to understand customer feedback, to simulate processes and many other things.

This is at the heart of the revolution of what some call "industry 4.0". Industry is a key pillar of the European economy – the EU manufacturing sector accounts for 2 million companies and 33 million jobs. Our challenge is to ensure that all industrial sectors make the best use of new technologies and manage their transition towards higher value digitised products and processes

(Oettiinger, 2015)

Conclusion

In my experience, most universities are behind the curve in the issues that are evolving fast and which challenge their values and ability to respond to societal needs. Some of their academics are in the vanguard and pressing urgently. There is an urgent need to ask the difficult questions about what values (if any) universities should base their teaching and research on in this environment. Do they have a duty to become more of the public conscience when their funders are largely focused on economic return to both the individual and the region? Just what is their role in the so-called public space? In addition to the moral and ethical perspectives, the ability to share information with anyone and with everyone will catch many unprepared for the implications that the new technology will deliver. Even today, mobile telephony links students to global information which many of the academics trying to educate them, especially where they have huge teaching loads and cannot keep up with their subject, are unaware of, leading to their personal credibility as academics potentially being found wanting.

There is an urgent need for the debate about these and many other issues among universities and their stakeholders to take place. The future is not what it used to be, and it is changing at an accelerating rate. Just what is the role of faith-based universities in developing the future, and how can they respond? We should not forget what Colin Lucas (ex Vice-Chancellor of Oxford) says in his reflections on universities in the twenty-first century:

Generation by generation universities serve to make students think . . . They learn to seek the true meaning of things: to distinguish between the true and the merely seemingly true . . . Universities alone are the bulwark against systems of pseudo-knowledge based on unverified sources and fantasies of meaning.

(Lucas, 2013, p. 372)

Acknowledgements

I am indebted to the invaluable help I have received in preparing this chapter from Dr. Alison Wood (no relation), Mellon/Newton Interdisciplinary Research Fellow at CRASSH, Cambridge University, and Nick Mulhern, the ACU librarian.

Notes

1 www.acu.ac.uk (accessed 2nd February 2016).
2 Private communication.
3 https://sustainabledevelopment.un.org/?menu=1300 (accessed 20th January 2016).
4 https://www.mona.uwi.edu/content/mission-statement (accessed 1st February 2016).
5 http://www.sgbau.ac.in/aboutus.asp (accessed 1st February 2016).
6 www.usp.ac.fj (accessed 1st February 2016).
7 http://www.uz.ac.zw (accessed 1st February 2016).
8 http://www.bhu.ac.in/aboutus/vision.php (accessed 1st February 2016).
9 http://www.strathmore.edu/en/about-strathmore/opus-dei (accessed 1st February 2016).
10 http://www.hua.edu (accessed 1st February 2016).
11 http://www.iiu.edu.pk/ (accessed 1st February 2016).
12 https://www.knust.edu.gh/about/knust/mandate (accessed 1st February 2016).
13 https://www.masdar.ac.ae/about-us/vision-mission (accessed 1st February 2016).
14 https://www.coursera.org (accessed 1st February 2016).
15 IoHE i.e. Institutes of Higher Education.
16 http://talloiresnetwork.tufts.edu/who-we-ar/ (accessed 1st February 2016).
17 https://www.capilanou.ca/WorkArea/DownloadAsset.aspx?id=42788 (accessed 13th November 2015).
18 Speech delivered 15th June 2015.
19 www.rd-alliance.org (accessed 4th March 2016).
20 As set out by the UK government in the following policy paper, published on 18th June 2013: https://www.gov.uk/government/publications/open-data-charter/g8-open-data-charter-and-technical-annex (accessed 2nd February 2016).
21 https://rd-alliance.org/groups/wheat-data-interoperability-wg.html (accessed 1st February 2016).
22 rd-alliance.org/groups/wheat-data-interoperability-wg.html (accessed 15th January 2016).
23 www.zooniverse.com (accessed 14th October 2015).

References

Barnett, R., 2011. *Being a University*. Abingdon: Routledge.
BIS (Department for Business, Innovation and Skills), 2013. *Research Paper 146 The Benefits of Higher Education Participation for Individuals and Society*. [online].

Available at: https://www.gov.uk/government/uploads/system/uploads/attachment_data/file/254101/bis-13–1268-benefits-of-higher-education-participation-the-quadrants.pdf. [accessed February 2nd 2016].

BIS (Department for Business, Innovation and Skills), 2015. *The Allocation of Science and Research Funding 2016/17 to 2019/20.* [online] Available at: https://www.gov.uk/government/uploads/system/uploads/attachment_data/file/332767/bis-14–750-science-research-funding-allocations-2015–2016-corrected.pdf. [accessed February 2nd 2016].

Burgelman, J.-C., 2015. Private Communication Presented at the European Competitiveness Council June 2015.

European Commission, 2009. *Preparing Europe for a New Renaissance EU23905.* Brussels: European Commission.

European Commission, 2010. *Riding the Wave – How Europe can Gain from the Rising Tide of Scientific Data.* Brussels: European Commission.

European Parliament, 2015. *Internationalising Higher Education PE.540.370.* [online] Available at: http://www.europarl.europa.eu/RegData/etudes/STUD/2015/540370/IPOL_STU(2015)540370_EN.pdf. [accessed February 1st 2016].

European Strategy and Policy Analysis System, 2012. *Citizens in an Interconnected and Polycentric World 2030.* Paris: Institute for Security Studies.

Ford, D., 2007. *Christian Wisdom: Desiring God and Learning in Love.* Cambridge: Cambridge University Press.

Garrett, G., and Davies, G., 2010. *Herding Cats.* Axminster: Triarchy Press.

Global University Network for Innovation, 2014. *Higher Education in the World 5.* London: Palgrave Macmillan.

Lucas, C., 2013. Looking Forward: Reflections for Universities in the Twenty First Century in Schreuder, D., ed. *Universities for a New World.* p. 372. New Delhi: Sage.

Mund, C., Conchi, S., and Frietsch, R., 2014. *Indikatorbericht Bibliometrische Indikatoren für den PFI Monitoring Bericht 2015.* Berlin, Bundesministerium für Bildung und Forschung.

Oettinger, G., 2015. *Speech at the European Data Forum November 17th 2015.* https://ec.europa.eu/commission/2014-2019/oettinger/announcements/speech-european-data-forum_en (accessed 5th July 2016)

Salmi, J., 2015. *Study on Open Science Impact, Implications and Policy Options.* Brussels: European Commission.

Toope, S., 2012. *Taking Action for Canada in the 21st Century.* [online] Available at: https://www.capilanou.ca/WorkArea/DownloadAsset.aspx?id=42788. [accessed November 13th 2015].

10 The universities we need

Stephen Heap

Introduction

What does the world need from its universities? This book began with Susan Durber outlining some of the issues the world faces. Subsequent chapters developed various points she made and suggested ways in which universities might help in facing the issues identified. This chapter draws together and builds on earlier chapters to argue society faces challenges universities can and should engage with as part of being a university. It further argues that, as universities engage, they should seek the good of society and individuals. Sadly, present changes in the higher education policy regime in England and elsewhere, discussed by Peter Scott and others, risk hindering rather than supporting universities in such work.

Questions about universities are important. Universities educate increasing numbers who, as students and graduates, will impact on society. They are likely to influence those students both academically and through the values and ethos for living they pass on. Universities make their mark not just on and through their students and graduates, however. They do so also through their research and as a voice in the public arena which will help mould the visions and policies by which individuals and societies live. Universities are, therefore, of significance. They help shape individuals and societies.

No doubt their importance can be overstated. There are many other forces influencing students, for example. Similarly, universities are but one locus of education, research and conversation about issues large and small. Let such things be recognised, but also let not the role of universities or their actual or potential influence be underestimated. In the United Kingdom alone, as Scott says, there are some 2.4 million students, amongst them nearly 50 per cent of young adults. What does the nature, curriculum and pedagogy of the universities within which they study pass on to those students about work, life, how to live well in the world and how to face the big issues of the day? What do universities communicate about purpose, meaning, values and the responsibilities students might have in the world in which they will live as graduates? What visions for living as individuals and as societies are universities embodying, either by dint of conviction or, perhaps, pragmatically in order to survive in the present policy and societal context? What of such visions are they speaking to their students and wider society?

Anyone concerned about the future shape of human living in and with this world may want to give thought to what universities are, and should be, passing on in such areas. This book is offered as a contribution to such thinking. Various of its chapters are written from theological perspectives. That does not mean they are written only for theologians, or for people who hold religious faith at all: they are for any with an interest in the good of society. They do, however, speak out of traditions important in today's world. As Durber and David Ford note, religion is a significant, even resurgent, force in the contemporary world. Further, as Ford writes, religions do have views on things happening in society, including in the university sector. The latter is part of an historic and continuing interplay between religious faith and universities. Such interplay is not surprising, for religions are concerned with what is, with the pursuit of truth and with what it means to live well in society, which things lead naturally to an involvement in education.

One famous product of that involvement is Cardinal Newman's classic *The Idea of A University* ([1852] 1982), which arises from Newman's essentially theological reflections on his experience of Anglican Oxford, his attempt to create a Catholic University in Ireland and changing ideas of what it meant to be a university at the time.

Religious faith and perspectives have led many others apart from Newman to engage with questions about what it is to be a university and to work to create universities or institutions which have become universities. In Britain that includes not only universities in the Cathedrals Group of Church Foundation Universities but, to name just a few, Bristol, Durham, Northumbria, Manchester, King's College London and University College London (UCL).[1] All had Christian involvement in their founding or the founding of the institutions from which they grew. UCL is an interesting case in which Jews, Christians and free thinkers associated with Jeremy Bentham worked together to create the new College.[2]

As in Britain, so elsewhere people of religious faith have been involved in creating universities. Significant in the overall story of universities is the Humboldt University in Berlin, opened in 1810. Much thought about what it means to be a university surrounded its founding, and it became a model for other universities. It was noted for a secular, reason-based approach to learning, yet the Christian theologian Friedrich Schleiermacher is recognised as one of the 'most influential figures' in its founding and became not the first but a subsequent Rector (Howard, 2006, p. 133). There was Christian involvement in founding many of the universities of the United States also. Yale, for example, begins its own account of its history with the words:

> The university traces its roots to the 1640s when colonial clergymen led an effort to establish a local college to preserve the tradition of

European liberal education in the New World. In 1701 the charter was granted for a school "wherein Youth may be instructed in the Arts and Sciences (and) through the blessing of Almighty God may be fitted for Publick employment both in Church and Civil State".[3]

Whilst in Britain, Europe and the United States, Christianity is the main faith engaged with questions of what it is to be a university, Jews have also been involved, as already noted, and some of the world's oldest universities originate within Islam. They include al-Qarawiyyin in Morocco, which both UNESCO and Guinness World Records describe as the oldest university in the world, founded in 859 CE. Another university which can trace its roots back long and deep in an Islamic context is Al-Azhar in Cairo, founded around 970 CE. Alison Scott-Baumann and Sariya Cheruvallil-Contractor remind us of the significant involvement of Islam in what today might be called higher education. John Wood also writes about Islamic and Christian foundations, as well as secular ones, and his reference to two Hindu universities is a reminder of the work of Hindus in establishing universities.

What all this shows is that religious groups have long been interested and involved in universities. Within contemporary Britain that continues, including as theologians and faith groups comment on university matters, as faith groups and universities work together in providing chaplaincy, and as some universities and associated institutions continue to live out a religious foundation as at least part of their identity. Usually in Britain their religious base is Christian, and some such are part of the already mentioned Cathedrals Group of Church Foundation Universities. There are also Islamic institutions (for example, Markfield Institute of Higher Education and Cambridge Muslim College).

In offering theological perspectives this book is not doing something new, therefore, but continuing a long-standing engagement.

Universities seeking the good: setting the scene

The book began with Durber's comments on key developments in the world. It is, perhaps as always, a world of opportunity and challenge. Durber indicates some of both. Scientific advance is meaning longer life and a better quality of life for millions; the worldwide web extends horizons, again for millions; numbers living in absolute poverty have fallen. There is much to rejoice in. The world also faces challenges, including how to live well on a fragile and threatened planet; how to live peacefully with difference; what to do about the huge gaps between rich and poor, powerful and powerless; how to respond to the vast numbers fleeing conflict; the significant disengagement especially of the young from traditional political processes; the changing loci of power; and the difficulties of calling power to account in a globalised world.

Such matters are of great significance for the future of humankind and are likely to remain so for the foreseeable future. They raise different sorts of questions. Some are about what works: what practical steps will effectively address climate change, for example? Other questions are about what *should* be done, about what is good, or right or best and how to decide those things in diverse societies. They are to do with how to create a good society, or a good economic order or how to make a good response to refugees, for example, and what is meant by 'good', a contested concept, as will be discussed later.

It is a central theme of this book that universities can make a contribution, alongside others, to addressing such issues. One way they can do so is through research, an important part of which is seeking solutions to specific problems. Part of research, however, is asking more fundamental questions, standing back and asking not just questions dictated by immediate ends, but rather, as Rowan Williams suggests, universities need 'to pose their own questions' about what is happening, and why, and what might be possible ways forward. They can, and should, look at the bigger picture.

Universities have other ways of contributing to society apart from research. Their work in helping to prepare people for democratic and global citizenship is discussed in this book. So is the stimulating, both in the university and wider society, of what Williams calls 'civil discourse' about the issues society faces. That includes discourse with 'the other'; vitally important in a diverse society. Such discourse must involve debate about difficult issues and universities can provide places for that, as Scott-Baumann and Cheruvallil-Contractor argue. Universities contribute to society also as they nurture people in the virtues, which Mike Higton writes about; the virtues needed for academic life and for living well in the world. In such and other ways, universities can help society address the issues it faces.

Part of what society has to face is questions about what are good or better, or best, ways forward; questions about ethics, values and purpose. They are difficult questions, as Higton indicates in his *A Theology of Higher Education* (2012). He argues that in contemporary society both what constitutes the good and how it might be decided what is good are contested. Discussion of what is good, he says, is 'perhaps the most notoriously broken form of discourse in our societies', often seen as 'lying in the realm of irrational private preference, rather than public discussion' (Higton, 2012, p. 226). Yet there does need to be 'public discussion', for there is an ongoing task of shaping society, as part of which questions about what is good need facing. We need 'serious, open, inclusive and critical *argument* about the good', says Higton (2012, p. 227 emphasis original). One of the places in which that can happen is universities. Universities can and should be catalysts for the debate, or argument, bringing to it their own commitments to questioning and exploration, plus the wisdom of their philosophers, theologians, ethicists and all from many disciplines who can work on questions of the good.

Within this chapter, the force of Higton's points are recognised. Debating what is good is difficult and contested, particularly so in the globalised context Wood points to in his chapter. That does not mean that views about what is, or might be, good should be withheld. Some such appear in this book. They are offered as a contribution to the debate Higton indicates is needed and which universities can support.

Before proceeding with the argument, a couple of caveats are in order. Firstly, to make clear that in arguing universities should be about debating the good, seeking and serving the good, preparing people for citizenship and nurturing in the virtues, it is not being suggested universities should be trying to create like-minded clones. Having space and freedom to disagree and put contrary cases is grounded in the very convictions and commitments which have long shaped universities. 'By its very existence', says Williams, 'the good university expresses certain philosophical commitments – to civil discourse, to liberty of expression, to careful and honest self-questioning, and to the possibility of creating trust through the processes of fair argument and exploration of evidence. This cannot be reduced to the narrow atmosphere of pressure-groups'. If it is being true to itself, the university will challenge totalitarian attitudes, not support them.

Secondly, whilst the claim is made that universities have often at least sought to serve wider society, it is not being claimed they have always done so, or, even less, always done so well. Universities are fallible. What is being said, strongly, is that society has certain needs, and universities do have the resources and responsibilities to contribute to identifying and facing those needs, including in such a way as to seek what might be called 'good'. Engaging in such a way with wider society is very much part of the tradition of being a university.

There is in such themes a rather bigger understanding of the work of universities than is sometimes in play today, including in higher education policy both in England and, as Wood shows, further afield. That point is simply flagged up at this point; it will be returned to. First, we take a longer view and consider how the idea of universities seeking the good of society keeps re-emerging.

Universities seeking the good: an enduring tradition

Nothing novel is being suggested in arguing that universities are to engage with the needs of society, be about the good of society and fulfil the particular roles suggested in this book. Having said which, it must be admitted that what it means to be a university is contested. That is unsurprising, given the nature of academic life. There are different ideas about what universities are for. One, found most famously in Newman, is that education is an end in itself, not for any external gain. However, one theme which keeps re-emerging in thinking and writing about universities is that there is an intimate relationship between being a university and pursuing the good of individuals and society. Even Newman, despite his particular commitment, did think, as Suzy Harris puts it, that 'a good liberal education would inevitably be of practical importance because it would result in cultivating the public mind'.

In drawing attention to universities working for what is, or might be, good, it is not being suggested other views on what universities are for should be ignored. There is in current policy a strong emphasis on universities serving the economy. Whilst such an emphasis on that area might properly be criticised, as it is in this book, it is clearly the case that the economy matters, and the university has a role in skills development for example, which itself can be a contribution to the good. The pursuit of truth, engaged in for its own sake, is so close to the heart of learning that it would be wrong to suggest it is not a fundamental part of being a university. If successful, it will also, happily, contribute to the pursuit of the good, for that pursuit will be aided by a clear knowledge of what is. Living in a good way with the world becomes more possible as the world is understood, or, as Higton puts it in his chapter, 'To live well requires well-ordered understanding'.

Examples of the interconnectivity between being a university and pursuing the good can be found in many places. The Humboldt University in Berlin, already referred to, was named after Wilhelm von Humboldt, the Secretary for Religion and Public Instruction during much of the time the university was being created. Higton (2012, p. 50) quotes von Humboldt as saying the new university was to be devoted to the 'moral culture' of the nation, its 'spiritual and moral formation'; the new University was to be about things thought good.

Similar themes about universities serving the good appear in United Kingdom higher education policy documents of not long ago. They suggest universities should be concerned about the good of individuals and societies, and that they should be so not as a bolt-on to other activities, such as serving the economy, but as part of being a university. That can be seen in the seminal policy documents to which Scott refers.

The 1963 Robbins report spells out four aims of higher education, tellingly described as 'general *social* ends' (Robbins, 1963, p. 6, emphasis added). They are: providing skills for work; promoting 'the general powers of the mind'; the 'advancement of learning'; and 'the transmission of a common culture and common standards of citizenship', which entails providing people with 'that background of culture and social habit upon which a healthy society depends' (Robbins, 1963, pp. 6–7). Robbins portrays universities as about skills for work and sustaining a 'healthy' society and citizenship.

The 1997 Dearing Report, *Higher Education in the Learning Society*, also discussed by Scott, again gives attention to what universities are for. The report sets out the following aims for universities:

- to inspire and enable individuals to develop their capabilities to the highest potential levels throughout life, so that they can grow intellectually, are well equipped for work, can contribute effectively to society and achieve personal fulfilment;

- to increase knowledge and understanding for their own sake and to foster their application to the benefit of the economy and society;
- to serve the needs of an adaptable, sustainable, knowledge-based economy at local, regional and national levels;
- to play a major role in shaping a democratic, civilised, inclusive society.

(Dearing, 1997, p. 13)

Therein are very clear statements of the idea that universities are for the creation of certain sorts of societies, presumably perceived as good.

All the above indicate that the ideas expressed in this volume, about universities serving the good of society by helping to create citizens (Williams), addressing questions of how to be a diverse and democratic society (Harris), nurturing virtues and the common good (Higton), being places for discussion of issues society finds difficult (Scott-Baumann and Cheruvallil-Contractor), are well within the parameters of common and enduring discourses about what it is to be a university. Such statements also indicate that something at least of the vision of what it is to be a university expressed by Elizabeth Stuart and Michael Holman when they write about citizenship and equipping people for service, for example, is mainstream to ideas of what it is to be a university.

Such discourses continue today amongst others who comment on the role of universities. Jon Nixon has written a trilogy of books, the latter two of which in particular deal with universities contributing to the good of society (2008; 2011; 2013). Higher education 'exists to ask what constitutes the public good' Nixon says (2011, p. 1). 'The purpose of higher education is to contribute to the common good and institutions of higher education should be organised in such a way as to further those public ends and purposes' (Nixon, 2013, p. viii). He regards such work as pressing in the wake of the financial crisis of 2007, 'which as it intensified was variously interpreted not only as an economic crisis but also as a moral and social crisis' which 'seriously threatened the social cohesion of supposedly advanced states' (Nixon, 2011, p. ix). He is arguing, therefore, both that the purpose of higher education *per se* is to contribute to the common good and that there are urgent contemporary reasons why the university must do such work now. He suggests two roles for the university in connection with the 'public good', rather redolent of themes in this book: 'first, it provides a dedicated space within which to debate what constitutes the public good; second, it supports the development of an educated public with the capabilities and dispositions necessary to contribute to that debate' (Nixon, 2011, p. x). They lead Nixon to suggest higher education is itself a public good (2011, p. x). In the third volume, he suggests there are big political and ideological questions about the role of the state and the individual behind some of the more specific questions society faces (Nixon, 2013, e.g. p. 6). They are questions universities can, and should, be concerned with.

Like Nixon, Stefan Collini (2012) is keen to affirm 'that higher education is a public good' (p. x). Collini is known for his assaults on current higher education policy, including the limited view of the role of universities in it. He quotes with approval Thorstein Veblen's comment that the university is 'a corporation for the cultivation and care of the community's highest aspirations and ideals' (Collini, 2012, p. 86). Universities are to seek the good of society.

Ronald Barnett has written extensively on what it is to be a university, including a recent trilogy in which he explores some possibilities for the future of the university (2011; 2013; 2016). In doing that, he touches on a number of roles and ways of being for universities. Within his work, Barnett indicates the potential, or even necessity, of universities engaging in issues to do with the good of society. He writes that the 'task of understanding the university is inherently an *ethical* project, for any such task, if it is to be taken seriously, has to incorporate an attempt to discern the possibilities that enable the university more fully to play its part in improving the world' (Barnett, 2016, p. 9, original emphasis).

Barnett seeks not only to understand the university but to imagine some futures for it, what he calls 'feasible utopias' (Barnett, 2011, p. 4). One such, whose 'time has come' (Barnett, 2011, p. 141), he says, is what he calls the 'ecological university' (Barnett, 2011, Chapter 12; 2013, Chapter 11). This is a university which will be ecological in the narrow sense of having a care for the environment, but Barnett has more than that in mind: it is a university which has a care for the wellbeing of the whole world, using its knowledge and wisdom for that wellbeing.

Ideas that universities are to seek the good of society and individuals are, therefore, present in a range of contemporary commentators. They appear also in the pages of *Times Higher Education* (THE) in immediately current debate. Amongst articles in THE during the time this chapter was being written, the following give a flavour. Edward Byrne, President and Principal of King's College London, wrote: 'UK universities must maintain their tradition of contributing to social progress not only locally and nationally but also globally'.[4] John Holmwood, Professor of Sociology at the University of Nottingham, was described as having 'called on universities to pay far more attention to the role [universities] can and should play in buttressing democracy' and quoted as saying that the 'contribution of the university to democratic life' has been 'almost entirely absent from discussions of the recent reforms', which he clearly regrets.[5] Joy Carter, Vice-Chancellor of the University of Winchester, writing shortly after a United Nations conference on climate change, called for universities to do more to 'help all our students to confront climate change . . . [as] a strong expression not only of our autonomy but also of our scholarly and ethical values and our noble purpose' and expressed 'a strongly held belief, which is shared across universities, in the power of higher education to do good for individuals, societies, nations and the world'.[6]

Similar commitments to universities serving the good of society and individuals emerge in some university mission statements. They are there in those quoted by Wood. The University of the South Pacific, for example, expresses its vision in terms of 'achieving excellence and innovation for sustainable development of the Pacific Island Countries'. The Banaras Hindu University includes in its mission 'to promote the building up of character in youth by religion and ethics as an integral part of education'. In England, the University of Winchester has as its mission '[t]o educate, to advance knowledge and to serve the common good'.[7] The University of Bristol says its mission is '[t]o pursue and share knowledge and understanding, both for their own sake and to help individuals and society fulfil their potential'.[8] Others seem to be heading in the direction of what Harris calls mission statements as marketing tools, for example by saying their mission is to be amongst the best universities.

How far such sentiments about serving the good have been lived out in practice has been questioned.[9] The fact that they are there, not just in the policy documents but, for example, in the submissions made to Dearing from individual universities (Fryer, 2005, pp. 75–76), suggests that here is something thought important. There is also some evidence of attempts to live them out in universities today. That can be seen in the mission statements quoted above, assuming they do accurately represent the mission of the university, in what Stuart and Holman say about Winchester and Heythrop, in the above quotations from recent articles in THE and in other material below about work at Aston and Newcastle Universities and University College London.

Present policy

The above confirms the view already expressed that nothing new is being proposed when it is suggested universities are to seek the good of individuals and society. What is being argued is that this vision of being a university is sadly lacking in the present reforms of universities and that it is actually vital for the present time. The reforms are, as Scott argues, shaped partly by trends in society as well as direct policy interventions. Whatever the exact balance, a shift towards a system geared to two principal aims, serving the economy and advancing social mobility, is being encouraged, with very little acknowledgement of the sorts of roles universities have traditionally been seen as playing in forming citizens and societies towards what is, or might be, good.

It is not only what universities are seen as being for in the present reforms which is noteworthy. The reforms also seek to shape the internal workings of universities in particular ways, towards courses which fit more closely the needs of the economy, treating students as consumers if not customers, and the development of a more competitive higher education system, with competition seen as the route to improving universities; in other words, a system run more according to the ways of the market. The documents bringing these changes are now explored in more detail.

The present reforms began with the 2010 *Report of the Independent Review of Higher Education Funding and Student Finance* (The Browne Report; Browne, 2010). Scott discussed in his chapter how it fits with previous developments in higher education policy.

Within Browne, there are occasional glimpses of a vision for universities somewhat in line with what is being argued for in this book. For example, Chapter One begins with the affirmation that '[h]igher education matters. It helps to create the knowledge, skills and values that underpin a civilised society'. However, the points about values and civilised society are hardly developed at all. Browne concentrates on two functions he sees universities as having; enhancing social mobility and strengthening the economy. That can be illustrated with reference to various parts of the Report, including Chapter One, which seeks to put 'The Investment Case for Higher Education' and does so in terms of universities '[s]ustaining future economic growth and social mobility in an increasingly competitive knowledge economy' (Browne, 2010, p. 14).

Browne thought more financial investment was needed in order for universities to do such 'sustaining'. To facilitate that, he proposed a shift in the main way of funding universities, away from a block grant given directly to universities towards higher fees which students would pay with a loan from the state. This system was accepted by government, though not quite as Browne envisaged. As Scott indicates, Browne suggested no cap on the fees universities could charge, but the government set a limit of £9,000 per year.

Other things are needed as well as investment, says Browne. For example, 'there needs to be a closer fit between what is taught in higher education and the skills needed in the economy' (Browne, 2010, p. 23). The curriculum, traditionally set by academics, Browne says should be changed to fit the needs of the economy. Nothing is said about what might happen to subjects which do not have what Browne might think of as a clear link to 'the skills needed in the economy', even if they are important in other ways. Browne also says universities are likely to better achieve the aims he sets for them if competition is introduced into the system, claiming 'Competition generally raises quality' (Browne, 2010, p. 2). Browne envisaged competition being introduced as students, armed with their loans and information about courses, purchased the course of their choice and universities would have to compete to attract students. No justification is offered for the claim about competition raising quality, a claim which is contestable since, arguably, a good deal of co-operation is needed in education, between disciplines, between students and staff, and between universities, for example in the case of major research projects.[10]

Scott argues that whilst much which was in Browne was in the same 'direction of travel as earlier reforms', Browne helped to formulate 'a coherent, and threatening, policy discourse'. The stage is set for the creation of a more 'marketised' and individualised higher education system focussed on important but narrow goals.

A brighter aspect of Browne is his concern for social mobility. He notes some success in widening participation, with increasing numbers attending university from previously under-represented groups. That trend has continued: young people from disadvantaged backgrounds were 10 per cent more likely to enter higher education in 2014 than in 2013, for example.[11] Whilst those from more affluent backgrounds are still much more likely to go to university than those from lower socio-economic groups, the increase from the latter, with all it can mean in terms of improved life chances and new opportunities to contribute to society is to be welcomed.

Whilst, as has been observed, the government did not accept all that Browne recommended, the 2011 White Paper *Higher Education: Students at the Heart of the System* (BIS, 2011a) does adopt the general tenor of Browne. It recognises that 'higher education is a good thing in itself' (p. 38) and that students may 'study a subject because they love it', but it draws particular attention to '[o]ne of the purposes of higher education [being] . . . to prepare students for a rewarding career' (p. 38) and calls for 'genuine collaboration' between universities and employers 'in the design and delivery of courses' (p. 39). It maintains both the shift in funding in the direction of fees paid by students, with the help of loans, and Browne's commitment to universities serving the economy and social mobility. On the latter, *Students at the Heart of the System* proposes the strengthening of the Office for Fair Access (OFFA). It also accepts the marketisation which was part of Browne; competition is good and students are paying 'consumers'. The individualistic approach seen in Browne continues, in contrast, for example, to Robbins's 'general social ends' for universities (1963, p. 6). In the new system, the individual student pays (with the help of a loan) and looks for a return on their investment. Given they are likely to have substantial debt to repay, and that they have entered universities in days when the rhetoric is around the economic benefits of university education, there may be a tendency to see that return in terms of a higher salary, rather than, for example, being equipped to serve the neighbour; indeed, this very point is in Browne who, envisaging more varied fees than actually emerged, wrote 'students will only pay higher charges if there is a proven path to higher earnings' (2010, p. 31). Continued enrolment on vocational courses associated with the caring professions, not likely to lead to high salaries, may indicate the human spirit does at least in some cases rise to higher ideals. Whether those who serve others should have to do so for comparatively low pay, and whether they should be saddled with a debt they cannot repay, even one which will eventually be written off, are both debatable points.[12]

The 2011 White Paper made further attempts at introducing competition as it sought to ease the way for 'alternative' or 'private' providers to enter the system. Scott comments on this in his chapter and notes that to date only a few such have entered 'the market'. They tend not to offer the breadth of subjects present in traditional universities. Some do, but most are involved in 'high-level training in vocational and professional fields', says Scott.

The 2015 Green Paper, *Fulfilling our Potential. Teaching Excellence, Social Mobility and Student Choice* (BIS, 2015) continues the emphasis on the economy, social mobility and choice. It seeks to further enable the entry of private providers as a source of choice and competition, with the hope such providers might focus on particular tasks such as 'offering programmes attractive to hard-to-reach communities' (BIS, 2015, p. 13). It will be interesting to see whether that happens if the proposed changes are introduced, and the nature of their educational offer. Will it be in line with the skills-based training model advocated by government, or seek the wider educational goals universities have traditionally been about? What impact will private providers have on existing universities which do seek to offer such wider education?

The Green Paper also prioritises work on improving teaching in universities and suggests a new regulatory framework to monitor teaching quality; points discussed by Scott in his chapter. It seeks 'greater emphasis on graduate employability' (BIS, 2015, p. 7) and says, 'Increasing productivity is one of the country's main economic challenges, and universities have a vital role to play' (BIS, 2015, p. 10), including by 'teaching students . . . transferrable work readiness skills' (BIS, 2015, p. 11). There is nothing about skills for citizenship and little about any wider role for universities in facing challenges other than the economic and those to do with social mobility. Where there are references to such a wider role, they are not developed. Thus, page 18 contains a reference to the 'economic and social benefits' of higher education but says nothing further about the social benefits. In a paragraph giving three reasons why 'the government intervenes in higher education', the third is because of 'the broader benefits to society of having a highly educated population' (BIS, 2015, p. 58), but again the idea of 'broader benefits' is left unexplored.

Following consultation on the Green Paper, another White Paper was issued in May 2016 under the title *Success as a Knowledge Economy; Teaching Excellence, Social Mobility and Student Choice* (BIS, 2016a). Scott discusses it in some detail. Much of it is about improving teaching in universities, facilitating the entry of new providers and redesigning the 'architecture' of the system, including creating an Office for Students to take over the responsibilities of a number of currently existing arms-length government bodies and act as a 'market regulator' (BIS, 2016a, p. 15). By now familiar ideas re-emerge. The purpose of universities is to advance social mobility and serve the economy, not least by equipping people with the skills for work; themes highlighted in the Paper's title. Increased competition and choice are again advocated as offering the route to improvement of universities. One section of the White Paper, headed 'Creating a competitive market', begins with the words 'Competition between providers in any market incentivises them to raise their game, offering consumers a greater choice of more innovative and better quality products and services at lower cost. Higher education is no exception' (BIS, 2016a, p. 8). The White Paper embodies the view that higher education is a market, education a product, students are consumers who should have choice and quality, with the whole system being geared towards enhancing social mobility and economic performance.

As in Browne and the earlier White and Green Papers, so in *Success as a Knowledge Economy* there are a few very welcome recognitions that 'Higher Education . . . (has) a wide range of societal benefits' (BIS, 2016a, p. 7). However, such references to any wider understanding of the nature and role of higher education are few, and those which do appear are not developed in the way references to the economy and social mobility are.

At the time of writing, a Higher Education and Research Bill drafted to implement those parts of the White Paper requiring legislation had been presented to Parliament but not debated (BIS, 2016b). A fairly technical document, it contained no bigger vision for higher education than the previous White and Green Papers.

In present policy, universities are seen as having two aims: serving the economy and advancing social mobility. They are important but limited aims. The documents do not deal with how universities can serve society in other ways, including by helping it face the sorts of challenges Durber identified. Whether the introduction of the methods of the market will produce improvements or not, time will tell. Various contributors to this book see dangers in them. Such points will be returned to after a deeper look into the sorts of universities we need.

The universities we need

That the policy does not give the attention once given to the contribution universities can make to the good of society is regrettable, for there is still work to be done, perhaps always will be, on such things as sustaining democratic, civilised and inclusive societies.[13] Indeed, given there are currently fundamental issues to be faced, including about the very future of the planet, there is a particular urgency for universities to engage with questions about the good of society at present.

To go into just a couple of matters in a little more depth, a democracy in which fewer and fewer even vote clearly has questions to address about the health of its democracy. Britain is at such a point. Durber refers to work about this by Ruth Fox of the Hansard Society. Fox writes that at the UK 2010 general election 'just 44 per cent of 18–24-year-olds voted' (Fox, 2015, p. 189). That is part of a trend of decreasing levels of voting, particularly amongst younger voters, which Fox relates to a deeper malaise in British democracy.[14] Whilst she thinks '[f]ew among us would relish the alternatives' to representative democracy (Fox, 2015, p. 185), she says there is widespread dissatisfaction with the present system; she quotes a Hansard survey showing only about a third of the public thinks it works well (Fox, 2015, p. 187). Fox explores some of the reasons for that. Interestingly, given what is happening to universities, she mentions the 'marketisation' of politics as one cause. She says parties offer not thought-out 'contending visions' (Fox, 2015, p. 191) of the national interest to which they are committed and for which they will argue, but increasingly engage in a 'marketing game' (Fox, 2015, p. 191) in which each party 'offers up promises to the public but rarely engages in open and forthright debate about the negotiations and compromises that are required to achieve those promises' (Fox, 2015, p. 191). That 'feeds the sense that people are being deceived, manipulated and kept in the dark' (Fox, 2015, pp. 191–192) and is one potent factor, amongst others, eroding the political process.

Whatever the precise causes, lower and lower levels of participation in voting and a widespread sense that the present system is not working are indicative of a malaise which needs addressing. This is a democracy which needs nurturing. It needs citizens who will engage. Universities have their part to play in addressing such needs. They have long been about preparing people for citizenship and engagement with society. They can be such today and, as indicated shortly, some try to be. A democratic society, facing the issues Fox suggests Britain does, needs help in revitalising its democracy. Universities can play a part, working to create citizens and to strengthen public engagement, that democracy might be nurtured.

British society, along with many others, is not only democratic, but also diverse. A society learning to live with diversity likewise requires nurturing. Diversity can enrich. It can also bring challenges, leading to some being characterised as what Scott-Baumann and Cheruvallil-Contractor call 'the different other', who can be 'pathologised'. Harris comments on such things in her chapter, suggesting diversity can raise questions about 'allegiances', about what to believe and commit to, and why, about what it means to be 'good', including what it means to be a good society. In Britain, it has raised questions about what it is to be British and what are British values; Scott-Baumann and Cheruvallil-Contractor write of how questions about such have been invoked in relation to debates around Islam. Maybe, as Harris suggests, seeking cohesiveness as may have happened in the past is not the way forward and a journey into the 'uncommon' is more appropriate. Whatever the route, there are questions to be faced. There is a need for learning from, with and about others, and for places which resource that; places which, as Harris puts it, stimulate '[c]ritical awareness, openness to different ways of thinking, and readiness for conversation'. Universities have been and can be such places, and society needs that of them. It needs universities which help society face the issues it does.

Unsurprisingly in what Christian theology calls a fallen world, there are problems to be faced. Universities, even universities which are themselves part of such a world, can make a contribution, with and alongside others, to facing those problems. They can, as Williams suggests, be about citizenship. They can, as Harris suggests, be about learning to live positively with diversity. They can, as Higton suggests, be about nurturing people in the virtues needed for flourishing civic as well as academic life. They can be places for the facing of difficult issues, as Scott-Baumann and Cheruvallil-Contractor indicate they have been and should be.

In short, universities can be a stimulus and focus for addressing the issues society faces, tackling them in the light of the learning of the ages and of today. In that, they are a rich resource for society, which it would be foolish to ignore.

In practice, at least some universities do seek to contribute to such needful work, facing questions about citizenship, the virtues and so on. They do so as they engage in research on a wide range of issues such as climate change, voting trends, food security, what the religions believe and how they might engage well with each other (to allude to points Ford makes). They do so as they make comment into the public arena, and as they involve members of the wider community in research and debate on key issues; something they are increasingly doing, says Wood.

At least some try to engage with questions of the good of society as part of educating students. Stuart wrote about what the University of Winchester does as it works for the common good, including seeking to develop students as global citizens. Amongst the things she refers to are modules which help students reflect on values, an award for those who engage in cross-disciplinary thinking about society's 'big issues', commitments to sustainability and ethical issues in the Business School, opportunities for students to volunteer as one way of raising social justice issues (including as part of degree courses) and organising the university in such a way as to reflect its convictions, with commitments to Fair Trade, an environmentally friendly campus and being a Stonewall Diversity Champion, for example.

Other universities engage similarly. In an article in THE, Julia King, Vice-Chancellor of Aston University wrote about initiatives in Aston, University College London (UCL) and Newcastle University to address what UCL called 'Grand Challenges' and Newcastle 'Societal Challenge Themes', as part of which Aston, for example, gave time in its second year timetable to 'teaching all students about the impact of climate change'.[15]

When universities do that, they are doing important work, helping students to engage with different views, with thinking about the world and what is happening in it, with questions about what is good, with questions of responsibility, including the responsibility of citizens.[16] They are also hopefully asking students to seek the truth of a situation, to virtuously engage with learning about some place, or question, or idea, or concept or value and to evaluate the different ways in which different people might regard something as 'true'. They are helping to create the graduates society needs if it is to tackle the issues it faces. They may even have some success in that; documents produced by the Department for Business, Innovation and Skills (BIS) suggest universities do impact in ways helpful to society, or at least that graduates show characteristics useful to society. BIS Economic Paper

Number 14 (BIS, 2011b) and BIS Research Paper Number 133 (BIS, 2013) speak of how graduates, compared to non-graduates, are, or were then, less likely to be involved in crime, more tolerant, more likely to volunteer and more politically involved, leading to societies with greater social cohesion and trust with less crime and more political stability.

The above is to look from the perspective of society and argue universities can and should be about the good of society. There are also arguments which suggest that to be true to what it is to be a university universities *need* to be about the good of the world, indeed that such a focus can save universities from serving that which they should not. That clearly matters to society also, for society will not want its universities devoted to what is damaging of the good. Higton (2012) gives a warning that unless universities are about 'the common good' (p. 216), there is a danger they will fall into serving the vicious and violent; 'overbearing state power' (p. 216), for example. In fact, he suggests this has happened at times in universities he considers in his book: Paris, Berlin and Dublin. Examples can be garnered from other places. Gerald Pillay writes out of his experience of being a member of 'a disenfranchised minority community in apartheid South Africa' (2010, p. 33). He says academics failed to speak out against apartheid, in which he clearly thinks they failed as academics and presumably as academic communities, as universities. It led him to reflect on 'the indissoluble link there is between intellectual pursuits and the public responsibility of the scholar' (Pillay, 2010, p. 34). Failure to exercise such responsibility can lead to at least tacit support for the 'overbearing state power' identified by Higton (2012, p. 216). Noam Chomsky made similar points in his famous 1967 paper on *The Responsibility of Intellectuals*. Written against the background of the Vietnam War and what he regarded as the less than absolute commitment of the powerful to speak the truth, he writes 'It is the responsibility of intellectuals to speak the truth and oppose lies'. The intellectual community has public responsibilities towards the good, and if it does not exercise them, it may support what is not good.

Thus universities can, should and need to be about the good, both for the sake of society and their own sake. At least some Christian theological perspectives would also support the idea that education should be about the good. The qualifier 'at least some' is required because there are different Christian views; as Stuart says, religious identities are contested. One way of approaching education from a Christian perspective is to think of education as about discovering and living with God's world, and doing so as those who are part of creation and who are called to love.[17] What love means is incarnated in the life of Jesus Christ. In Christian thinking, what Jesus called the great commandments to love God and neighbour are to be lived out in all parts of life, professional and personal, public and private. Within this purview, education becomes an expression of love; love which helps the student and staff member grow, love which seeks the truth, love which desires the best for the world and all its people. Such an education, as an expression of love, will be committed to listening and valuing, to academic freedom and debate, to exploring how the world looks to the other. It will not be about imposing a dogma (religious or otherwise) or seeking to control either the student or the world, but about creating space for exploration and growth.

That is not a way of saying anything goes, or all views are equal. It arises from prioritising Christ-like love. It affirms the dignity of human-kind, with all its diversity. It affirms the importance of caring for creation. It recognises such affirmations create questions, about when it becomes unloving to express certain opinions and when, or if, it becomes loving to stop them being expressed, for example. It also may affirm, as does Higton (2012), that education is to be seen in the context of the Kingdom of God, 'the fulfilment that God has for God's creatures' (2012, p. 145) in the coming 'kingdom of heaven' (2012, p. 149). Whether such a *telos* is shared or not, this Christian view emphasises that education is about the good, about truth, learning to listen, to value, about exploring how the world looks to the other and about seeking the best for the world and its people. Such an approach would seek the good of individuals and society, and some of it at least may be shared by those who are not committed to Christian faith.

Present policy and the universities we need

There is clearly a mismatch between the vision for universities spelled out in the last section and the way present policy is seeking to shape the sector. Certainly the policy does not articulate the sort of vision being advocated here. It is too soon to know exactly how all the policy changes will impact, though there are some danger signals emerging. Some concerns were raised in the section on current policy. Others were flagged up in earlier chapters and are summarised here.

They include fears that the commitment to the ways of the market in pres-ent policy may not be helpful to the maintenance of the sorts of universities society needs. This is a matter Stuart raises when she writes out of experience at Winchester that '[t]he marketisation of higher education with its emphasis on competition between institutions, league tables and attempts to construct the student as consumer brings its pressures to bear on a values-driven insti-tution which to survive has to compete and this can place burdens on indi-viduals who may feel conflict between those pressures and our values'. Stuart clearly finds the marketisation of higher education creates conflicts for a university, and its staff, committed to the common good.

Scott makes a similar point when he says 'the habits of solidarity and com-monality characteristic of a public system of higher education may . . . decay as notions of "publicness" are eroded by the enthusiasms for the "market"'. That is clearly of concern if universities are to serve the good of the public realm, in solidarity with wider society.

Scott actually lists a number of 'the more likely consequences of the current reforms in higher education in England'. One is that '[t]he delicate balance between higher education, of a liberal or scientific character, and professional training . . . could be upset', a matter of concern particularly if the professional training becomes emphasised to the detriment of a liberal education which helps to create reflective citizens, for example. Scott also writes about a likely 'extension of political control over higher education' as a result of the reforms, for '[t]he lust to measure achievement, drive up standards, promote transparency is insatiable'. Whilst any realisation of such a future 'can be attributed as much to deeper structural forces as to the deliberate effects of policy', says Scott, policy obviously plays its part in creating a possible, but not inevitable, 'for many dystopian future'.

Scott-Baumann and Cheruvallil-Contractor raise their own concerns about the present reforms, not unrelated to some of those raised by Scott. The reforms are, Scott-Baumann and Cheruvallil-Contractor say, creating 'rapidly changing understandings of what the function of universities should be.' They ask the question: 'are they [universities] institutions of learning that produce scholars, thinkers, conscientious citizens and loyal dissenters *or* are these institutions that produce efficient but unquestioning employees to staff global conglomerates that satisfy our collective capitalist materialist demands?' If the reforms produce the latter rather than the former, that is clearly a huge step away from the sorts of universities it is argued here society needs.

Wood raises a similar point when he questions how far universities working in the new policy framework are able to prepare people for living in the world as it is, with its increasing population and diminishing resources. Universities should be geared towards preparing students for citizenship in such a world, rather than focusing on narrowly economic ends which may not be realisable in the world as it is.

Some contributors look more closely at specific areas of the work of a university. Williams does that, raising a point similar to one raised by Scott about the balance between skills training and a liberal education. Williams writes, 'The most difficult challenge in the Western university world today is how the university avoids being completely dominated by this external pressure to produce and to offer functional training'. His concern is that the work they can and should do about things such as citizenship and general 'civil' discourse about the good of society may be squeezed out due to the emphasis on providing skills for the economy.

Holman's contribution raises questions about the future of small and specialist institutions, at least about the future of those which specialise in some areas; in Heythrop's case, theology and philosophy. This is part of a wider concern that the reforms may erode recruitment to and fail to support subjects which are important for society but which may not immediately appear to be in line with Browne's statement, taken up by the White and Green

Papers, that '[t]here needs to be a closer fit between what is taught in higher education and the skills needed in the economy' (2010, p. 23).

The subjects which suffer may include arts and humanities, as people may not perceive a link between them and the needs of the economy. (Whether that perception is accurate is another matter, in saying which it is not the intention to suggest economic are the only or best criteria by which to judge the value of a subject area). Holman writes of a 'move away from some humanities subjects to those which students and their parents regarded as more useful for employment'. Like Scott, Holman sees this as associated with bigger trends than higher education policy. It has to do, he suggests, with the financial crisis of 2008, but he also notes students becoming 'more consumer-minded', the latter certainly encouraged by the policy changes, including the idea that students may assess the value of a course by the salary level they think it is likely to lead to.

Figures from the Higher Education Statistics Agency comparing enrolments in various subject areas in 2013–14 and 2014–15 indicate that at undergraduate level sciences increased and, with two exceptions in the table referenced, arts and humanities decreased.[18] Holman gives figures showing decline in recruitment to theology and religious studies.

The latter must be a matter of concern in days when religions impact significantly on society, for good and ill, and in days when there is a need for 'religious literacy'. Society needs the religions to be studied and understood, including for the wellbeing of society.

Any move away from the arts and humanities generally is also serious because, as Ford suggests, universities need to be about wisdom and offering wisdom from various sources to a world facing complex issues. That includes both religious and secular wisdoms. Such wisdoms can be gained from studying not just theology and religious studies, but the arts and humanities generally, alongside the sciences. Literature, history, philosophy, languages and many other subject areas can all illuminate something of what it is to be human in society and be sources of wisdom for living well in the world. If such subject areas decline, then the world loses insights into its condition and is the poorer for that.

Another matter Scott touches on in terms of enrolments is 'that the increase in fees has dealt a devastating blow to part-time students', with numbers enrolling on such courses dropping dramatically. The Government has given extra help to such students, but it has not thus far offset the fees rise. Such a drop is not likely to help the social mobility agenda; some who might once have benefited from higher education are now being deterred.

The above indicates some of the concerns raised in the book about higher education policy. There are also pressures on universities from other policy areas, such as the Prevent programme, or interpretations of it, say Scott-Baumann and Cheruvallil-Contractor. They suggest the 'assertive' and 'aggressive' language around the programme and the guidance given to universities about 'monitoring' for example 'effectively renders the sector fearful of encouraging, fostering and hosting critical debate'. It discourages universities from being places for the debate of difficult issues.

Thus, there are forces at work which give little attention to long-held notions about universities working for such things as the public good, the common good, the health of democratic societies, and the creation of citizens who will operate effectively for the good of such societies. Indeed, there are forces at work which see universities as about little more than producing workers for the global economy and which are trying to organise universities around market principles which may reduce the number and type of courses, erode important values and attitudes in universities and hinder the interdisciplinary and inter-university working needed for tackling complex issues. They may cause universities to be less than they can be, less than they are at present. Some universities do valiantly work to be the universities society needs, but unsupported by present policies, which will, no doubt, have their effects in time. They may create universities which do not rise to the challenges society needs them to face. There may even be dangers that students and others will be shaped in unhelpful directions, for example into believing that human beings are individuals designed for competition and consumption, living first for their own good.

Therein is the concern, that we are in danger of creating universities which do not serve either their students or society adequately. For society does have urgent questions to be addressed ultimately about what sort of society we wish to be, what we will name as good in our life in society, what sort of society we will seek as we do economics, create (or lose) wealth, respond to conflict, develop different ways of communicating and shape ways of living in culturally, ethnically and religiously diverse societies. Equally, society needs citizens equipped for living in and shaping societies facing such questions. Universities have their part to play in such work, but that is taken little or no account of in present policy.

The universities we need: looking forward

There is within present higher education policy a limited view of what it is to be a university, a limited view of education and, perhaps, a limited view of what it is to be human, for human beings are not only economic beings. We are, rather, beings who live in relationships and societies. Through our learning, imagination and hard work we have taken enormous steps forward in things such as health care, poverty reduction and methods of communication. Durber wrote of such in her chapter. She also highlighted some of the fundamental questions humankind faces about the survival of the planet, the sustaining of democracy, how to regulate power and how to live well in diverse societies. Ultimately, we face questions about the ends and purposes of human life and human societies, questions about what we will call a good life and how we will seek what we call good.

Universities can help with such work. They have long done so. Their role in wider society was acknowledged in previous generations of policy documents. There are still those who seek to work to that bigger vision of what it is to be a university. Given the importance of the matters faced, and the contribution universities can make, it seems strange indeed, almost beyond belief, that the work universities have done, can do and actually do in such areas is hardly recognised at all in present policy documents.

That omission, along with aspects of what is in the policy, does pose challenges, as already noted. Despite that, this is not a book which preaches doom. It does say doom is a danger, but it can be avoided. As Scott puts it, a 'dystopian' future for the university is not inevitable. As Barnett affirms, 'the university has possibilities in front of it' (2011, p. 1). One of the possibilities, the 'feasible utopias', he considers has already been mentioned; the 'ecological university' (Barnett, 2011, Chapter 12; 2013, Chapter 11). That is the term Barnett uses to speak of a university which centres its life on what Barnett calls the 'wellbeing' of the whole world, using its knowledge and wisdom for that wellbeing. He suggests it is a way of imagining the university 'whose time has come', for 'the world needs its universities to be ecological' (2011, p. 141) in the bigger sense of tackling the issues which matter for the world's wellbeing.

Fortunately, there are people within and without universities who continue to work for such, who are committed to the struggle of seeking a good society and enabling the university to play its role in creating such a society. That can be seen in the work of people such as Barnett and others who have contributed to or been quoted in this book. It can be seen in the story of the University of Winchester with its commitment to creating global citizens. It can be seen in the mission statements and articles from THE quoted earlier, with their concern for universities helping to nurture democracy and tackle big issues such as climate change. It is still possible to do such work, and there are those who are committed to doing it.

They do it unsupported by the policy framework, which is not as it should be. Indeed, the policy may threaten what is being done.

If this was only about universities, perhaps it would not matter as much as it does. It is not only about universities, however. It is about the good of society. The world does face difficult issues. The life of the planet is threatened. Failure to live creatively with difference can lead to societies not at ease with themselves and the most appalling violence. There are important issues to be addressed which universities can help with.

Scott argues that universities are shaped in part by trends in society as well as policy. Maybe the present policy is in part a reflection of wider trends. If what has been argued in this book is correct, and society does need universities which will help it face the challenges it does, then a counter-trend is needed, a wider movement of concerned citizens who will speak out in favour of the universities we need. Faith groups will have a role in that: as Ford, Stuart and Holman show, faith can lead to rich views of what it means to be a university and, as shown earlier, there is a long history of faith groups engaging with universities. Students, whose future is at stake, will have a role also. So will those who work in universities as academics, managers and support staff. So will unions and the campaign groups formed to address issues around universities. But it needs to be wider than that. What this book is about is the good of society and the universities society needs to support it in seeking the good. This is a matter for society, therefore. It is a matter for all concerned about the good of society, for all who know there are issues to be faced which need facing well, virtuously, intelligently, with wisdom and knowledge. Universities are one focus for such work. They need to be understood and supported as such. Failure in that may lead to them becoming less than we need.

As this is about society, so there needs to be a more general raising of voices from across society, the telling of a different story about what it is to be a university, an older, richer, fuller and more relevant story, with letters to MPs and newspapers, comments on Facebook and Twitter and all the usual means of drawing attention to arguments, pointing to the dangers of the present policy and, more importantly, putting the positive case for the universities we need, for the good of society.

The universities we need are places where important and difficult issues can be faced. They need to be about citizenship, living with difference, the virtues, tackling specific issues such as climate change, or how power can be called to account in a globalised world. They need to be places where secular and religious wisdoms and many intellectual disciplines can be drawn on to help society not just face immediate challenges but dream dreams and see visions of better ways of living. The universities we need will be about seeking a world of justice and peace, where there is a valuing of creation and all its peoples, a world Christians might speak of in terms of the Kingdom of God, at least part of which can be owned as good by others and spoken of in different ways also. The contrast between such a view and that which dominates Browne, the White and Green Papers, and the present Higher Education and Research Bill is great. It is rich fare indeed in comparison with what they offer. It speaks more of the universities we need than they ever will. It speaks of universities which face the challenges society faces and which commit to seeking the good of all. Such are the universities we need.

Notes

1 The full list of Cathedrals Group members can be found at http://cathedralsgroup. org.uk/Members.aspx (accessed 27th January 2016).
2 The UCL story is told in Harte and North (2004, pp. 30ff), for example.
3 http://www.yale.edu/about-yale/traditions-history (accessed 9th February 2016).
4 Edward Byrne, *In Praise of Ambition* Times Higher Education 28th January 2016, p. 30.
5 Matthew Reisz, *Democratic role of sector 'waning'* Times Higher Education 21st January 2016, p. 32.

6 Joy Carter, *It's time for the academy to wake up and smell the greenhouse gases* Times Higher Education 24/31 December 2015, p. 30.
7 http://www.winchester.ac.uk/aboutus/missionandvalues/Pages/MissionandValues.aspx (accessed 17th January 2016).
8 http://www.bristol.ac.uk/university/governance/policies/vision/mission.html (accessed 17th January 2016).
9 For example, by Fryer, R.H. (2005).
10 Higton (2012), chapter 7 discusses the 'sociable' nature of education, suggesting, 'Competition is only a secondary reality' (p. 203).
11 https://www.ucas.com/corporate/news-and-key-documents/news/record-number-students-placed-ukuniversities-and-colleges (accessed 20th February 2016).
12 The health of a system based on debt may itself be questionable. Debt is perceived negatively in various religious traditions. It is certainly the case that the loans have not been repaid at the anticipated levels. Interestingly, Cable (2010, p. 18) points to the dangers of debt and suggests unsustainable personal debt was a major factor in the 2007 economic crisis.
13 Cf Dearing (1997, p. 13).
14 At the time of writing, in terms of voting rates the Scottish Independence referendum was the exception.
15 Julia King, *Collective Wisdom*. Times Higher Education, 29th October 2015, p. 30.
16 Leesa Wheelahan (2012), commenting on such things, helpfully draws on Durkheim's distinction between 'sacred' and 'secular' knowledge, secular being that needed for everyday living and sacred 'the knowledge that it [society] uses to think about itself' (Wheelahan, 2012, p. 40). Universities need to be about both.
17 Rowan Williams addressed something of this at a lecture at Rikkyo University in Japan in 2009. http://english.rikkyo.ac.jp/aboutus/philosophy/spirit/canterbury/ (accessed 8th February 2016).
18 https://www.hesa.ac.uk/sfr224 (accessed 7th April 2016), table 5.

References

Barnett, R., 2011. *Being a University*. Abingdon and New York: Routledge.
Barnett, R., 2013. *Imagining the University*. Abingdon and New York: Routledge.
Barnett, R., 2016. *Understanding the University*. Abingdon and New York: Routledge.
BIS (Department for Business, Innovation and Skills), 2011a. *Higher Education: Students at the Heart of the System*. London: HMSO. [online] Available at: https://www.gov.uk/government/uploads/system/uploads/attachment_data/file/31384/11–944-higher-education-students-at-heart-of-system.pdf. [accessed February 1st 2016].
BIS (Department for Business, Innovation and Skills), 2011b. *Economic Paper Number 14*. [online] Available at: http://webarchive.nationalarchives.gov.uk/20121212135622/http://bis.gov.uk/assets/biscore/economics-and-statistics/docs/s/11–1007-supporting-analysis-for-higher-education-white-paper.pdf. [accessed February 5th 2016].
BIS (Department for Business, Innovation and Skills), 2013 *Research Paper Number 133*. [online] Available at: https://www.gov.uk/government/uploads/system/uploads/attachment_data/file/251011/bis-13–1244-things-we-know-and-dont-know-about-the-wider-benefits-of-higher-education.pdf. [accessed February 5th 2016].
BIS (Department for Business, Innovation and Skills), 2015. *Fulfilling our Potential: Teaching Excellence, Social Mobility and Student Choice*. London: HMSO.

[online] Available at: https://www.gov.uk/government/uploads/system/uploads/attachment_data/file/474227/BIS-15–623-fulfilling-our-potential-teaching-excellence-social-mobility-and-student-choice.pdf. [accessed February 1st 2016].

BIS (Department for Business, Innovation and Skills), 2016a. *Success as a Knowledge Economy: Teaching Excellence, Social Mobility and Student Choice.* London: HMSO. [online] Available at: https://www.gov.uk/government/uploads/system/uploads/attachment_data/file/523396/bis-16-265-success-as-a-knowledge-economy.pdf. [accessed May 31st 2016].

BIS (Department for Business, Innovation and Skills), 2016b. *Higher Education and Research Bill.* London: HMSO [online] Available at http://www.publications.parliament.uk/pa/bills/cbill/2016-2017/0004/17004.pdf. [accessed June 5th 2016].

Browne Report (Independent Review of Higher Education Funding and Student Finance), 2010. Securing a Sustainable Future for Higher Education. No publication details given.

Byrne, E., 2016. In Praise of Ambition. *Times Higher Education*, 28th January 2016, p. 30.

Cable, V., 2010. *The Storm: The World Economic Crisis and What It Means.* London: Atlantic.

Carter, J., 2015. It's Time for the Academy to Wake Up and Smell the Greenhouse Gases. *Times Higher Education*, 24th/31st December 2015, p. 30.

Chomsky, N., 1967. *The Responsibility of Intellectuals.* New York Review of Books, February 23rd 1967. [online] Available at: http://www.chomsky.info/articles/19670223.htm. [accessed February 12th 2016].

Collini, S., 2012. *What Are Universities For?* London: Penguin.

Dearing Summary Report (National Committee of Enquiry into Higher Education), 1997. *Higher Education in the Learning Society.* London: HMSO.

Fox, R., 2015. Improving the Health of Our Representative Democracy in Sentamu, J., ed. 2015. *On Rock or Sand? Firm Foundations for Britain's Future.* pp. 185–212. London: SPCK.

Fryer, R.H., 2005. Universities and Citizenship: The Forgotten Dimension? in Robinson, S., and Katalushi, C., eds. *Values in Higher Education.* pp. 74–106. Vale of Glamorgan, UK: Aureus.

Harte, N., and North, J., 2004. *The World of UCL 1828–2004.* London: UCL Press.

Higton, M., 2012. *A Theology of Higher Education.* Oxford: Oxford University Press.

Howard, T.A., 2006. *Protestant Theology and the Making of the Modern German University.* Oxford: Oxford University Press.

King, J., Collective Wisdom. *Times Higher Education*, 29th October 2015, p. 30.

Newman, J.H., 1982; 1852. *The Idea of a University.* ed: Svaglic, M.J., Notre Dame, IN: University of Notre Dame Press.

Nixon, J., 2008. *Towards the Virtuous University.* New York and Abingdon: Routledge.

Nixon, J., 2011. *Higher Education and the Public Good.* London and New York: Continuum.

Nixon, J., 2013. *Interpretive Pedagogies for Higher Education.* London and New York: Bloomsbury.

Pillay, G., 2010. Leading a Church University: Some Reflections in Wright, M., and Arthur, J., eds. *Leadership in Christian Higher Education.* pp. 33–57. Exeter: Imprint Academic.

Reisz, M., 2016. Democratic Role of Sector 'Waning'. *Times Higher Education*, 21st January 2016, p. 32.

Robbins Report (Committee on Higher Education), 1963. *Higher Education: A Report by the Committee Appointed by the Prime Minister Under the Chairmanship of Lord Robbins, 1961–63*. London: HMSO.

Wheelahan, L., 2012. Accessing Knowledge in the University of the Future in Barnett, R., ed. *The Future University: Ideas and Possibilities*. pp. 39–49. New York and Abingdon: Routledge.

Williams, R., 2009. *The Mission of the Anglican University in the Present Age*. [online] Available at: http://english.rikkyo.ac.jp/aboutus/philosophy/spirit/canterbury/. [accessed February 8th 2016].

Contributors

Sariya Cheruvallil-Contractor is a Research Fellow in Faith and Peaceful Relations at the Centre for Trust, Peace and Social Relations, Coventry University, UK. She specialises in the sociology of religion, with particular emphasis on democratic research methodologies that work with and for research participants, to capture the nuance and complexity of societal diversity, pluralism and everyday lived experiences of religion or belief. She is the author of *Muslim Women in Britain: Demystifying the Muslimah* (2012), co-author of *Religion or Belief, Discrimination and Equality: Britain in Global Contexts* (2013) and *Islamic Education in Britain: New Pluralist Paradigms* (2015) and co-editor *Digital Methodologies in the Sociology of Religion* (2015).

Susan Durber is a minister of the United Reformed Church, serving in Taunton, and Moderator of the Faith and Order Commission of the World Council of Churches. She has served pastorates in Manchester, Salford and Oxford and was Principal of Westminster College, Cambridge. From 2013–2016 she was Theology Advisor for Christian Aid. She has published collections of prayers, and books and articles on parables and on preaching.

David Ford, OBE, is a Fellow of Selwyn College and Regius Professor of Divinity Emeritus in the University of Cambridge. He is a co-founder of the inter-faith practice of Scriptural Reasoning (www.scripturalreasoning. org). He was awarded the Coventry International Prize for Peace and Reconciliation in 2012 and an OBE for services to theological scholarship and inter-faith relations in 2013. He is co-editor of *The Modern Theologians – An Introduction to Christian Theology since 1918* (2005), and among his authored books are *The Drama of Living* (2014), *The Future of Christian Theology* (2011), *Christian Wisdom: Desiring God and Learning in Love* (2007) and *Shaping Theology: Engagements in a Religious and Secular World* (2007).

Suzy Harris is Professor of Education at the University of Roehampton and Director of the Philosophy of Education Research Centre;

she was also Head of Digby Stuart College 2011–13. She has held visiting positions in Madrid and Barcelona. Her research interests are in higher education policy and practice; questions of language and translation in relation to the university; Newman and Wittgenstein.

Stephen Heap is a Baptist minister, currently a Visiting Professor at the University of Winchester and lecturer and consultant for the Cardiff Centre for Chaplaincy Studies. Most of his work has been in and around universities, as chaplain, occasional lecturer, governor and, latterly, the Church of England's National Higher Education Adviser. He has also been a local minister and Director of a Christian Education Centre. He is the author of the Grove Booklet *What Are Universities Good For?* (2012) and various articles on universities and chaplaincy.

Mike Higton is Professor of Theology and Ministry at Durham University, where he oversees the 'Common Awards' partnership, in which the University validates much of the ministerial training of the Church of England and the Methodist Church of Great Britain and some similar training in other churches. He is the author of several books, including *A Theology of Higher Education* (2012), *Christian Doctrine* (2008), *Difficult Gospel: The Theology of Rowan Williams* (2004), and, with Rachel Muers, *The Text in Play: Experiments in Reading Scripture* (2012). From 2011 to 2013 he was co-leader, with David Ford, of the Templeton-funded 'Religion and the Idea of a Research University' project at the University of Cambridge, and he is a member of the Theological Reference Group of the Church of England's Education Office.

Michael Holman is a Jesuit priest who since January 2012 has been principal of Heythrop College, a specialist philosophy and theology college in the University of London. Before ordination, he studied in both Britain and the United States. His first years of ministry were spent mostly in secondary education, and from 1995–2004 he was headmaster of Wimbledon College, a Catholic secondary school maintained by the Jesuits. From 2005–2011 he was provincial superior of the Jesuits in Britain

Peter Scott is Professor of Higher Education Studies at the UCL Institute of Education. From 2011 until 2015 he was Chair of the Council at the University of Gloucestershire. Previously, he was Vice-Chancellor of Kingston University (1998–2010), Pro-Vice-Chancellor and Professor of Education at the University of Leeds. He was editor of (what was then) *The Times Higher Education Supplement* from 1976 until 1992. He is the author of several books on the development of mass higher education, the governance and management of universities and new patterns of knowledge production.

Alison Scott-Baumann is Professor of Society and Belief at the School of Oriental and African Studies, University of London. Having been a schoolteacher, educational psychologist and teacher educator, she returned in the 1990s to her first love, philosophy, and is known internationally for her work on Paul Ricoeur. Concurrently she developed an interest in applying philosophy to matters regarding social justice, which involves evidence-based research on Islam and Muslims in Britain. Subsequently, the government commissioned Alison in 2008 to review imam training, and she has also researched Arabic, higher education for Muslim women and collaborative partnerships between universities and Muslim colleges. She also works on feminist issues. In 2015, the Arts and Humanities Research Council awarded Alison a significant research grant to look at re/presenting Islam on campus, with regard to gender, interfaith activities and radicalisation (2015–2018).

Elizabeth Stuart is Deputy Vice-Chancellor and Professor of Christian Theology at the University of Winchester. She has written ten books on the theology of sexuality and gender and has also published in the theologies of death and liturgy.

Rowan Williams is Master of Magdalene College, Cambridge. His career began as a lecturer at the College of the Resurrection, Mirfield, from where he moved to Westcott House, Cambridge, in 1977. After ordination and serving as Honorary Assistant Priest at St George's Chesterton, he was appointed to a University lectureship in Divinity. He was elected a Fellow and Dean of Clare College, Cambridge in 1984 and in 1986 became Lady Margaret Professor of Divinity in Oxford, before becoming Bishop of Monmouth, and, from 2000, Archbishop of Wales. From 2002 to 2012 he was Archbishop of Canterbury. Dr. Williams is a noted poet and translator of poetry. He has also published studies of Dostoevsky, Arius, Teresa of Avila and Sergii Bulgakov, together with writings on a wide range of theological, historical and political themes.

John Wood, CBE, FREng, is a materials scientist and has held many academic positions, finally as Principal of Engineering at Imperial College. He holds honorary chairs in materials and nanotechnology at Imperial College, UCL and Brunel University London at present. He is currently Secretary-General of the Association of Commonwealth Universities and co-chair of the Global Research Data Alliance. He is an adviser to many governments and the European Commission on research, innovation and international research infrastructures, having chaired the European Research Board (2008–12), and remains on that board to advise on Open Science. He has held a number of company directorships and among those current are M4 Technology and Bio-nano Consulting, and he is also a consultant to CERN in Geneva. He is a Reader in the Church of England.

Index